CHARLES MASSON
of
AFGHANISTAN

EXPLORER, ARCHAEOLOGIST, NUMISMATIST
AND INTELLIGENCE AGENT

CHARLES MASSON
of
AFGHANISTAN

EXPLORER, ARCHAEOLOGIST, NUMISMATIST
AND INTELLIGENCE AGENT

Gordon Whitteridge

Orchid Press
Bangkok 2002

Gordon Whitteridge
CHARLES MASSON OF AFGHANISTAN
EXPLORER, ARCHAEOLOGIST, NUMISMATIST AND INTELLIGENCE OFFICER

First Edition by Aris & Philips, Ltd., Warminster: 1986
Second Edition: 2002

© Orchid Press 2002

Orchid Press
P.O. Box 19,
Yuttitham Post office,
Bangkok 10907, Thailand

Cover: the Great Buddha at Bamian, height 55 m; first described in Chinese sources in the 6th century AD. Photograph by courtesy of UNESCO and Andrine.

This book is printed on acid-free long life paper which meets the specifications of ISO 9706/1994

ISBN 974-524- 020-6

CONTENTS

LIST OF ILLUSTRATIONS

Colour Plates

Black and White Plates

ACKNOWLEDGEMENTS

The library of the British Ambassador's Residence in Kabul was well-stocked with books on Central Asia including a first edition of Charles Masson's *Narrative of Various Journeys in Balochistan, Afghanistan and the Panjab*. But it was not until after the founding of the Society for Afghan Studies and the setting up under its auspices of the British Institute of Afghan Studies in Kabul that I read the whole of Masson's four volumes in the 'Oxford in Asia Historical Reprints' series. His interests, particularly archaeology, numismatics and ethnography, paralleled those of the Society and the Institute. His careful recording of ancient sites throughout his travels was impressive. It struck me that Masson could be regarded as the Father of the British Institute in Kabul and I suggested to the Council of the Society that I should write his biography as the first part of a larger study designed to reappraise his work as a pioneer of Central Asian antiquities. This suggestion was accepted and my warm thanks are due to the Council of the Society for Afghan Studies (now incorporated in the Society for South Asian Studies), for sponsoring and encouraging the project. I am grateful to several fellow-members of the Council for reading my manuscript and offering valuable criticisms and suggestions in their special fields: Basil Gray, Peter Fraser, Dr David Bivar, and Dr David MacDowall whose knowledge of pre-Islamic coinage was of great help in a subject about which I knew very little. My thanks also to Dr Svend Helms for reading the manuscript and giving advice on publication, to T. Richard Blurton for answering my queries about Buddhist sects, and to Warwick Ball for the sketch-maps of Masson's archaeological sites.

I am grateful to the staff of the India Office Library and Records for their willing assistance. It would be impossible to write a biography of Charles Masson without a close study of the Masson Collection of Manuscripts in the Library and the admirable introductory essay by E.H. Johnston to the catalogue of that collection in which he set out the full details, previously not known, of the mystery surrounding Masson's early life.

My thanks are due to Mrs I.F. Pollock of the Guildhall Library, London, for her extensive research into James Lewis's background, to the Librarian and Secretary of the Royal Society for Asian Affairs for the use of special books in the library, and to the staff of the Indian Institute, Oxford, for their help. The staff of the Departments of Coins and Medals and of Oriental Antiquities of the British Museum have been good enough to enable me to examine their collection of Masson's coins and relics.

My brother and sister-in-law, Professor David and Dr Gweneth Whitteridge, besides reading the manuscript and giving me sound advice, put me up for many weeks at an early stage of writing it, and so did my sister Marcelle and her husband Robert Furtado. Miss Joan Morris typed the first draft efficiently. To my wife, Jill, I am greatly indebted for her constant encouragement and for typing the revised version.

If this book should be instrumental in gaining a belated entry for Charles Masson in the Dictionary of National Biography, I should be well content.

Illustration plates 1, 3, 6(a) and 9 appear by permission of the British Library, 11 by permission of the National Army Museum, London and 12 by permission of the National Portrait Gallery. Plates A, B and C appear by permission of and © Copyright The British Museum; my thanks also to the individuals mentioned.

SPELLING

The transliteration of Afghan and Central Asian proper and place names always presents difficulties when dealing with authors writing in the first half of the 19th Century. Masson's spelling in his published works was surprisingly modern, for example Karachi whereas Alexander Burnes has Curachee. In order to avoid too many variations in the text I have kept to Masson's spelling throughout hence *Mohamed* wherever it occurs, except in the case of the Shah of Persia where the modern Muhammad Shah has been used. Shah Shuja-ul-Mulk has also been preferred to his Shah Suja-al-Mulkh and Kabul to his Kabal. When quoting from his contemporaries, their own spelling has been retained.

If any fool this high samooch [cave] *explore*
Know that Charles Masson has been here before

Written on the wall of a cave above the niche of
the large Buddha at Bamian and discovered by
the French Archaeological Delegation in the 1930s

CHAPTER 1

EARLY LIFE AND
MILITARY SERVICE IN INDIA

What's become of Waring
Since he gave us all the slip
Chose land-travel or seafaring,
Boots and chest or staff and scrip,
Rather than pace up and down,
Any longer London-Town?

Robert Browning
Waring

L ondon-born Charles Masson told his British host in Persia* in 1830
that he was a U.S. citizen from Kentucky who had taken ten years
to travel leisurely overland from Europe to India via Herat and
Kandahar. Yet when he stayed for several weeks at Lahore with General Allard, the French officer engaged by the Maharaja Ranjit Singh
to train his Sikh cavalry, the former found that his guest spoke fluent
French, though with a slight accent, and thought he was an Italian. He
also wrote good French as can be judged from a letter to Allard from
Kabul in 1837.[1] Furthermore, in his book of verse published in 1848,
Masson included a number of verse translations of French poetry which
serve to show that he was familiar with contemporary French litera-
ture.[2] An English friend writing to him from Calcutta said:

Bayley,† in one of his conversations with me was very minute in his en-
quiries about your country etc., remarking from the manner in which you
wrote French and Italian he had always thought you were a Frenchman.[3]

Some French authorities have evidently thought so too, since there is
an entry for Masson in a 19th century 'Biographie Nationale' which
assumes he was French: and indeed Charles Masson could be a perfectly good French name. On the other hand, he does not figure in our
own Dictionary of National Biography: another case of a prophet who

---

* Major David Wilson, British Resident at Bushire.
† Deputy Secretary to the Government of India.

is not without honour except in his own country. Who then was Charles
Masson? Why did he encourage the belief that he was not an Englishman? And what interest has he for us today?

Charles Masson was in fact an alias. He was born James Lewis on
16 February 1800, and was baptized at the church of St Mary the Virgin, Aldermanbury, London on 23 March 1800.[4] His father was George
Lewis, oilman, of 58 Aldermanbury, and a member of the Needle
Makers Company, whose marriage to Mary Hopcraft had taken place
at Croughton, Northants, on 6 March 1799.[5] She came of a family of
substantial yeoman farmers of Rowlers Farm, Croughton, who subsequently achieved affluence as brewers.

Efforts to discover what school the young James Lewis attended
have proved unavailing. We only know that he did not go to any of
the major London schools such as Westminster, Charterhouse, Merchant Taylors, etc., although one of his correspondents assumed that
he had been at Harrow with G. T. Vigne.* This was not so, but that he
went to a good school is very likely. Had his school been known it
might have provided a clue to the subjects he had been taught. He is
known to have learned Latin and to have had some Greek. We have
already seen that his French and Italian were good enough for him to
be taken for an Italian by a Frenchman and for a Frenchman by an
Englishman. That his written French was good is one thing, but that
his spoken French was fluent is quite another. The first could be acquired by diligent study, but the second is hardly likely to have been
well developed at school in his time any more than it is today. A so-
journ in France, perhaps lengthy, and in Italy would therefore be indi-
cated, yet his father's means seem inadequate for such a programme.
Possibly James Lewis managed to obtain jobs on the continent. It is
tantalising not to be able to provide a single detail of his first 21 years
other than his birth and parentage.

The first documented facts of his adult life are provided by the Embarkation Lists of the Honourable East India Company.[6] On 5 October, 1821, Lewis enlisted in the Company's armed forces initially for
the infantry, though his actual service was in the artillery. Nothing is
known of his reasons for enlisting. However, it was not unusual for
men of some education to enlist in the Company's artillery in view of
the relatively good pay and the excellent prospects of promotion to

---

* G.T.Vigne, author of *A Personal Account of a Visit to Ghuzni, Kabul and Afghanistan.* He accompanied Masson on a trip to Begram.

clerical appointments. He sailed for Bengal on the *Duchess of Atholl* on 17 January 1822 and served in the 3rd Troop of the 1st Brigade of the Bengal European Artillery from 6 July 1822 till 4 July 1827.[7] During that time 'he attracted the particular notice of Major-General Hardwick, when he was the Commandant of that Corps, and was employed by him in arranging and depicting his zoological specimens...'.[8] He fought at the seige of Bharatpur which fell in January 1826 and in the follow-ing year deserted from his regiment at Agra together with a fellow-soldier, Richard Potter. They travelled westward on foot towards the Indus traversing the formidable desert of Bikanir and reaching Dera Ghazi Khan in December 1827. There they parted company,* Potter (now calling himself John Brown) going to Lahore with a view to en-tering Sikh service, Lewis (now Charles Masson) to Peshawar, Jalalabad and Kabul. Masson himself is silent about any travelling companion—though one senses from his narrative that he had one. Besides chang-ing their names, both men gave themselves out to be Americans at some point for cover purposes, though Masson seems not to have made such a claim until his visit to Persia in 1830. In fact he did not need a specific cover until then; the rough tribesmen he encountered could not distinguish between one European nation and another, and few had heard of the United States. The two deserters appear to have got the idea from Dr Josiah Harlan, a genuine American physician of their own age from Philadelphia, with whom they fell in at an undisclosed but early stage of their travels through the Punjab. However, Masson grew to dislike Harlan and the two Englishmen left him to go their own way. No doubt they had absorbed enough information from him about the United States and the American way of life to lend colour to their stories. At the same time, Harlan had learned rather too much about the deserters for comfort.

Harlan later told the Reverend Joseph Wolff, who was staying with him in June 1832 at Gujerat where he had succeeded in getting himself made governor of that place and province by the Maharaja Ranjit Singh, that on his first journey to Peshawar 'he was accompanied for some time by a Mr Mason [sic] who afterwards travelled about in Persia as an American'.[9] Harlan had been appointed to the Bengal establishment as a temporary surgeon to serve in Burma during the war of 1824-26, but the appointment was terminated when the

---

* According to C. Grey, *European Adventurers of Northern India 1785-1849* p. 184: but he gives no authority for the statement.

emergency was over. He was on leave at Ludhiana when he lost his job and at first tried to enter Sikh territory but having failed went to Kabul instead. An official report of 15 October 1827 from Captain Claude Wade, the Political Assistant at Ludhiana, the British frontier post, gives the details:

> Dr Harlan, lately an officiating surgeon on the establishment, who came to Ludhiana a short time ago with permission to cross the Sutlej, has now left Ludhiana, with a view to proceeding to Peshawar, via Bahawalpur. Dr Harlan's principal object in wishing to visit the Punjab was in the first place to enter Ranjit Singh's service, and ultimately to pursue some investigation regarding the natural history of that country, but failing in his attempt to procure a passport from the Maharaja he has taken the route via Bahawalpur, and will endeavour to cross the river at that place. Previous to his departure, Dr Harlan proposed to communicate his progress to me as opportunities might offer, and should his communications contain anything of interest to the Government, I shall consider it my duty to report.[10]

This was the journey when Harlan encountered Masson and Potter, though Masson never mentions the fact.

There appear to be no clues to why Masson deserted. Desertion was in fact not uncommon at that time and seems to have affected the Company's artillery more than the other arms. This was particularly the case with the Bengal Artillery for desertions from it, both during and after the siege of Bharatpur, were fairly frequent. The 1820s were quiet years from a military point of view, apart from the first campaign in distant Burma. He may simply have become bored with soldiering. Moreover as a ranker with an educated background he may well have found the lack of cultural stimulus intolerable. In any case, he wanted to travel. His youthful imagination had been excited by the writings of Colonel Wilford on Bamian[11]—they were, he says, enshrined in his memory—and as it is certain that he had already studied with some thoroughness the routes of Alexander the Great on his Persian and Indian campaigns he may have had at the back of his mind a desire to explore Afghanistan in particular.[12] These interests may even have led to his enlistment in the first place. He certainly took great pains in due course to try to identify Alexander's routes and battlefields, and he became absorbed in the antiquarian problems posed by the 'marvels of Bamian'.

In his introduction to the 1974 reprint of the Narrative of Various Journeys,[13] Gavin Hambly suggested that Masson was probably a social outcast for whom enlistment under an assumed name was an escape from crime, debt or family misfortune. He wondered whether Masson actually did travel overland to India as he claimed, and even whether the name James Lewis was not also an alias. Although some private soldiers found it expedient for a variety of reasons to enlist under an assumed name, Masson only changed his name *after* deserting. There is no evidence to suggest that he in any way approximated to Kipling's

> Gentlemen rankers out on the spree,
> Damned from here to Eternity.

Even though the austerity of his life in Central Asia was originally forced upon him, he accepted it so readily and without any signs of regret that it is difficult to imagine that he had ever been prone to excess. He seems to have been indifferent to alcohol; indeed he became a connoisseur of water, often noting its varying qualities in different places. He appears to have had little or no interest in sex and certainly did not indulge in any liaisons.

Whereas Masson's motives for enlisting and deserting can only be guessed at, that he came by sea to India is well-attested. The Embarkation Lists prove the point, as does a letter from his ship-mate, Charles Brown, who later called himself Brownlow and whose name appears on the same List. This letter dated Calcutta, 11 August 1835, addressed him as 'My dear Lewis', and referred to the 'many hours which you lightened of their misery by your society when we were fellow-travellers on board the "Duchess of Atholl"'. The writer went on to say that he was aware of recent documents which had passed through the hands of the Bengal Government (i.e. Masson's pardon), and rejoiced that this news had restored his friend to the land of the living, a report having circulated that he had committed suicide soon after quitting the service of the East India Company. Brownlow gave news of former army friends now living in Calcutta, including George Jephson (formerly Morton) who wished to be remembered to him, and ended by congratulating him on his 'restoration to Society'. The envelope containing Brownlow's letter has also been preserved: it is addressed to Charles Masson, Esq., c/o Captain Wade at Ludhiana and so neatly links his real and assumed names.[14] As for the conjecture that James Lewis was also an assumed name, his baptismal certificate and other family papers rule that out.

Brownlow had bought his discharge from the army in 1826 and had joined a firm in Calcutta. George Jephson had become head of the Office of the Adjutant-General. The three men henceforth corresponded

with some regularity. From the warm tone of their letters it is evident
that James Lewis had impressed them very favourably in the past.
These letters make it clear that both his correspondents were also educated and cultured men. They were to prove helpful in various ways
to Masson in the future.

The *Narrative of Various Journeys* is silent about the author's immediate past. He deliberately avoids all reference to it by skipping such
preliminaries as the starting point and purpose of his travels. He opens
his story without preamble:

> ... *in the autumn of 1826 having traversed the Rajput States of
> Shekhawati, and the kingdom of Bikanir, I entered the desert frontiers of
> the Khan of Bahawalpur; and passing successively the towns and castles
> of Pularah, Mihr Char, Jam Char, Marut, and Moz Ghar, arrived at the
> city of Bahawalpur.*

This date, 1826, is incorrect; it should be 1827. The Bengal Muster Rolls
must be regarded as authoritative on this point. In addition Masson
left a manuscript list of certain dates where in every case the year as
originally written has been corrected to a year later. For example, the
entry for Dera Ghazi Khan has been altered from December 1826 to
December 1827.[15] Corroborative evidence is provided by the date of
Captain Wade's letter of 15 October 1827 about Dr Harlan's departure
for Peshawar. The false date was originally intended to conceal the
real facts when Masson needed a cover story. But it was not corrected
in his published work in spite of the truth being known in British India; he may have assumed that it was unknown to the general public
in England. Be that as it may, the 1826 date has been perpetuated not
only in the opening sentence of the *Narrative of Various Journeys* but
also in its full title and has misled writers on Masson ever since. Retaining the false date meant that a whole year was unaccounted for
which together with the paucity of dates made it difficult to follow
the sequence of his journeys.

Masson's desertion from the army remained a crucial factor in his
life even after his Royal pardon in 1835. It provided the initial impetus
to put as much territory as possible between himself and British India
in order to minimise the risk of being detected. The pretence of
American citizenship and of having reached India overland had the
same object in view. Masson spent extended periods of time in the
company of British army officers and East India Company officials in
Persia, none of whom appear to have suspected that their companion
was a deserter from the ranks.[16] It is remarkable that he escaped

detection. Certainly he must have kept a very tight rein on his tongue if only to avoid letting slip a remark, so easily done, disclosing familiarity with British India—which he was not supposed to have visited—or with the Indian Army. At the same time he had to keep up his American *persona* and be careful not to reminisce about London and his boyhood there, or indeed about any actual personal experiences prior to 1827. Such enforced reticence became a habit which remained with him even after the need no longer existed, with the result that in his books he makes no mention at all of his family and early life in England. It is only among his unpublished papers that one finds evidence even of his ex-army friends. No wonder that he has been described as the most enigmatic of the European explorers of the northwestern borderlands of the Indian sub-continent.[17]

Years later when he severely criticised the policies and competence of the leading Political Officers, Sir William Macnaghten, Sir Claude Wade and Sir Alexander Burnes, especial resentment was aroused in certain circles by the knowledge that the author of these writings was a pardoned deserter. In general it was felt that he was brazen in presuming to criticise his betters.

CHAPTER II

THE POLITICAL BACKGROUND
TO MASSON'S JOURNEYS

The number of Oriental names which it is
necessary to introduce — the repetition of in-
cidents ... of conquest and re-conquest, of
treachery and counter-treachery, of rebellions
raised and suppressed — creates a confusion
in the mind of the European reader.

Sir W.J. Kaye
History of the War in Afghanistan

Before giving some account of Masson's journeys, especially those in Afghanistan, and of his antiquarian activities during his long residence in Kabul, it will be well to look at the broad political situation of the region in 1828, the year of his arrival in the country.

In the Punjab, the great Maharaja Ranjit Singh had brought the Sikh empire to the zenith of its power and the Sikh army to a pitch of efficiency little short of that of the British Indian army. He played so important a part in the next decade that it is worth quoting three contemporary impressions of that outstanding figure. Masson, who saw him in 1829, writes:

... in person the Maharaja is a little below the middle size, and very meagre. His complexion is fair, and his features regular, with an aquiline nose. He carries a long white beard, and wants the left eye. Though apparently far advanced in years, I believe he has not completed fifty. On the right side of his neck a large scar is visible, probably the effect of a wound. In his diet he is represented to be abstemious, but has always been perniciously prone to copious cups of the strongest spirits which, with his unbounded sensuality, has brought on him premature old age, with a serious burthen of infirmities: for some ailment, he makes daily use of laudanum. Simple in his dress, which is white linen, he wears on his arm the celebrated diamond Koh-I-Nur, of which he deprived Shah Sujah al Mulkh, who had promised it to him, but first

Plate 1(right). Maharaja Ranjit Singh.

attempted to dupe him, and then to withhold it altogether... To sum up his character as a public man, he is a prince of consummate ability, a warrior brave and skilful, and a good but crafty statesman. In his private or individual capacity, he has many shining qualities; but they are obscured by many failings and by habits so grossly sensual that they can scarcely be excused by the knowledge that they may be attributed to the barbarous period at which he was born, or by the fact that in such respect he is not worse than many of his compatriots.[18]

(In passing it may be remarked that Masson's account of the rape of the Koh-I-Noor is more favourable to Ranjit than most which depict him as having extorted it from Shah Shuja when he was a fugitive and at his mercy.)

Lord Auckland's nephew and military secretary, Captain William Osborne, describes the Maharaja as he found him in 1838:

Ill-looking as he undoubtedly is, the countenance of Runjeet Singh cannot fail to strike everyone as that of a very extraordinary man; and though at first his appearance gives rise to a disagreeable feeling almost amounting to disgust, a second look shows so much intelligence, and the restless wandering of his single fiery eye excites so much interest, that you get accustomed to his plainness, and are forced to confess that there is no common degree of intellect and acuteness developed in his countenance, however odd and repulsive its first appearance may be.

His height is rather below the usual stature of the Sikhs, and an habitual stoop causes him to look shorter than he really is. He is by no means firm on his legs when he attempts to walk, but all weakness disappears when he is once on horseback. He has still a slight hesitation of speech, the consequence of a paralytic stroke about three years ago; but those about him assert that his health is much improved within the last twelve month. His long white beard and moustachoes give him a more venerable appearance than his actual age would lead you to expect; and at fifty-eight years of age he is still a hale and hearty old man, though an imaginary invalid...

It is hardly possible to give an idea of the ceaseless rapidity with which his questions flow, or the infinite variety of subjects they embrace...[19]

Emily Eden, Lord Auckland's sister, neatly sums him up: 'He is exactly like an old mouse, with grey whiskers and one eye.'[20]

Lying between British India and the Afghan territories, the Sikh kingdom under Ranjit Singh was for thirty years in strong and friendly hands. It became one of the few really successful buffer states in history,[21] not least because Ranjit Singh knew and accepted, even if with some reluctance, the limits placed by the British on his territorial ambitions. Till his death in 1839 the maintenance of good relations with the Maharaja remained a fixed principle of British policy.

Sind, though still a nominal dependency of the Afghan rulers who continued to claim tribute but rarely received it and then only after military pressure, had been virtually independent for more than 20 years. It was divided among the various branches of the Talpura clan into a number of petty independent states each headed by one of the Amirs of Sind who had proved 'too indolent to strive for supremacy and too foolish to unite'.[22] In their anxiety to be left alone the Amirs were extremely wary of European travellers and above all loath to allow exploration of the Indus river and valley by the British, fearing, rightly as it turned out, that familiarity with their country would lead by degrees to substantial encroachment by their powerful neighbour British India.

In Afghanistan, Dost Mahomed Khan had achieved supremacy in the city and province of Kabul as recently as 1826 after a bitter struggle with his numerous half-brothers. He was slowly beginning to bring order in his limited domains out of the chaos which had subsisted for nearly a decade as a result of the break-up of the Durrani Empire, and it was not till 1834 that he felt strong enough to assume the title of Amir.

The Durrani Empire had been created by Ahmad Shah Abdali, chief of the Sadozai clan of the Abdali tribe. He was originally the commander of the Afghan mercenaries who formed the bodyguard of Nadir Shah of Persia, but after the latter's murder by his Persian troops in 1747, Ahmad Shah took advantage of the confusion that followed to seize the royal treasure. The spoils included the Koh-i-Noor diamond which had been looted from the Mughul Emperor when Nadir Shah sacked Delhi in 1739. Ahmad Shah and his men fought their way out of the camp and hastened to Kandahar where, thanks to his forceful personality and to his newly acquired wealth, he was elected the first King of the Afghans. To mark his elevation he took the resounding name of Dur-i-Durran or 'Pearl of Pearls' whereupon the Abdali tribe became known as the Durrani. Besides being a good administrator, he took care to seek the advice and consent of his Council of chiefs. Unfortunately neither of these traits was to be inherited by his sons or grandsons. But above all he was a fine soldier who fully appreciated that the only way to achieve a degree of unity among the diverse races, languages and religions of his turbulent people was to lead them in wars against their neighbours. Ahmad Shah Durrani was fortunate in his hour inasmuch as the Mughul Empire had been much weakened by Nadir Shah's campaigns and by internal commotions, while on his western frontier the death of the Persian autocrat was immediately followed by prolonged anarchy throughout Persia. Ahmad Shah soon captured Kabul and thus finally broke Mughul rule in Eastern Afghanistan which had lasted since the time of the Emperor Babur, with the exception of a brief interlude under Nadir Shah. He likewise destroyed Persian control of North-Western Afghanistan by the capture of Herat. By extending his conquests north-eastwards to encompass the Cis-Oxus territories as far as Badakshan he gave Afghanistan approximately her present boundaries in the west and north. For the first time Afghanistan became a separate entity, ruled by one of her own people.

Turning his attention to India, in the course of three campaigns he captured Lahore in 1751-52 and was only deflected from advancing on Delhi by the action of the Emperor of Delhi in marrying his daughter to Ahmad Shah's son Timur, with the Punjab as dowry. His fourth invasion resulted in the sack of Delhi in 1757, while his fifth was marked by the catastrophic defeat of the Marathas at Panipat in 1761. The Mughul Empire was by then no longer an effective power. Ahmad Shah proved, however, unable to consolidate his gains. His Afghan tribesmen were too individualistic, too unsophisticated and ignorant: they knew how to conquer but not how to rule. Nevertheless, when he died in 1773, the vast Durrani Empire extended over present-day Afghanistan and Pakistan (including Baluchistan to the sea), Kashmir, as well as parts of India, Iran and Soviet Turkestan. But even he had had to relinquish some of his conquests, notably central Punjab to the Sikhs whilst retaining Peshawar and the northern Punjab.

During the reign of his son, Timur Shah, the Sikhs started to nibble at the Afghan possessions in the Punjab, while Sind succeeded in becoming practically independent, as we have seen. Timur Shah moved his capital from Kandahar to Kabul, a more central location both politically and strategically, and at his death in 1793 the Empire was still of considerable extent. He left twenty-three sons, but failed to nominate an heir, and the next twenty-five years were filled with the frantic jealousies and feuds of rival claimants to the throne, until the Durrani Empire finally collapsed. The in-fighting between the Sadozai princes was further complicated by the growing influence of the powerful Barakzai (or Muhommadzai) clan of the Durrani tribe, headed by Payindah Khan.*

Zaman Shah (1793-1800), the fifth son of Timur Shah, was fortunate enough to be in Kabul when his father died and with the backing of Payindah Khan succeeded to the throne. Payindah Khan was rewarded by being made vizier or chief minister. But soon the new King was attacked by one disappointed brother from Kandahar and later by another, Shah Mahmud, from Herat. Having dealt with both, he conducted desultory campaigns in the Punjab but never advanced beyond Lahore. Ineffective though they were, they raised the spectre of the devastating raids of Ahmad Shah's formidable Afghan horsemen forty years before and caused the authorities in British India to realise how ignorant they were of affairs in Afghanistan. In 1799, Zaman Shah confirmed Ranjit Singh in his tutelary possession of Lahore. This move did no more than legitimise a *fait accompli*, but it enhanced the prestige of Ranjit Singh who was then only nineteen and at the beginning of his spectacular career. He finally threw off Afghan suzerainty soon after. Zaman Shah was unwise enough to dismiss Payindah Khan and in 1799 had him executed at Kandahar. The victim left twenty-two sons, the eldest of whom, Fath Khan, escaped to Persia where he incited Shah Mahmud who had fled there from Herat, to rise once more against Zaman Shah. In 1800 the latter was deposed in favour of Shah Mahmud, blinded and exiled. Fath Khan's first essay in king-making resulted in his appointment as vizier.

Shah Mahmud, (1800-1803 and 1809-1818) reigned for a mere three years before he was ousted by yet another brother, Shah Shuja-ul-Mulk (1803-1809 and 1839-1842). It was to Shah Shuja that the well-known mission of Mountstuart Elphinstone was sent in 1809 by Lord Minto, the Governor-General, with a view to securing his goodwill against a possible invasion of India by Napoleon. But the King's authority was already threatened by Shah Mahmud who was approaching Kabul with an army. The lavish mission was therefore received at Peshawar, the winter capital. A treaty was signed but lapsed within weeks with the downfall of the King. In any case Afghan monarchs were not interested in the designs of the far-off French. Much the best and most lasting result of the mission was Elphinstone's *Account of the Kingdom of Caubul*, the first thorough study of that remote realm. It has been described as 'the greatest and most readable volume we possess on

---

* Also known by his title of Sirafraz Khan: he is thus named by Masson.

the Afghan country and the Afghan people. It is of an amazing accuracy still today.'[23]

Equally, it is regarded by Afghans as the most sympathetic of all European writings about their country, according to my Afghan friends. All this despite the fact that Peshawar, then the richest portion of the Kingdom, was only the winter resort and the British Envoy and his suite had no opportunity of traversing the Khyber Pass and penetrating into the heartland of Afghanistan. The Mission was on its way back to India and on the point of leaving Durrani territory when the news came that Fath Khan had helped Shah Mahmud to defeat Shah Shuja at Nimla and so regain the throne.

After various attempts to recoup his fortunes, Shah Shuja was obliged to go into exile at Ludhiana where he joined his brother, the blind Zaman Shah. Both former monarchs were given pensions by the British. Shah Shuja's very existence was to have a divisive effect on his faction-torn country. His intrigues and moves to regain his throne rumbled on for years before and during Masson's time until he was restored to the throne in 1839 by British forces in the First Afghan War.

Despite the obligations of Shah Mahmud to Fath Khan who had twice put him on the throne, but whose loyalty had become suspect, he and his son Prince Kamran had the Barakzai vizier blinded and subsequently murdered in 1818. His many brothers immediately took up arms against the Sadozai who were forced to take refuge in Herat. In this fashion the Sadozai dynasty came to an inglorious end that year. Masson, describing this momentous event, writes that the affairs of Afghanistan had become very complicated, and the utmost energy would have been required to sustain it under the pressure of attacks from the Persians on the one side, and the Sikhs on the other. The seizure of Fath Khan was the 'prelude to the enactment, in rapid succession, of as many strange events, and of as many enormous crimes and perfidies as can be found in the annals of any country'.[24]

Henceforth, in spite of strenuous efforts by Prince Kamran, he and Shah Mahmud with other members of the Sadozai clan were to be confined to the Herat district. The murdered Fath Khan's brothers divided the rest of the country between them, four taking over the Peshawar valley and five, Kandahar, while Dost Mahomed Khan held Ghazni, then gradually extended his control to Kabul. Thus it was that the kingdom disintegrated, torn to pieces first by the struggles for power among the Sadozai and then by the blood-feud which developed between them and the Barakzai brothers. The Barakzai in turn fought for primacy among themselves. Inevitably, once the central control had been removed, the outlying parts of the Durrani Empire also collapsed under irresistible external pressure. In 1828, what is now Afghanistan was still in a state of anarchy and split into three main principalities with ever-shifting boundaries. Furthermore Balkh had been seized by the Amir of Bokhara, while Kunduz under its Uzbek chief, together with other smaller territories in Afghan Turkestan, maintained a precarious independence.

Exceedingly convoluted though the situation in Afghanistan had become as a result of the events related above, it needs to be understood since the personalities concerned figured so largely in Masson's story and played important roles in the developments leading up to the First Anglo-Afghan war.

Four Afghan cities were of crucial importance: Peshawar, Kabul, Kandahar, and Herat. Peshawar was held by four Barakzai brothers all born of the same mother: Sultan Mahomed Khan, Saiyad Mahomed Khan, Pir Mahomed Khan and Yar Mahomed Khan. The Vale of Peshawar was and is inhabited by Sunni Pathans (Pushtuns), i.e. of the same faith and race as the majority of Afghans. The city itself had long been the winter capital and was regarded as quintessentially Afghan. By the Treaty of Amritsar in 1809, the British had given Ranjit Singh a pretty free hand in lands up to and beyond the Indus, other than Sind. He took advantage of the break-up of the Durrani Empire to control Peshawar from a distance after 1819 by allowing the Barakzai sirdars to remain there in return for an annual tribute and the dispatch of one or more of their sons as hostages at his court in Lahore. In effect therefore the Barakzai brothers held Peshawar entirely at the pleasure of the Maharaja. This arrangement lasted until Shah Shuja was about to launch his campaign of 1833-34 to regain his throne. His pressing need for Sikh support and for permission to march through their territory, forced him to conclude a treaty which formally ceded substantial Afghan territory, including Peshawar, to Ranjit Singh, if he could dispossess the Barakzai sirdars. So, on 6 May 1834, while Shah Shuja and his army were struggling through the Bolan Pass en route to Kandahar, Ranjit Singh foreclosed on his bargain, sent an army under Hari Singh to seize Peshawar and drive out the sirdars. Masson was there at the time and gives a vivid eye-witness account (see Chapter IX). With a small force the Sikh general had thus possessed himself of a region which, some years before, Ranjit Singh in person, with twenty-five thousand men, had not ventured to retain. As Masson remarks: 'True it is, that since that period the spirit of the Mahomedans had become dejected by repeated defeats, and that there was, as there universally is, treachery in the Durrani camp and councils.'[25]

The principal object of clan treachery, Dost Mahomed Khan, was in no position to go to the aid of Peshawar as he was busy defeating Shah Shuja at Kandahar (2 July 1834). The loss of Peshawar infuriated Dost Mahomed, but an attempt to retake it the following year petered out when Sultan Mahomed Khan and his brothers went so far as to accept lands in the vicinity of the city from the hands of Ranjit Singh. Henceforth, the Amir of Kabul and the Maharaja were implacable enemies, while relations between the Amir and his half brothers, the Peshawar sirdars, became more strained than ever. The loss of Peshawar and the refusal of the British Governor-General to disturb his good relations with the Maharaja by bringing pressure to bear on him, to restore the city to the Afghans, were the main causes of Dost Mahomed Khan's eventual disillusion with the British, his flirtation with the Russians and the failure of Alexander Burnes's mission in 1838. These were all factors which led to the First Anglo-Afghan War. It should be said that the Afghans have never become reconciled to the loss of their beloved Peshawar and its adjacent districts which later became part of the Northwest Frontier Province. As *terra irridenta* that province is the corner-stone of successive Afghan Governments' agitation for an autonomous Pushtunistan which has so bedevilled Afghan-Pakistan relations since Independence to the present day. A striking instance of the Afghan obsession occurred when King Zahir Shah paid a semi-official visit to Pakistan in 1967 (which was intended to be a bridge-building exercise) and flatly refused to include Peshawar in his itinerary.

The Kandahar sirdars were Fur (or Poor) Dil Khan, Kohim Dil Khan, Rahim Dil Khan and Meher Dil Khan; the eldest, Shir Dil Khan, had died in 1826. They were all full brothers, but only half-brothers of the Peshawar sirdars and of Dost Mohomed Khan. Masson points out 'how curiously they were separated into groups, affected by their maternal descent. A history of the Barak Zai family would illustrate the advantages and disadvantages of polygamy.'[26] The brothers quarrelled among themselves and when Masson visited Kandahar he found that two separate Durbars were held each week, one by Fur Dil Khan and the other by Kohim Dil Khan.[27]

The Kandahar sirdars were as ill-disposed towards Dost Mohamed as were the Peshawar sirdars. especially after he took Kabul. Both groups sometimes combined to put pressure on him, by force of arms if necessary. Occasionally they came to each other's aid in the face of Persian and Sikh threats. For centuries Kandahar had oscillated between Persian rule and domination by the Mughul Emperors. In 1738, Nadir Shah of Persia captured and destroyed the fort and city* and laid out a new city on a new site. But with the accession of Ahmed Shah Durrani in 1747 it became the capital of his Empire. The Persians, however, had never given up their claim to Kandahar and Herat and their efforts to regain these territories further disturbed the Afghan scene during Masson's time.

Herat, as has been said, was now the last stronghold of the Sadozai clan who were not only enemies of the Barakzai but even hostile to their own kinsman Shah Shuja. Shah Mahmud died in 1829 and was succeeded by Kamran, a stronger character until enfeebled by debauchery and the opponent most feared by Dost Mahomed Khan. Herat was the key to Afghanistan: it was soon to become a thorn in the flesh of Governors-General of India and of British Cabinets in London, the cause of conflicts and alarms for years to come.

---

* They were excavated by the British Institute of Afghan Studies, 1974-78.

CHAPTER III

THE GREAT GAME IN ASIA

When everyone is dead the Great
Game is finished, not before.
Kipling
Kim

Anarchy in Afghanistan, unrest in Persia and endemic misrule in the Khanates of Transoxiana, were of dubious value to the security of British India. A foreign power might well take advantage of such conditions to create trouble in India. There had been a brief flurry of concern when Napoleon was in Egypt and turned his eyes towards the East, and again when the Treaty of Tilsit in 1807 made Russia an ally of France. But from 1829 onwards, the security of British India became a matter of serious debate in London and Calcutta. Alarm as to Russia's intentions in Central Asia and beyond was sparked off in that year by the Treaty of Adrianople which followed the defeat of Turkey by Russia. The Duke of Wellington regarded it 'as the death blow to the independence of the Ottoman Porte and the forerunner of the dissolution and extinction of its power'. Earlier Russian successes against Persia which had led first to the loss of Georgia, then to the exclusion of Persian vessels from the Caspian, and finally to the humiliating peace of Turkmanchai in 1828, had already caused uneasiness in London. It began to look as if both Turkey and Persia would before long either become Russian protectorates or would suffer dismemberment with large portions being absorbed by Russia. This unwelcome development came closer as regards Turkey with the Treaty of Unkjar Skelessi (1833) and seemed to pose a sharper threat to British India. The support of the Turkish Empire against Russian encroachment now became, and remained during the rest of the century, a major British interest. It is in the interaction of British policy towards Russia in the Near and Middle East that the explanation of much that happened in the two Afghan wars is to be found. If, argued Palmerston, Russia could alarm the British in India by moves in Persia, why should not the British in India alarm the Russians by moves in Afghanistan? Similarly the Russians could bring pressure to bear on the British in Europe by making their flesh creep in India. Both sides, the one through the possession of interior land lines, and the other through sea-power, were able to threaten the other in either direction. Events in one theatre cannot therefore be understood without reference to events in the other; the Afghan wars were essentially a part of the Eastern Question.[28]

A direct invasion of British India by Russia in the 1820s was not the most serious threat, but rather Russian expansion in Turkey, Persia and Central Asia. Wellington told Lord Aberdeen that the Russians:

> ... *having the desire ... to mix themselves up as principals in every concern, and having a real interest in none, I am not quite certain that they are not the most inconvenient for us to deal with in friendly terms of any power in Europe.*[29]

Lord Ellenborough, President of the Board of Control of the East India Company in 1828, wrote 'that Russia will attempt, by conquest or by influence, to secure Persia as a road to the Indus, I have the most intimate conviction. It is evident that the latter and surer mode, that of influence, is the one she now selects.'[30] Officials in British India, with some notable exceptions, did not believe that there was a real danger of a direct Russian invasion. They were far more concerned lest the spread of Russian influence in Persia and Afghanistan should cause unrest in India, particularly among her Moslem inhabitants, but also among the Princes.[31] Increased military expenditure to meet the internal threat might be disastrous to the finances of British India. In other words, the British began to play the Great Game in Asia in 1829, less to prevent the invasion of India than to prevent bankruptcy and rebellion.[32]

This distinction between actual invasion and the long-range effects of growing Russian influence, political and commercial, was not always drawn by those concerned. The soldiers tended to think in terms of military campaigns which would bring the Russians by stages either across the Khanates of Central Asia to the Oxus, the Hindu Kush and Kabul, and finally to the Indus, or through Persia, Herat and Baluchistan. The civilians, especially the Evangelicals and Utilitarians, were firm believers in the civilising value of commerce. According to Cobden 'Commerce is the grand panacea... Not a bale of merchandise leaves our shores but it bears the seeds of intelligence and fruitful thought to the members of some less enlightened community...'[33] British—and Indian—manufactured goods were therefore to be pushed as hard as possible in all directions, even to Central Asia where they might succeed in ousting the Russian competition, bringing enlightment to Bokhara and Khiva, and perhaps enlisting their help in stemming the Russian advance.

Both views were somewhat naive. From a military standpoint, Russia in the 1820s was still some 1800 miles from the Indus. Of graver import, the route lay across vast deserts, long stretches of semi-arid tracts and over formidable mountains, with extremes of temperatures throughout. It would have been impossible for an army of the requisite size to live off the land since surplus foodstuffs were rarely available. Immense supply trains would therefore be essential. Moreover lack of water for men and animals was an ever-present hazard. In Afghanistan proper, to move artillery by any route was a tremendous task. These conditions were either unknown or scarcely appreciated in London and only guessed at in Calcutta and even in Teheran. Hence it was possible for Sir John Macdonald, the British Envoy to Persia to write in 1829 to Sir Robert Gordon, his colleague in Constantinople, that the Russians would easily conquer Transcaspia, and that as soon as they had captured Bokhara 'the way is short and easy from the Oxus to the Indus. The Russians would be astonished at the facility of their conquests.'[34]

As for the Benthamites' faith in commerce, they had given little thought to the question of how the recipient States were to pay for the imports from Britain and India: in reality they had few commodities to offer in exchange and moreover were extremely poor, as Afghanistan still is to this day. Ellenborough, however, saw the point and confided to his diary that 'what the Bokharians are to send us in return I do not well see, except turquoises, lapis lazuli, and the ducats they receive from Russia'.[35] Lord Heytesbury, the British Ambassador at St. Petersburg, tried to inject a note of realism into the debate. In a despatch to Lord Aberdeen of 18 January 1830, he wrote:

> There cannot be the slightest doubt that the attention of the Russians has of late been very much directed towards India, and that the establishment of commercial relations at least, with the several intervening States between the Caspian and the Indus, has been for many years a primary object.

After giving some examples of Russian interest in visitors from those countries he said:

> But whatever wild thoughts may be germinating in the heads of the Russians generally, the Emperor and his Government have, I am convinced, too thorough a consciousness of the real weakness of the country to entertain for an instant serious thought of ever embarking in so

gigantic an enterprise as the marching of an Army to India ...

He went on to suggest that there was nevertheless cause to fear the disruptive influence of Russian agents, who 'invariably outstrip the orders of their Government'. To counter them it would be expedient to place British agents in Kabul and Bokhara.[36]

However, aroused by the fears caused by the Russian successes in Persia and Turkey, and further stimulated by public debate about Russian designs on British India, Ellenborough began to realise that detailed knowledge of Central Asia and of Afghanistan was sadly lacking. Maps too were quite deficient. 'What we ought to have is *Information.* The first, the second and the third thing a government ought always to have is *Information,*' he wrote to Sir John Malcolm, the Governor of Bombay.[37] Accordingly, after a seminal conversation with the Duke of Wellington on 16 December 1829, he set about obtaining reliable military, political, commercial and geographical intelligence on the countries between the Caspian and the Indus. Specifically he was keen to have the Indus surveyed, believing that by employing steamships it could become a great highway for the transport of British goods to the frontiers of Afghanistan and thence to the countries north of the Oxus where commerce was to perform its beneficent role.

On 12 January 1830, Ellenborough's views were transmitted by the Secret Committee of the Directors of the East India Company to the Governor-General:

> We can neither feel justified in reposing upon the good faith and moderation of Russia, nor in permitting the apprehensions her policy and her power are calculated to excite to be altogether done away by reflection upon the difficulties she would have to encounter in the attempt to approach the Indus... We dread therefore, not so much actual invasion by Russia, as the moral effect which would be produced amongst our own subjects and among the Princes with whom we are allied, by the continued apprehension of that event. We look with dismay on the financial embarrassment in which we should be involved by the necessity of constant military preparations, not only to meet a European army in the field but to preserve tranquility in our provinces and in our tributary states. If such should be the consequence of any approximation of the Russians to the north of India, it is our interest to take measures for the prevention of any movement on their part beyond their present limits. But the efficiency of such measures must depend upon their being taken promptly, and you cannot take them promptly unless you are kept constantly informed of everything which passes on the Russian frontier in Asia, in Khiva, and in Bokhara...[38]

The same despatch announced the gift of English carthorses to Ranjit Singh. They were to be shipped from England to Bombay, thence up the Indus in a suitable vessel to Lahore accompanied by an 'able and discreet officer'. Lieutenant Alexander Burnes, who was then assistant to the British Resident in Cutch, Colonel Henry Pottinger, was selected by Malcolm for the task of implementing Ellenborough's commercial policy and satisfying his need of intelligence. This he accomplished with credit after considerable initial difficulties with the Amirs of Sind who were quick to perceive that the expedition to Lahore was simply an excuse to survey the Indus and to spy out the land in general.

Shortly after his return to British India, Burnes offered to travel to Bokhara, unaware of London's new interest in Turkestan, and his offer was immediately accepted. Early in 1832 he started on the travels which made him famous. So began the first officially sponsored British journey into Central Asia and the first practical manifestation of the Great Game.

The Russian reaction may be seen in the reference by the Russian Foreign Minister in a despatch to the Russian Ambassador in London to the:

> ... indefatigable activity displayed by English travellers to spread disquiet among the people of Central Asia, and to carry agitation even into the heart of the countries bordering on our frontier whilst on our part we ask nothing but to be admitted to partake in fair competition the commercial advantages of Asia. English industry, exclusive and jealous, would deprive us entirely of the benefits which it pretends to reap alone; and would cause, if it could, the produce of our manufactories to disappear from all the markets of Central Asia: Witness the remarks of Burnes, and the tendency of English travellers who have followed his steps on the road to Bukhara and to the very gates of Orenberg.[39]

CHAPTER IV

EARLY 19TH CENTURY TRAVELLERS IN CENTRAL ASIA

*And see the land, what it is, and the people that
dwelleth therein ... and what cities they be that
they dwell in, whether in tents, or in strong holds...*

Numbers 13: 18-19

During the 1820s, Central Asia north of the Oxus had begun to be penetrated by a few European travellers, while others had traversed Persia and Afghanistan en route to India. An early traveller among the Khanates of Transoxiana was the Russian, Count Muraviev, who reached Khiva in 1819. He later wrote that the possession of that city could give Russia command of the riches of Asia. 'It would become the point of reunion for all the commerce of Asia, and would shake to the centre of India the enormous commercial superiority of the dominators of the sea.'[40] A Russian diplomatist, Baron Meyendorff, who had accompanied a mission to Bokhara in 1820, claimed for Russia the right to develop and civilize the states of Turkestan.[41]

William Moorcroft, a veterinary surgeon in the East India Company service, had a limited brief in 1811 to study stockbreeding methods in untrodden Himalayan and Tibetan regions. But his ardent desire was to visit Turkestan in order to buy some of the renowned breed of horses to be found there which it was his great ambition to domesticate in India for the benefit of the Army. His last journey in 1819-25 undertaken without official backing took him therefore eventually to Bokhara and the steppes of Transoxiana. It earned him the distinction of being the first Englishman since the 16th century to get so far.

According to a manuscript note of Masson's written in 1833, a surprising number of Europeans had visited Kabul in recent years including a Frenchman; a Dutchman; John, an English artilleryman; Moorcroft; Alexander Burnes and his companion Dr J.G. Gerard; the wildly eccentric Reverend Joseph Wolff; and Dr Martin Honigberger, the personal physician of Ranjit Singh.[42] Of this group the last-named four succeeded in reaching Bokhara as of course had Moorcroft. Also on Masson's list were the Neapolitan officer Avitabile and the French officer Court, on their way in 1826 to join Ranjit Singh's forces in which they both later rose to the rank of General. Dr Harlan is mentioned as having stayed for a year with the Nawab Jabar Khan in 1828. In 1822, too early for Masson's list, two other officers who subsequently became Generals in the Sikh army, Ventura and Allard, had travelled from Persia to Lahore via Kandahar and Kabul. In the course of time Masson met nearly all the men he named.

One of the first British travellers to take the overland route from England to India through Russia and Persia was Lieutenant Arthur Conolly of the Bengal Cavalry. Setting out in 1829 he tried to reach Khiva from Asterabad, but was forced to turn back half-way. Consequently he travelled via Meshed and Herat, bypassing Kandahar because of the notorious rapacity of the sirdars, and thence over the Bolan Pass to Shikarpur.[43] His travels and his stay at Herat had two results. He became convinced that the likeliest Russian invasion route would be through Persia and Herat, thereby turning the flank of the Hindu Kush, rather than via Khiva and up the Oxus to the high passes of that formidable range. On his return to India he assisted Charles Trevelyan in writing reports on Central Asian politics and trade which influenced the development of British policy there. Secondly, he was appalled by what he had seen of the traffic in slaves, mostly Persians but also Russians, in Turkestan. A deeply religious man, he tried hard during the Anglo-Afghan war to persuade the Governor-General to mount a virtual crusade to free the slaves in Transoxiana and at the same time remove a Russian motive for intervention. Conolly was reluctantly allowed to try his hand with the Uzbek Khans. He went to Khiva, Kokand and Bokhara where he was imprisoned and eventually executed. Although Masson and Conolly were both in Persia in 1830 they did not meet until 1840. Masson did not warm to the other man.

William Moorcroft and his companion George Trebeck perished in 1825 in Afghan Turkestan, another area famous for its horses. News of their fate was widely reported and long remembered. Alexander Burnes makes numerous references to them and visited Moorcroft's grave at Balkh and Trebeck's at Mazar-i-Sharif, the first and only traveller to do so. Masson records seeing their names written on the wall of a cave at Bamian. In 1838, Dr Lord and Lieutenant Wood, temporarily detached from Burnes's mission, also visited Mazar-i-Sharif and recovered most of Moorcroft's books. Moorcroft's difficulties and miserable end did at least teach his successors a sharp lesson. He had travelled with a large sum of money to buy horses, as well as valuable merchandise to support his role of merchant. This inevitably gave rise to exorbitant demands for transit dues wherever he went and eventually aroused the cupidity of the infamous slave-dealing Murad Beg of Kunduz who treated him abominably. Burnes consequently took great care to travel as inconspicuously as possible. Indeed, soon after leaving Lahore, he and his party gave away their tents, beds and boxes and broke their tables and chairs. He relied mainly on letters of credit, while his ready cash was either sewn into his clothes or distributed among his companions and servants. In pursuance of some admirable written advice from General Court, the party discarded all their European clothes and adopted Afghan costume, including 'ponderous turbans'.

In the Preface to his *Travels into Bokhara* Burnes draws particular attention to his chosen mode of travel:

> *I determined to retain the character of a European, accommodating myself in dress, habits, and customs, to those with whom I should mingle. The sequel has proved that the design had much to recommend it, though the character involved us in some difficulties. I adopted the resolution, however, in an utter hopelessness of supporting the disguise of a native: and from having observed that no European traveller has ever journeyed in such countries without suspicion and seldom without discover... I did not, then, hesitate to appear among them*

Plate 2. *In the Hazarajat, Central Afghanistan.*

*in their own garb, and avow myself a foreigner. By all the accounts
which I collected, it did not appear to me that there was any just cause
for apprehending personal injury or danger; but I received little con-
solation from my friends in India, who referred to the fate of our predecessors, poor Moorcroft and his party, as our inevitable lot.*[44]

Burnes and Gerard did sometimes declare themselves Armenians, while
the master of the caravan once or twice gave out that they were Hindus.
Masson had no need to take any special precautions during his early
travels either as regards money or costume since he was virtually des-
titute. As he remarks when first setting out from Peshawar to Kabul
by the unfrequented, because dangerous, Khyber Pass:

[Sadadin] *very much wished me to accept assistance, both in money
and garments, but I excused myself, as I had experienced I could do
without the first, and as to the last, I had purposely abandoned what I
had, to save the Khaibaris the trouble of taking them.*[45]

He was soon proved right. As a rule he wore the clothes of the country
and was in fact urged by Afghan friends to do so, not as a disguise,
but in order to be inconspicuous.

He never tried to pass as a Moslem—always a dubious ploy, sometimes a highly dangerous one, as in the case of Lieutenant Eldred
Pottinger. In 1837 this officer traversed the rugged central route
through the Hazarajat from Kabul to Herat (where he was to distinguish himself during the siege). Already somewhat unconvincingly
disguised as a horse-dealer, he had more or less familiarised himself
with Sunni gestures at prayer, but was caught out when in the company of some Shias and narrowly escaped being murdered. Dr
Honigberger had the opposite experience. A seasoned traveller who
spoke fluent Arabic, he was accustomed to Shia practices, but when
he reached Sind by sea he was obliged, in order to avoid detection at
prayers of the Sunni rite, to hint that both he and his servant were
suffering from a loathsome complaint which rendered them unfit to
associate with pure and orthodox Moslems.[46] The Reverend Joseph
Wolff coming from Bokhara had successfully slipped past Murad Beg,
unlike Moorcroft, but at Doab at the foot of the Hindu Kush he gave
his name as Haji Yousuf to a group of Hazaras and their mullas. For
passing himself off in this way as a Moslem who had made the pilgrimage to Mecca, he was at first threatened with death, but then allowed to purge his sin by surrendering all his possessions and every
stitch of clothing.

When Arthur Conolly sought to disguise himself as a merchant, equipped with trade goods and spices, for his attempt to reach Khiva, he was robbed of most of his stock and money and only escaped death by the efforts of his quick-witted and persuasive, though peppery, companion Saiyad Keramat Ali, of whom more will be said. Conolly thereafter travelled as a poor man and a Christian, disputing with mullas as he went. His religious prejudices, common to evangelicals of the time, are evident from his references to the 'arch-imposter' Mahomet, and to the 'gross and idolatrous' superstitions he found among the Russian Orthodox in Moscow. Joseph Wolff deliberately sought out mullas in order to preach the Gospel and dispute the teachings of the Koran. The amazing thing is that neither man suffered as a result— that they both fell among thieves was another matter. Indeed Wolff, following Conolly's route in part a year or two later, met mullas who remembered him with affection. It is impossible to imagine a similar immunity in today's Islamic Republic of Iran. Masson found that it was a positive advantage on occasion to declare himself a *Feringhi* (European) and a Christian:

> *Such is the reputation of the Pathans inhabiting these countries* [Marwat and Bannu], *that faquirs and mendicants are deterred from entering them. Placing my trust in Divine Providence, I resolved to commit myself amongst them... I found a company of individuals, seated in a small hut, or shed. One of them conversed with me and questioned me as to my country and religion. On being answered, an European and Christian, he informed his companions that Hazrat Isa, or our Saviour, was an assil or genuine Pathan. This agreeable communication ensured for me a hearty reception, and excited a little curiosity, to gratify which a fire was kindled that my features might be the better observed. The best entertainment the village afforded was produced, and in such quantities that I was compelled to cry quarter. The assertor of our Saviour's Pathan lineage, who proved to be a Saiyad, made himself particularly busy, and provided me with a snug place to sleep in, and plenty of warm clothing.*

Of another occasion Masson writes:

> *... in my progress to this place* [Kundi] *I encountered a man, who drew his sword, and was about to sacrifice me as an infidel Sikh. I had barely the time to apprise him that I was a Feringhi, when he instantly sheathed his weapon and, placing his arm around my waist in a friendly mode, conducted me to a village near at hand, where I was hospitably entertained.*[47]

He was often taken for a Moghul in Sind, there being a tradition in that country that some Moghuls were as fair as Englishmen.

CHAPTER V:

MASSON AS EXPLORER AND GEOGRAPHER.
I: FIRST JOURNEYINGS

Kai Lung professed to have no fear,
remarking ... that a worthless garment
covered one with better protection than
that afforded by an army of bowmen.

Ernest Bramah
The Wallet of Kai Lung

The local and international scene into which Charles Masson walked,
literally, and where he wandered or resided for the next ten years
was described in Chapter II. At first sight he was ill-equipped to play
a noteworthy role in his new environment: absent without leave and
on the run, almost penniless with barely a change of clothes, on foot
and ill-shod, and moreover ignorant of the local languages. But he
had learned Hindustani during his time in the Indian Army and this
helped him to communicate as is clear from his account of his first
meeting with Dost Mohamed Khan at Ghazni who asked what language he should speak:

> *... and being told I could not converse in Pashto or Persian, he spoke in*
> *those languages to those near him, and they repeated to me what he*
> *had said in Hindustani for I found that although he well understood*
> *that dialect, it was hardly thought becoming in a Durrani sirdar to*
> *hold communications in it.*[48]

Masson later learned Persian, presumably becoming fluent in it during his ten months' stay in Persia and the Persian Gulf. He specifically
states that he picked up a smattering of Pushtu on the march, indeed
he eventually acquired enough Pushtu to understand an overheard
conversation between certain ruffians which enabled him to avoid a
dangerous trap which might have cost him his life.

His *Narrative of Various Journeys* is not wholly easy reading. It is not
his style that is at fault, quirky though it is, but rather the multiplicity
of unfamiliar Islamic names of individuals (who keep popping up in
different contexts) which tax the memory, as well as names of

innumerable 'castles', obscure hamlets, hills and other topographical points, which cause confusion. Yet inasmuch as he is frequently intent on painting the historical background of contemporary events and unravelling the appallingly complicated relationships and intrigues of the leading personalities amongst whom he moved, the plethora of proper names is easily justified. As for the place names, he was attempting to provide as much geographical and topographical information as possible. He also constantly employs Persian words, while all too many plants and trees are given local, instead of botanical, names.

A common complaint has been about the scarcity of dates through-out his writings. Worse still, he provided no maps which would have clarified his wanderings especially where he doubled back on his tracks. He supplied one eventually with the fourth ('Kalat') volume of 1843, in response, as he says, to public demand. The 1974 reprint of the first three volumes has a perceptive Introduction by Gavin Hambly. Unfortunately it is marred by numerous errors of fact. Nevertheless, this Introduction does give the background story about Masson's ser-vice in the Indian Army, his desertion and assumed name. Lacking this information, readers of the early editions must have been as mys-tified by the anonymity of *the Narrative of Various Journeys*, as surprised by the absence of the subjective accounts of personal suffering and fine descriptive writing, common in earlier books of travel.

Masson, however, occasionally displays his feelings as for instance on first seeing the river Indus, and later the snow-clad Safed Koh range in Afghanistan. His narrative moreover becomes noticeably more vivid when he is describing his arrival in or return to Afghanistan. Like other travellers since, he was delighted with the marked change of temperature as the road climbed steadily towards the 6,000 ft. high plateau of Kabul. He was entranced by the capital and its surroundings.

In spite of occasional obscurities, Masson provides a vast amount of valuable geographical information, vivid descriptions of men and places, as well as a fascinating tale of travel and adventure. Sir Tho-mas Holdich gives a most appreciative account:

> *Before British Indian administrators had seriously turned their atten-tion to the Afghan bufferland and set to work to fill up 'intelligence' material at secondhand, there was at least one active European agent in the field who was in direct touch with the chief political actors in that strange land of everlasting unrest, and who has left behind him a record which is unsurpassed on the Indian frontier for the width of its*

scope of inquiry into matters political, social, economic and scientific, and the general accuracy of his conclusions... It must be remembered that the Punjab and Sind were almost as much terra incognita in 1830 as was Afghanistan...'

Holdich goes on to say that Masson lived with the Afghans, partook of their hospitality (indeed depended on it for his daily bread), studied their ways, discussed their politics and their history, and placed himself on terms of familiarity with his hosts 'in a way which has never been imitated since'. The very fact that he walked much of the way, by preference even when he had a horse, was often penniless and without baggage, brought him exceptionally close to the people and to the ground. It helped, too, that he so obviously had no ulterior motive for his journeyings—the nomadic life was everything.

Fifty years elapsed, says Holdich, before the footsteps of Masson could be traced with certainty. Not till the conclusion of the Second Anglo-Afghan war in 1881 and the final reshaping of the surveys of Baluchistan, could it be said exactly where he wandered during those strenuous years of unremitting travel. Considering the circumstances under which his observations were taken and recorded, they are marvellously accurate in geographical detail.[49]

Holdich is peculiarly well qualified to assess Masson's merits as a geographer since he was a distinguished frontier survey officer who had seen much of Afghanistan during the Second Anglo-Afghan war and later as a member of the Russo-Afghan Boundary Commissions of 1886 and 1895 which finally settled that frontier. His account of Masson's achievements was the first to rescue the explorer's reputation from the oblivion into which it had fallen.

Masson begins his story with his arrival at Bahawalpur, the capital of the State of that name. He stayed some weeks there and elsewhere in the State and was well treated by the notables. They were, however, puzzled what to make of a man who had no business to transact. At Ahmedpur he was assigned to the care of Rahmat Khan, a Rohilla officer and a former soldier of fortune, who had some experience of Europeans in British India. They became firm friends and Masson paid several visits to him during the next few years. After recovering from a bad bout of fever, Masson was received by the handsome young Khan of Bahawalpur who sent him three double-handfuls of rupees most of which stuck to the fingers of the court officials. He was impressed with the luxuriant cultivation of the country and its abundant game. He was equally pleased with the inhabitants:

> *Although I had suffered much from fever and its consequences, during my stay at Ahmedpur and its neighbourhood, I had every reason to be gratified with the civility of all classes of the people; and I found them always disposed to be communicative on points within their knowledge.*

While still at Ahmedpur, he learned that the Khan of Bahawalpur's chief minister intended to move with an armed force of some 3,000 men, horse and foot, with 6 guns on Dera Ghazi Khan in order to exact the tribute due from the petty chief of Sang Ghar near by. As this was the route Masson intended to take, he marched with it. The expedition crossed the Indus opposite Dera Ghazi Khan and his first view of that river, famous for its association with Alexander the Great, moves him to write:

> *It was not without emotion that I approached the river Indus, hallowed by so many historical recollections and now the boundary, as once possibly the parent seat of the Hindu races. I found it, perhaps, nearly as low as it could ever be; still its bed was most extensive, and at the point we crossed must have been three miles in breadth. There were two or three boats at the ferry, but the wide expanse of sand, and the scanty reeds and shrubs fringing the opposite shores, gave a feature of loneliness to the prospect which required the strength of associations to relieve. Numerous, on the borders, were the tracks of tigers which, from such tokens, must be very common although they are seldom seen and, I learned, seldom do harm. I felt, however, a deep interest of another kind, in reflecting on the people and scenes I was about to leave behind, and on the unknown lands and races the passage of the river would open to my observation. If a feeling of doubt for a moment clouded my mind, one of pride at having penetrated so far removed it, and encouraged me to proceed farther.*[50]

Three or four miles beyond the river the force entered the important town of Dera Ghazi Khan which was situated in the midst of extensive date groves and gardens. Masson remarks that only a few years before it had been the residence of a Durrani governor but was now in a depressed condition. He also notes that the Mahomedan inhabitants complained much of their misfortune in being under Sikh domination, while the Hindus joined with them in deprecating the rapacity of the Bahawalpur chief, who farmed the revenues from Maharaja Ranjit Singh. Both parties also united in regretting that the Durrani power had passed away. Amongst their former governors they affectionately

remembered the Nawab Jabar Khan, extolling his liberality and his
humanity.[51] The Nawab was the half-brother of Dost Mahomed Khan;
his title derived from his former governorship of Kashmir. He was to
play a prominent part in Masson's life in Afghanistan. Christmas Day,
1827, was spent in Dera Ghazi Khan and Masson enjoyed the luxuries
of fresh grapes, pears and apples brought by the traders from the
orchards of Kabul.

At Dera Ismail Khan, further up the river, he was handsomely entertained by the chief of that district for several weeks, but the weather
beginning to grow sultry, and inactivity becoming irksome, his
thoughts turned towards Kabul and its bracing climate. He trudged
on hoping to fall in with a caravan of Lohani merchants, but he could
obtain no reliable information. After various detours in the company
of Sikhs and merchants he found himself back again in the vicinity of
Dera Ismail Khan. He determined to strike across the hills alone despite the dire warnings from acquaintances of the lawless character of
the tribes he would encounter. Fortunately perhaps he met a party led
by a Saiyad of Peshawar on their way to that city. In their company he
gained the summit of a range of hills from which:

> ... the plains of Marwat and Bannu burst upon the sight. The numer-
> ous villages, marked by their several groups of trees, the yellow tints
> of the ripe corn-fields, and the fantastic forms of the surrounding moun-
> tains, presented, in their union and contrast, a splendid scene. In front
> and to the west, the distant ranges exhibited a glorious spectacle, from
> their pure whiteness, diversified by streaks of azure, red and pearly
> grey. These beautiful and commanding features of the landscape were
> enhanced by the charm of an unclouded sky. I was lost in wonder and
> rapture on contemplating this serene yet gorgeous display of nature... [52]

The party stopped briefly at Bannu, but the next stage, a very long
one of thirty-six miles, caused Masson's feet to blister so severely that
after one more day's march he was obliged to drop behind. He dragged
himself painfully to Hangu where he stayed for a while. When his feet
had recovered, he proceeded alone to Kohat, a walled town with a
considerable bazaar. Between Bannu and Kohat he had found the scenery very beautiful, the land well cultivated, numerous fruit trees and
abundance of water. On the way, he had met a force led by Pir
Mahomed Khan, one of the Peshawar sirdars, who had just taken possession of Kohat and was about to attack Hangu. These manoeuvres
were directed, as in the past and in the future, against the growing
power and prosperity of Dost Mahomed Khan in Kabul. On his return

to Kohat from Hangu, where the chiefs had fled across the hills to Kabul, Pir Mahomed Khan hastened back to Peshawar taking Masson on his elephant. Masson's host at Peshawar was Saleh Mahomed whom he had met in Kohat:

> *Saleh Mahomed did everything in his power to make my residence at Peshawar as agreeable as possible, and people of all classes were most civil and desirous to oblige. I made a great number of acquaintances; and there seldom occurred any diversion or spectacle that I was not called to witness. The change also from a life of wandering to one of repose was not in itself disagreeable; and every scene had the charm of novelty to recommend it. The inhabitants, if not so civilized as to have lost their natural virtues, were abundantly more so than the rude but simple tribes I had so long been conversant with; and as a stranger I had only to experience their good qualities. I had ample reason to be satisfied with them.*[53]

The city had suffered considerably from the Sikhs. The Balla Hissar, once the favourite residence of Shah Shuja, was in ruins and its fine gardens which the Mountstuart Elphinstone mission had admired were in a neglected condition.

By this time Masson had become confident of his ability to travel long distances on foot and alone, if necessary, though he always attached himself to a caravan or a single companion, if possible. Indeed he often waited many wearisome days for a party to start. He must also have become aware that he possessed the happy knack of making friends with indigenous people of high and low degree. As he pursues his journeys he provides a potted history of every place of some importance together with an outline of its commerce, industry, agriculture and revenues. He notes local strongholds as well as ancient monuments and is careful to give distances between towns and between his route and prominent landmarks. He follows this pattern throughout the voluminous pages of his narrative. Holdich justly remarks that:

> *Nothing seems to have come amiss to his enquiring mind. Archaeology, numismatics, botany, geology and history—it was all new to him—an inexhaustible opportunity lay before him. He certainly made good use of it.*[54]

It was June 1828 when he arrived at Peshàwar and he seems to have stayed for at least a month. At length he made acquaintance with an equally penniless and footloose Pathan who offered to accompany him to Kabul. They chose to follow the Khyber Pass route—a bold decision in view of its evil reputation. In fact, conditions had deteriorated of late. The sections of the Afridi and Shinwari tribes who inhabited the eastern and western parts of the hills overlooking the pass were notorious for their ferocity and their long-indulged habits of rapine. Under the Sadozai princes they had received an annual allowance of Rs. 12,000 on condition that they kept the pass open and abstained from plunder. The Barakzai sirdars, however, to whom the attachment shown by the tribes to Shah Shuja had rendered them very suspect, cancelled the subsidy, with the result that they threw off all restraint and effectively closed the pass to the traders of Peshawar and Kabul.

After cautiously crossing the Peshawar plain and keeping at first to by-paths into the hills, they struck the high road of the Khyber near Ali Masjid. Here they fell in with the first people they had met en route, some twenty men sitting in the shade of the rocks; most of them were elderly and of venerable aspect who received the travellers hospitably. News of the arrival of a European soon spread and many persons came, afflicted with disorders and wounds. At that time every European was expected to be a doctor and Masson had to assume the role and make the most of his very limited knowledge. His remedies were mostly simple, with an emphasis on cleanliness which seemed to be neglected on principle. He had sufficient success to ensure him a welcome whenever he was called upon to administer to the sick. Moreover the tribesmen here as elsewhere considered their hospitality well repaid by stories of the outside world and personal contact with a member of a race so much heard of, but so little known.

He was struck by a massive monument at Ali Masjid called the Padshah's Tope:

> ... it is in good preservation and consists of a massive rectangular base, on which rests a cylindrical body, terminating in a dome or cupola; it is erected on the summit of an eminence. I have noted the existence of another in the plain of Peshawar, and I have heard of others in the Punjab. The inhabitants of these parts refer these structures to former Padshahs, or Kings, sometimes to Ahmed Shah, but I judge their antiquity to be remote. The stones employed in the Khaibar monument are of very large dimensions, and the whole has a grand and striking aspect.[35]

Years were to elapse before it was recognised as a typical Buddhist stupa in Gandhara style. Indeed Masson was not yet aware that he was on one of the main Buddhist pilgrimage routes. Equally he did not dream that in the course of time he would systematically reveal the antiquity of similar Buddhist remains which lie thickly around Jalalabad and the valleys adjoining the Khyber route to Kabul.

He met with various incidents: at times treated hospitably; on one occasion robbed. It was Afridi tribesmen, generally regarded as fiercer than the Shinwaris, who had been so much in need of medical treatment, whereas to his surprise it was two ruffians of the latter tribe who pounced on him and his Pathan companion. They took the Englishman's wrap, but returned his book on being told it was a pious volume. The Pathan's knife was wrenched from the band of his trousers. All that remained to the travellers were thirty or forty copper coins in a water-bottle which the robbers missed, and some bread. That incident apart, Masson managed to establish 'a close, if not absolutely friendly intimacy with the half-savage people of those wholly savage hills. An intimacy such as no other educated European has ever attained...'[56] This tribute is well deserved. His character and personality, combined with his obvious poverty, were essential factors in his preservation. On the other hand, he was fortunate in his time. For the next decade or so, that is until 1839, an Englishman could generally count on the respect and goodwill of the people, other than the wildest tribesmen. Thereafter the Anglo-Afghan War created a totally different attitude on the part of the Afghan towards the British.

Masson was impressed by the extensive remains of ancient forts and buildings on the crests of the hills throughout the length of the Khyber which suggested to him that their founders must have been much more enlightened and opulent than the present inhabitants. He regrets the impossibility of inspecting them or the great number of artificial caves cut into the hillsides. His account of his traverse of the famous Pass ends:

> I missed my chaddar [wrap] at night, for its employment was to cover me when I slept, yet, on the whole, I was pleased with my passage through the Khaibar. My companion had instructed me on all occasions to appear pleased and cheerful, a salutary counsel, and one which stood me in good stead, as did the indication of perfect tranquility, and implicit confidence in the good faith of those I fell in with.

Shortly after clearing the pass, he crossed Afghanistan's present-day frontier near Dakka and proceeded westwards towards Jalalabad through semi-desert plains bordered by the Kabul river on its way to Ahe Indus. Opposite the village of Bassowal (Basawal) high steep hills confine the stream; Masson noticed that at their eastern extremity were a series of caves with triangular entrances. At Bassowal and beyond

he found quantities of potsherds strewn over a wide area. In course of
time, Japanese archaeologists were to establish that Bassowal had been
a large Buddhist centre in the 4th and 5th Centuries AD with over one
hundred caves, most of them carved and decorated, not unlike those
at Bamian with which Masson later became familiar.[57] But he was on
the wrong side of the river to examine them and in any case they were
then quite outside his experience.

He passed a tope on an eminence. It was very picturesque and the
scenery was so agreeable that his Pathan companion asked him
whether there were any spots so charming in his own country. The
following evening he reached a small village where a party of men
were resting in the shade of some trees and was invited to join them.
The chief man proved to be Khalil Khan who farmed the customs at
Jalalabad under the Governor, Mahomed Zeman Khan. He urged
Masson to spend two or three days with him:

> ... we were ferried across the stream in a boat and I found the Khan's
> castle, a very neat and commodious one, seated amid the most luxuri-
> ant fields of sugar-cane and lucerne, and with good gardens, and fine
> groves of trees attached. In the immediate neighbourhood were many
> other handsome castles, and the country around seemed quite a garden.

Khalil Khan and his family were most kind and civil. A neighbouring
landowner who was related to the sirdars of Peshawar and Kandahar,
also entertained Masson at his 'handsome seignorial castle'. At no great
distance away, the Kunar river joins the Kabul river. The Kunar drains
the mountainous region of Kafiristan (Land of the Infidel), renamed
Nuristan (Land of Light) after Amir Abdur Rahman subdued the country in 1895 and forcibly converted the infidels to Islam. Masson's com-
parative proximity to this mysterious land whilst staying with Khalil
Khan led him to make enquiries about its inhabitants, the Siaposh
Kafirs, or black-clad infidels, as they were then called. Of their origin,
languages, religion and customs almost nothing was known: they were
in fact Asia's greatest ethnological mystery and remained so for the
next seventy years. They excited curiosity by their success in main-
taining their independence for over two thousand years: Alexander
the Great spared them; the otherwise triumphant march of Islam made
no impact; and they even forced Tamberlane to call off his determined
campaign against them. But what intrigued Europeans most was the
prevalence of Kafirs with blue eyes and red or blond hair. Masson was
fascinated by the subject as were other travellers of his time:
Mountstuart Elphinstone, Alexander Burnes and Dr J.G. Gerard. All

of them had of course had a classical education and were thus inclined to accept the legend that the blond Kafirs were descended from Alexander the Great's soldiers. Each published his gleanings and his views about these strange tribes.

Various local people, Hindu and Moslem, were brought for questioning to Masson who listened to their 'wondrous tales' with little benefit. He also spoke with several Siaposh youths who were no better informed, having been kidnapped as children and who were anyway of low intelligence. He devotes a whole chapter to the results of his enquiries then and later about these 'singular and secluded people'. One singularity was known: they used chairs and stools in preference to a rug on the floor. As for their seclusion, the precipitous and heavily wooded interior with its numerous valleys and defiles was accessible only on foot. Strangers were forcibly driven off by the inhabitants who limited their contact with the outside world to the bare minimum necessary to obtain by barter essential articles such as salt and cotton piece goods. Hence the lack of any reliable information about them, but as Masson remarks, 'when no one knows, all may conjecture' and we need not follow him in his speculations. Suffice it to say that even today, despite intensive research, the racial origins of the Nuristanis are not known for certain, while the dialects of the separate tribes which in many cases are mutually unintelligible from valley to valley, have still not been fully studied.

Jalalabad was but a few miles distant. Exceedingly hot in summer when Masson first visited the town, it was a favourite resort of Afghans in winter. No sooner was he recognised as a *Feringhi* than many hastened to announce his arrival to the Nawab Jabar Khan whose good feelings towards Europeans was well known. The Nawab, of whom Masson had heard high praises at Dera Ghazi Khan, had recently arrived in Jalalabad with his troops to guard the town from invasion by the Peshawar sirdars. He received Masson civilly. Wonderment was expressed how he had got through the Khyber at which the Nawab remarked that he had nothing to lose. And in truth Masson was in rags by then. Nevertheless he refused pecuniary help, but did accept an offer of a good guide and a horse as far as Kabul. His stay was brief and the little party of three moved up the highly cultivated and well watered valley of Jalalabad. Masson was charmed: 'Few countries can possess more attractive scenery, or can exhibit so many grand features in its surrounding landscape. In every direction the eye wanders on huge mountain ranges.' To the south was the noble barrier of the Safed Koh (White Mountain); he had previously seen the range from the other side near Bannu and had extolled its snow-clad beauties. To the north beyond the Kabul river were the mountains of Laghman province with those of Kafiristan behind.

Two days travelling brought them to the village of Havizangani where they found a group of men sitting under a clump of fine mulberry trees. They presented Masson with an enormous heap of the fruit: 'I had eaten the mulberries of Kohat, Hangu and Peshawar but had never before seen or tasted fruit comparable to the present. I needed no encouragement to enjoy the treat.' One of the group, the headman of a near-by village, told him that he had ten wives and wished to be given an aphrodisiac; he became importunate when Masson was unable to oblige him. The travellers had become conscious of moving into a purer and cooler atmosphere, but at Havizangani:

> ... the change was extremely sensible, and I was in high spirits at the certainty of having reached the cold country. Neither was I less delighted at the novelties shown in the aspect of the country, and its vegetable productions... I was never tired of roving about the low hills in our neighbourhood, and found everything new and pleasing...[58]

Alas, disaster struck that night when his book which had survived the perils of the Khyber, was stolen while he slept.

Masson pushed on steadily to Kabul, but stayed only two or three days in the neighbourhood because cholera was raging. Furthermore, Dost Mahomed Khan was encamped outside Ghazni with an army in order to counter an attack aimed at Kabul by his half-brother Fur Dil Khan of Kandahar. Masson therefore determined 'to lose no time in proceeding to the Sirdar's camp, being as curious to witness the proceedings of an Afghan army as desirous to escape from the baleful influence of contagion and disease'. He was well received by Haji Khan (of the Kakar tribe), Governor of Bamian, to whom he had been recommended. The latter introduced him to Dost Mahomed Khan and Masson records his opinion of that controversial personality:

> The assumption of authority by Dost Mahomed Khan has been favourable to the prosperity of Kabul, which, after so long a period of commotion, required a calm... He is beloved by all classes of his subjects, and the Hindu fearlessly approaches him in his rides, and addresses him with the certainty of being attended to. He administers justice with impartiality, and has proved that the lawless habits of the Afghan are to be controlled. He is very attentive to his military; and, conscious much depends upon the efficiency of his troops, is very par-

ticular as to their composition. His circumscribed funds and resources hardly permit him to be regular in his payments, yet his soldiers have the satisfaction to know that he neither hoards nor wastes their pay in idle expenses.

Dost Mahomed Khan has distinguished himself on various occasions, by acts of personal intrepidity, and has proved himself an able commander, yet he is equally well skilled in stratagem and polity, and only employs the sword when other means fail. He is remarkably plain in attire, and would be scarcely noticed in durbar, but for his seat. His white linen raiment afforded a strange contrast to the gaudy exhibition of some of his chiefs... In my audience of him in the camp at Ghazni, I should not have conjectured him a man of ability, either from his conversation or from his appearance... A stranger must be cautious in estimating the character of a Durrani from his appearance merely; a slight observer, like myself, would not discover in Dost Mahomed Khan the gallant warrior and shrewd politician...[59]

The impending hostilities arose from a concerted plan by the sirdars of Peshawar and Kandahar to attack Dost Mahomed Khan from the east and the west. Pir Mahomed Khan's earlier foray against Hangu and Kohat had opened the campaign; an advance on Jalalabad was due to follow, hence Nawab Jabar Khan's presence there. In the event, negotiations took place that were so adroitly conducted by Dost Mahomed Khan and his friends that he lost not an inch of the territory demanded from him, though he did agree to pay Fur Dil Khan forty thousand rupees. The Kandahar troops hastily retired, while one of the Peshawar sirdars who had marched with them quietly returned to that city. The rupees were never remitted.

Cholera had accompanied the Kabul force and was causing serious loss among the troops and the inhabitants of Ghazni:

My curiosity led me to visit the tomb of the celebrated Sultan Mahmud,* and in the courts and gardens belonging to it was displayed a revolting spectacle of disease and misery. Crowds of poor wretches had crawled in to them, anxious, possibly, to resign their mortal breath in the sacred spot — the dying were confounded with the dead — and almost all were in a state of nudity; either that the miserable sufferers had cast off their own garments or, as likely, that amongst their fellow men there had been found those base enough to profit by their forlorn state, and to despoil them. Ghazni has numerous ziarats, or shrines, and all of them were now so many charnel houses.

---

* Sultan Mahmud, AD 998-1030, the outstanding ruler of the Ghaznavid dynasty.

From Ghazni, Masson and his Pathan companion (whom he never names) continued their journey to Kandahar on foot, but were savagely treated by some Ghilzais near Karabagh and had difficulty in avoiding the attention of others of the same tribe.[60]

He remained a considerable time in Kandahar where he was hospitably received by one or other of the Barakzai chiefs. Kandahar is renowned for its fruit: figs, plums, apricots, peaches, pears, grapes and melons, but Masson considered its pomegranates were unsurpassed. He next intended to make for Herat and spend the winter there. His Pathan companion, however, was so terrified of the accounts he had heard of the plundering bands along the route that he declined to accompany him and parted from Masson to go on pilgrimage to Mecca. Nevertheless, Masson started out for Herat alone, but he only covered twelve miles before he was robbed of all he possessed. He never did manage to visit Herat despite his claim to have done so (see p. 11). Retracing his steps to Kandahar, he then left for Shikarpur by Quetta and the Bolan Pass route, and it was on this journey that he nearly lost his life. He committed the error of allowing the caravan with which he was to travel to precede him, trusting to his being able to catch it up en route. He fell amongst the Achakzai thieves of the plains, and being everywhere known and recognised as a *Feringhi*, he passed a very rough time with them. They stripped him of his clothing in exchange for a ragged pair of pyjamas, beat him and took his money, leaving him:

> ... destitute, a stranger in the centre of Asia, unacquainted with the language—which would have been most useful to me—and from my colour exposed on all occasions to notice, inquiry, ridicule, and insult ... It was some consolation to find that the kafila [caravan] was not far off; and with my new companions I proceeded, without apprehension of further plunder, having nothing to be deprived of.[61]

But that night he nearly died of cold and exposure:

> The cold increasing as the night advanced, I suffered much from the want of clothing: my companions, on preparing for sleep, furnished me with a quantity of wood, to enable me to keep the fire alive at night, over which I was to sit; I did so, with my knees drawn up to my chin; nevertheless the severity of the cold was seriously felt. Towards morning, my situation being observed by a Mogal soldier in the service of Khadar Khan [the leader of the caravan] he came and threw over my shoulders a postin, or great-coat, if I may so express myself, made of the skins of dumbas, or large-tailed sheep, the leather excellently prepared, and the fleece well preserved. They are the general winter

habits of all classes in Khorasan, and are certainly warm and comfortable.

I endeavoured to rise and return thanks, when I found that, what with the heat of the fire in front, and the intensity of the cold behind, my limbs were contracted, and fixed in the cramped position in which I had been so long sitting. I now became alarmed lest I should not be able to accompany the kafila; nor should I had it started early in the morning as kafilas generally do; but this, with a view to the convenience of the women, did not march until the sun was high above the horizon. This was a fortunate circumstance, as the solar heat gradually relaxed the stiffness of my limbs, and as I became warm in walking the pain lessened. I know not whether to impute my misfortune here to the presence of the fire or to the cold. My legs and arms were covered with blotches, and at their respective joints were reduced to a state of rawness. The latter evil disappeared in a few days, but the pains in the limbs continued to distress me exceedingly for four or five months, and have not wholly left me to this day, and probably never will. The present of this postin was undoubtedly the means of my preservation, as I never should have been able to have passed another night in similar nudity: and the cold, I afterwards found, increased for the next eight or ten marches.[62]

At Quetta his pains grew so intense that he was obliged to remain there. He was very hospitably treated, in particular by a wealthy Brahman of Bikanir who gave him some clothes. When he was sufficiently fit to travel he was allowed to join a large caravan. With it he traversed the notorious Bolan Pass, dreaded for the roughness of the track, its narrow defiles and its length of sixty miles:

I could have enjoyed this march under other circumstances, but what with its length, and the ill condition I was in, it proved a penible one to me. The constant crossing of the river, and the necessity of tramping so often barefoot, nearly exhausted me, and my feet at the close of the journey were sorely blistered.

His condition did not, however, prevent him from noting in detail the geography of the region and the relative importance of the various passes, of which the Bolan is in a direct line of communication between Kandahar and Sind. It also marks the boundary between the cold and the hot countries:

... the natives here affirm that all below the Pass is Hind, and that all above is Khorasan. This distinction is in great measure warranted, not only because the pass separates very different races from each other, speaking various dialects, but that it marks the line of a complete change

of climate and natural productions. As we near Dadar we behold the
akh, or milky euphorbia; no plant is more uniformly found at the verge
of the two zones: belonging to the warmer one, it stands as a sentinel
overlooking the frontier, over which apparently it may not step.[63]

Once again sickness obliged him to lose contact with the caravan and
again he was set upon. Twice an exchange of shoes was demanded,
but when the one-sidedness of the transaction was realised, he was
allowed to keep his worn-out pair. Eventually, after losing his way
more than once and being taken for an Uzbek by a party of Baluch
soldiers, he caught up with the caravan. This was fortunate as a few
marches further on they had to cross the Dasht Bedari, a desert tract
of infamous repute owing to the numerous robberies and murders
committed on it by predatory bands. The leader of the *kafila* determined to make but one march across it starting at sunset and moving
throughout the night and the following day. Once during the day, a
cloud of dust was observed. The *kafila* was halted, the men with
matchlocks assembled, and the horsemen took up position in front;
the camels were also concentrated and made to kneel. It was a false
alarm; the dust, being merely the effect of a whirlwind, subsided, and
the journey was resumed. The unusually severe march across the Dasht
Bedari again aggravated Masson's pains caused by the bitter night
beside the camp-fire and he could not manage the final stage to
Shikarpur all at once. He therefore went quietly on from village to
village alone, well treated by the peasantry, a mild and unassuming
people, until he reached Shikarpur.

Holdich writes:

There are several points about this remarkable journey which might
lead one to suspect that romance was not altogether a stranger to it,
were it not that the route itself is described with surprising accuracy.
He could hardly have carried about volumes of notes with him under
such conditions as his story depicts, and it might very well have hap-
pened that he dislocated his topography or his ethnography from lapse
of memory. But he does neither; and the most amazing feature of
Masson's tales of travel is that in all essential features we knew little
more about the country of the Afghans after the second war with Af-
ghanistan than he could have told us before the first.[64]

CHAPTER VI

MASSON AS EXPLORER AND GEOGRAPHER. II: FURTHER JOURNEYS BY SEA AND LAND

> *The Master of the Caravan:*
> *But who are ye in rags and rotten shoes,*
> *You dirty-bearded, blocking up the way?*
>
> *The pilgrims:*
> *We are the Pilgrims Master: we shall go*
> *Always a little further: it may be*
> *Beyond that last blue mountain barred with snow.*
>
> James Elroy Flecker
> *The Golden Journey to Samarkand*

The wealthy city of Shikarpur (which figures frequently in Masson's story) was the gateway to Baluchistan and the West. It had been a great centre of trade under the Durranis and was still an important commercial and manufacturing town. Renowned for its banking system, its financial credit had extended far into Central Asia. European travellers in remote places were glad to be able to borrow money from its agents against a promissory note. But in Masson's time much of that credit had disappeared with the capitalists who supported it—chiefly Hindu bankers who migrated to the cities of Multan and Amritsar as the Sikh power in the Punjab became an ever more powerful factor in frontier politics. Leaving Shikarpur in February 1829, he crossed the Indus at Sakkar and from Rohri on the east bank he moved across northern Sind towards Fazilpur in Bahawalpur with an intermediate stop of a month at Khairpur. A feature of this stage was the universal hospitality offered by the villagers to Masson who, moreover, passed unmolested throughout. At Fazilpur he called on his old friend Rahmat Khan, now in charge of the castle there. He was much cosseted: new clothes to replace his much-patched postin, a bed to lie on, and good food, for his host was somewhat of an epicure. About a month spent with his friends at Fazilpur so entirely set him up that he grew impatient to resume his journey to Lahore 360 miles away. Rahmat Khan was over-generous. Having spent his last rupees on a nautch, he had to borrow from the Hindus of the bazaar in order to present two rupees to his guest. On Masson's arrival at Lahore he still had half a rupee left although he had lived very well for weeks on the road! Meanwhile he noted the extraordinary extent of ancient ruins around Uch and related its importance to the days of Arab ascendancy. At Multan he found an amazing number of old Moslem tombs, mosques, and shrines around the city. The heat, though, was excessive. At Kamalia, a small town on the left bank of the Ravi and some 80 miles short of Lahore, he believed that he was in a part of the country which had been the scene of some of Alexander the Great's exploits.[65] And again at Haripah he was convinced that he had found the site of the battle of Sangala as described by Arrian.[66]

On the outskirts of Lahore he accidentally encountered General Allard, conversed with him in French and was invited to stay at his splendid establishments (see page 11). He remained with the General during the rainy season and was apparently no longer troubled about being recognised. Was he not now thought to be a French-speaking Italian? He did, however, decline Allard's offer of an introduction to the Maharaja Ranjit Singh lest he should be invited to join the Sikh service and so lose his freedom of action. Although he does not say so, there was a more cogent reason for his caution. Such an appointment would have been reported by the local British-paid newswriter to Captain Wade at Ludhiana who was sensitive about the Europeans recruited by Ranjit Singh, particularly if they turned out to be deserters from British India.

Allard lived in great style as did the other European general officers stationed in Lahore: his immediate neighbour Ventura who had converted a Moslem tomb into a harem; Avitabile; and Court. Masson cast an eye on their mansions: Avitabile's was 'painted in a singular and grotesque fashion'. His host was an educated and cultured man whom Masson describes as universally and deservedly respected. Of the others, Ventura and Court were to have an important, if indirect, influence on Masson because of their excavations of the stupas at Manikyala the following year. The flamboyant General Avitabile became Governor of Peshawar from 1835 to 1843. When Burnes withdrew his ill-fated Mission from Kabul in 1838, he and Masson stayed with Avitabile; Allard and Court were fellow guests. During the First Anglo-Afghan War which started at the end of that year, General Avitabile rendered signal services to the British forces by his firm control of Peshawar and the approaches to the Khyber Pass, and to individual British officers by his unbounded hospitality.

About Lahore, the capital of the Punjab and of the territories of Ranjit Singh, Masson had much of interest to say. He admired the principal mosques, but deplored the condition of the Shalimar Garden where the gay pavilions and other buildings had suffered from the depredations of the Maharaja who had removed much of the marble and stones to embellish the religious capital of Amritsar. As was his habit, he included a short history of the Sikhs and their religion, as well as an account of the remarkable rise of Ranjit Singh. Masson also gave details of the revenues and reserves of the Sikh state, and a table showing the various branches of the Army with their strengths, locations, and the names of their commanders, of whom two were Englishmen. The 'highly respectable appearance' of the Maharaja's troops was noted and their uniforms, personal weapons, and pay were described. Masson attempted to assess their military value, but concluded that on the few occasions they had seen service, their enemies had not been of a calibre to establish a criterion.[67]

When he finally left Lahore he was in easier circumstances and had purchased a horse. He rode south towards Multan in the company of a young Sikh sirdar who had taken a great liking to him. Falling sick with a fever, Masson spent a month in Multan, still with the sirdar and his entourage. From there he largely retraced his steps and revisited several of the towns he had known on the outward journey, including Fazilpur where he again stayed with Rahmat Khan. Near Larkhana his horse broke down, but meeting a fruit merchant of Kabul who was delivering supplies to the Hyderabad Amirs and had a government boat at his disposal, Masson dropped down the Indus to Hyderabad. There he spent the winter of 1829-30 agreeably enough.

In the spring he decided to gain the port of Karachi with a view to making his way to Persia as best he could. Accordingly, he went by boat to Tatta, a town of great antiquity and renown, but then in decline. From Tatta he walked to Karachi where he had the great satisfaction of seeing the sea for the first time for many years. The harbour brought to his mind another item of classical interest: 'there being little doubt that it is the port of Alexander, which sheltered for some time the fleet of Nearchus, the first European admiral who navigated the Indian seas'. Burnes, too, found his thoughts turning to the deeds of Alexander the Great when he first saw the Indus delta the following year. It is difficult, he says, to describe the enthusiasm one feels on first beholding the scenes which have exercised the genius of Alexander. 'A town or a river, which lies on his route, has acquired a

celebrity that time serves only to increase; and while we gaze on the
Indus, we connect ourselves, at least in association, with the ages of
distant glory.'[68]

Charles Masson sailed from Karachi to Muscat and thence in an
Arab craft to Bassadore, then a British station, where he was cordially
welcomed by the few of his countrymen residing there. After a time a
cruiser of the Honourable Company called at the port and her officers
were kind enough to offer him a passage to Bushire where he stayed for
a few weeks:

> ... under the hospitable roof of the late lamented Major Wilson, at that
> time the Resident; and a gentleman of a mind so superior, that to have
> possessed his friendship and esteem is a circumstance of which I shall
> never cease to be proud. I there drew up, from materials in my posses-
> sion, and from recollection, a series of papers relating to my journeys,
> and the countries through which I had passed, which were forwarded
> to the Government of Bombay, or to Sir John Malcolm, then the gov-
> ernor. I was not aware that such use would be made of them, nor am I
> quite sure I should have wished it; and I doubt whether it has not
> proved more hurtful than beneficial to me. I may justly lament that
> these documents should have been artfully brought forward in sup-
> port of unsound views and ambitious projects. I may also be dissatis-
> fied, in a less degree, that the information they contained has served
> the purposes of men wanting the generosity to acknowledge it.[69]

This complaint was directed at Burnes. These papers were subsequently incorporated in the *Narrative of Various Journeys Vol. 1.**

Major David Wilson forwarded his guest's papers under cover of a
lengthy despatch dated 11 September 1830 to the Chief Secretary to
the Government of Bombay. It opened by reporting the arrival on 13
June of an American gentleman and related Masson's invented story
of his ten years' travels from the United States through Europe and
Russia to Persia and Afghanistan (see p.11). It drew attention to various
interesting aspects of the papers ranging from Masson's search for
Alexander the Great's route through the Punjab and his success in
digging up Greek coins including one of the conqueror himself, to his
views on Ranjit Singh and the Sikhs, the navigation of the Indus, and
the wretched condition of Sind. Wilson also stated that he had strongly
recommended Masson to proceed to Tabriz for the purpose of meeting

---

* An earlier version appeared in the *Proceedings of the Bombay Geographical Society,
Vol. V 1840.*

the British Minister to Persia and offered a letter of introduction:

> ... *conceiving that Sir John Macdonald was peculiarly well qualified, both from his pursuits and situation, to direct Mr Masson's future enquiries to objects in these countries that require elucidation. I conceived likewise that the envoy might have been authorised to employ individuals for such purposes and to provide them with the necessary means which I had not.*

He ended by saying:

> *The papers now forwarded were given to me by Mr Masson with no injunction or understanding of concealment; he is perfectly aware that I would not hesitate to communicate their contents to any of my friends. I have likewise reason to think he would be flattered provided he were given the credit... I should not consider myself justified in communicating them without permission for general publication. I did not think it necessary to state directly to Mr Masson that I should send copies of these papers, some of which were drawn up at my suggestion, and avowedly to be communicated to some distinguished individuals for the information of the Government, and although he must have been aware that a public officer, situated as he knew me to be and making the enquiries I did, must have done so with a view to the good of the service.*[70]

This passage merely reflects normal official practice and is a sufficient answer to Masson's complaint.

Wilson could have no notion of the far-reaching effect of his action in forwarding the narrative of an 'American gentleman's' travels. For it was these reports that first drew the attention of the British authorities in India to Masson's existence and to his exceptional knowledge of the area between the Indus and the Persian Gulf. It was inevitable that these papers would lead to Masson's unmasking. They would have been in time to be read by Sir John Malcolm before his departure in December 1830 after a distinguished career. The Bombay Government was bound to have sent a copy to Colonel Henry Pottinger, the Resident in Cutch, since he was in charge of intelligence work south of the frontier and was the main source of information on Sind. His assistant was Alexander Burnes who had been posted to Cutch that year. He probably read Masson's reports before he set off on his journey to Bokhara; he was certainly shown them in Persia by Sir John Campbell in 1832 and in London by Lord Ellenborough.[71]

Meanwhile, Major Wilson's letter of introduction to the British Envoy to Persia ensured a welcome at Tabriz for Masson. Having left the

Residence on 23 July 1830, he writes:

> *From Bushir, a two months' journey led me to Tabrez, the capital of*
> *the late Abbas Mirza* [the Heir-Apparent], *but then desolated by the*
> *plague. Before setting out, the sad intelligence of the decease of the*
> *envoy, Sir John Macdonald, had reached Bushir, and I found Major,*
> *now Sir John Campbell, in charge of the mission. My obligations to*
> *this gentleman are more than mere words can express, and far greater*
> *than might be seemly to relate in these pages — yet, I may be permitted*
> *to record, that if my subsequent labours have proved advantageous to*
> *science, it was owing to his generosity that I was placed in the posi-*
> *tion to prosecute them. With Sir John Campbell were Mr now Sir John*
> *McNeill* and Captain Macdonald, nephew of the much regretted en-*
> *voy. Nearly, or quite two months I enjoyed the society of the friendly*
> *circle at Tabrez, at the hazard of acquiring a distaste for the rough*
> *pleasures of a rude and rambling life. I then accompanied Captain*
> *Macdonald to Baghdad, where for some days we profited by inter-*
> *course with Colonel Taylor, the Resident, and passed down the Tigris*
> *to Bassorah* [Basra], *having been joined by the late Captain Frank*
> *Willock.‡ From Bassorah we gained Karak* [Kargh Island], *which*
> *has since become remarkable from its occupation by a force from*
> *Bombay,† and then crossed over to Bushir, where I had the satisfaction*
> *to meet Major David Wilson, who was preparing to proceed overland*
> *to England. Captain Macdonald arranged to return with him, and*
> *Captain Willock and myself took our passages, in a merchant vessel of*
> *Bombay for Muskat, and a pleasant course of eleven days brought us*
> *to anchor in its haven. We took up our abode at the house of Reuben*
> *ben Aslan, agent of the Bombay government; and a few days were*
> *agreeably passed in visits to the Imam and in intercourse with the*
> *inhabitants. Captain Willock hired a vessel to convey him to Mandavi*
> [in Cutch] *and I took my passage in an Arab* bagala [coaster] *des-*
> *tined to Karachi. I sailed the day preceding that fixed for the departure*
> *of Captain Willock, in April 1831, and that excellent and kind-hearted*
> *gentleman accompanied me to my vessel, and remained with me until*
> *it was put under weigh. We parted, never to meet again.[72]*

So end Masson's brief remarks on his travels in Persia, the Persian
Gulf and the pashalic of Baghdad which had occupied some ten
months. During that time he had met and become a close acquaintance,

---

* McNeill succeeded Campbell in 1836.

‡ Captain Willock, R.N. had travelled with Conolly from St Petersburg to Tabriz.

† Sent to put pressure on Persia to lift the siege of Herat.

in some cases a friend, of British personalities in the region who were to play important roles in the formulation of policy with regard to the defence of India; notably Campbell, McNeill and Taylor. From these contacts Masson acquired a broader conspectus of British policy in the whole region than had been possible hitherto. In addition he had lived at close quarters with the cultivated Major Wilson and had had the run of his library and later of the Tabriz Residency library. Indeed at Tabriz he had had the help of John McNeill in brushing up his Greek in case his researches required it. He had hobnobbed with a number of British army officers and Company officials without betraying his origins and had established the story of his U.S. citizenship: altogether a remarkable achievement for a ranker and deserter. Above all, he had acquired a generous patron in Sir John Campbell who took a keen interest in his work and sent him money at intervals: in a letter to Campbell in 1834 he acknowledged the receipt of two sums of Rs. 500 and said 'for so much goodness I have to return you my very best thanks'.[73]

From 1831 on, Masson's life took on a new aspect. He was no longer a fugitive, penniless, travelling on foot, and in rags as he had once described:

> My postin, many years old, was so full of rents, and so rotten, that I was every day occupied two or three hours in repairing it, and the variously coloured threads employed gave it a singular and ludicrous appearance. To add to the unseemliness of my habiliments, the dress bestowed upon me by the Brahman at Shall [Quetta] was fairly in tatters, and my shoes were absolutely falling from my feet.[74]

He now had a little money, enough to mitigate the rigours of travel; he could afford to hire a horse or camel as required and to obtain some respectable clothes for special occasions, though he remained indifferent to his dress.

Helped by strong north-westerly winds, the vessel on which Masson had embarked at Muscat made the voyage to Karachi in seven days. But he was not permitted to land owing, as he subsequently discovered, to the presence at one of the mouths of the Indus of two Europeans anxious to proceed to Lahore by the river route. They proved to be Lieutenant Alexander Burnes and another young officer, intent on delivering the British Government's gift of shire horses to Ranjit Singh (see p. 18). Burnes was in fact in great trouble. Twice he was refused entry, denied provisions and even fresh water, and each time was obliged to return to Cutch. A vigorous correspondence with the Amirs

of Sind ensued. At the third attempt Burnes finally succeeded in obtaining permission to proceed up river with the horses and the heavy
carriage, deliberately added on the advice of Colonel Pottinger in order to ensure that the consignment went by water. The Amirs' main
concern was to deny knowledge of the Indus to foreigners. Their immediate objection, however, was based on their absurd notion that
the English were able to carry about regiments of soldiers in boxes.
Masson subsequently learned that having no boxes with him, the opposition in his case had been withdrawn as tantamount to a breach of
hospitality. Permission to land came too late as he had already left in
the Arab coaster for Urmara on the Makran coast. The violent north-
westerlies, which were now against him, made it a lengthy passage.
From Urmara he hoped to reach Kalat but the road was too dangerous to travel alone and no caravan appeared in the course of a month.
He therefore sailed to Sonmiani in another Arab vessel whose home
port it was. As a reputed physician he was held to be a privileged
person and was not even asked to pay for his passage.

At Urmara and Sonmiani he sustained himself by practising medicine:

> *I made some unexpected and extraordinary cures, for if I felt myself*
> *safe, and knew the disorder I had to treat, I did not neglect the oppor-*
> *tunity to do good, and my fame so much increased that I was visited*
> *by patients from the distant hills. I had a singular case from the hills,*
> *of a personable female, the wife of a wealthy Lumri, part of whose face*
> *had become white. The husband proffered two camels if I could by my*
> *skill induce the return of the original tint. I remarked that the lady*
> *would look better if she became white altogether. They both smiled but*
> *were not to be persuaded that black was not a preferable hue.*[75]

His stay at Sonmiani was becoming tedious when a party of Afghan
merchants arrived from Karachi who offered to take him with them to
Kalat, their home town. One of the group was the portly and good-
natured Kalikdad who was to prove the staunchest of friends. This
journey through Las Bela and Eastern Baluchistan to Kalat and the
neighbourhood of Quetta traversed unknown country which remained
unmapped for the next fifty years. However, in such experienced and
agreeable company, the journey proved uneventful and he was able
to make a list of twenty-eight different trees and plants which he saw
on the road.[76] Masson took an immediate liking to Kalat and to the
relatives and friends of his travelling companions, in particular Faiz
Ahmed, a cousin of Kalikdad. One of them accompanied Masson on a
lengthy excursion to Chahiltan, a peak near Quetta from the summit

of which he had a magnificent view. In one quarter he saw the 'bleak, sterile plain' of Dasht-i-bedaulat, which was later to cause difficulties for the Army of the Indus.

He resumed his stay at Kalat but before long he realised that winter was about to set in which ruled out a move to Kandahar; furthermore he was suffering from a severe attack of dysentery. Consequently he sought a milder climate and decided to accompany Kalikdad who was starting on his annual business trip to Sind. The route this time was via the Mulla Pass which Masson describes as 'not only easy and safe, but may be travelled at all seasons'. From Jhal the caravan proceeded to Sehwan, whose antiquity allowed him scope for much speculation, thence through lower Sind, passing many ancient structures of huge stones (locally known as 'gots', i.e. kot or fort), the origin of which he was unable to determine. Other constructions he noted, such as the cylindrical heaps on the hills, were no doubt Buddhist since he was traversing a province which is full of the traces of Buddhist culture. On nearing the coast, Kalikdad turned off for Karachi while Masson, preferring Sonmiani, hired a Bulfut (Lumri) camelman to conduct him there. They shared a camel for the three days' march. As the owner was in the habit not only of taking opium himself but also of giving it to his camel, the morning's ride was sometimes perilously lively.

Masson lived on the best of terms with the inhabitants of Sonmiani, as on his former visit but fearful lest a long stay might impair his health he anxiously awaited an opportunity to proceed again to the north. At length he was able to join a large caravan bound for Kandahar. As far as Kalat it followed very much the same route that Masson had taken before, but there it divided and he continued with the Afghan contingent to Kandahar on a road new to him. It was spring 1832 and he noted vast numbers of red and yellow wild tulips and many varieties of the *Orchis*. He made the journey by camel in a *kajawa*, (panniers slung on either side of a camel), an uncomfortable way of travelling, but one which ensured him a good view of the country and a degree of privacy to take surreptitious notes and compass bearings. The Achakzai tribesmen, some of whom were with the caravan returning to their country from Bombay, behaved with unexpected modesty and good faith, and belied their notorious characteristics of truculence and treachery. In spite of a cordial reception by his Kandahar friends, Masson tarried only until he could find a caravan bound for Kabul. The stages to Ghazni were packed with incidents and the extraordinary greed of the Ghilzai tribes, who live along the road, leaves

one astonished that enough was left of the merchandise for worth-
while business in Kabul. Masson ends his account of their behaviour
thus:

> ... *we had a laughable instance of the furtive instinct of our Ghilzai
> friends afforded by a child of some seven or eight years of age, who had
> detached a camel from the line, and was leading it off before our faces.
> He was detected, but what could be done to so juvenile an urchin?*

Masson was struck by the desolation and degradation of Ghazni. He
could hardly believe that it was the magnificent capital of the
Ghaznavid empire in the 11th and 12th centuries depicted by contemporary writers: 'We look in vain over the city for any traces of the
splendour which once marked the capital of the great Sultan Mahmud.'
Every visitor to Ghazni has had the same feeling of incredulity, but it
only testifies to the appalling destructive capacity of the hordes of
Genghis Khan. Happily Italian archaeologists have in recent years
uncovered two major sites which begin to give some notion of Ghazni's
former glory. Masson continues:

> ... *about a mile distant from the town is the village of Rozah* [Rausa];
> *contiguous to which is the sepulchre and shrine of the mighty Mahmud.
> This has been suffered to dwindle away into ruin, and the broken fig-
> ures of marble lions, with other fragments, alone attest the former
> beauty of its courts and fountains.*[77]

The shrine is today unpretentious despite some reconstruction and
the re-creation of a garden, but the tomb itself, of finely carved marble,
is intact. In Masson's time, the two famous 12th century Minarets could
still be climbed by interior steps though with difficulty and were then
taller than they are now.

CHAPTER VII

KABUL AND BAMIAN

I told him [the Shah of Persia] *that
Cabool was the paradise of our travels.*

Alexander Burnes
Travels into Bokhara

A few days before Charles Masson's arrival in Kabul on 9 June
1832, three Englishmen* had visited the city: Lieutenant Burnes,
Dr Gerard and the Reverend Joseph Wolff. The first two men were, as
we know, on their way to Bokhara; Wolff was on route to India from
Bokhara. The latter had already noted under the date of 23 April 1832:
'We arrived at Saighan; here I learned that two English gentlemen
had arrived at Peshawar with fifteen servants, who were going to re-
claim the property of Mr Morecroft's (sic) party at Mazaur (sic)'[78] —an
interesting example of the efficiency of the local bush telegraph. In
Kabul, Wolff had predicted earthquakes followed by civil dissensions
and these things having come to pass shortly afterwards, his reputation as a prophet was established not only in Afghanistan but also in
India whither it preceded him.

As soon as Masson had found comfortable lodgings in the Armenian quarter close by the Balla Hissar (the citadel which also contained
the royal palace) he called on Haji Khan and was invited to accompany the force that he planned to take in the autumn to the Hazarajat
and to his fief of Bamian in the heart of the Hindu Kush. Masson accepted as he much wished to see the celebrated antiquities of Bamian.
In the meantime he had the whole summer to explore the city and its
environs. He gives a detailed description of the delicacies obtainable
in the bazaars, not least blanched rhubarb, lamb and lettuce. Blanched
rhubarb he says:

---

* Masson writes 'Englishmen' in accordance with contemporary usage, but Burnes
and Gerard were Scotsmen. Wolff was a German Jew who became a Roman Catho-
lic. He was expelled from Rome for erroneous opinions, became an Anglican priest
and missionary and married the daughter of an earl. In 1843 he returned to
Bokhara to ascertain the fate of Stoddart and Conolly.

... is much eaten in its natural state, simply with the addition of salt, and is largely employed in cookery with meat. It affords a grateful, acidulated relish, and is held to be particularly sanative. It serves a variety of uses, and dried is preserved for any length of time... The day of my arrival was distinguished by the presence in the bazaar of cherries, the first-fruits of the year; a day or two after apricots were seen, and in four or five days they were succeeded by mulberries. Cherries, I observed, were of three varieties; and to the Emperor Babur is ascribed the merit of their introduction into Kabul and to which he lays claim in his memoirs. Apricots are of very numerous varieties, as are mulberries; and all exist in profusion ... [Black grapes] appear about the end of June, and continue until the end of July, when they are replaced by the many varieties for which Kabul is famous, until the close of autumn, following each other in due succession. Apples, pears, peaches, quinces and water-melons follow. Besides all these fruits, there are walnuts, almonds and pistachio.

He concludes:

It is scarcely possible that Kabul can be surpassed for the abundance and variety of its fruits, and, perhaps, no city can present, in its season, so beautiful a display of the delicious treasures supplied by nature for her children.[79]

He made excursions in the course of which he inspected various ancient remains and, of course, the tomb of the Emperor Babur whose wish it was to be buried in his beloved Kabul. The numerous burial grounds attached to the city attracted Masson's attention: the different sects, he notes, having their distinct ones, and even the different classes of the same sect. Many of the head-stones were several centuries old, in particular one with a sculptured mitre denoting a Georgian bishop of the 16th or 17th century. Another mitre on a stone in the Armenian cemetery 'points to the rank of the person deposited beneath it, although tradition is silent as to him or to his age'. Masson continues:

But the more curious, and to Englishmen the most interesting gravestone to be found about Kabul, is one commemorative of a countryman, and which bears a simple epitaph and record, in large legible Roman characters. The monument is small, and of marble, not of the very frequent description of upright head-stone, but of another form, which is also common, and which imitates the form of the raised sod over the grave... It is rather confusedly engraved around the sides of the stone, but runs as follows:

Here lyes the body of Joseph Hicks the son of
Thomas Hicks and Eldith who departed this lyfe
the eleventh of October 1666.

*The date carries us back to the commencement of the reign of
Aurangzeb, when Kabul was held by one of his lieutenants. This monument was one of the first objects of curiosity brought to my notice at
Kabul, and residing immediately within the gate of the Balla Hissar
near to it, I had it in sight whenever I left my house on a stroll.*

A knowledgeable grave-digger informed Masson that he understood
from his predecessors that the monument commemorated an officer
of artillery who stood so high in the estimation of the Governor that
they were buried close to each other on a contiguous mound. This
mound and the monument raised over the Governor were pointed
out to Masson by the grave-digger who declared that before his time
the Hicks memorial had been removed and placed over the grave of a
Mahomedan: 'such transfers, however indecorous or indelicate, being sometimes made'.[80]

Inasmuch as Masson was a careful observer and constantly passed
the Hicks monument, one would think that his rendering of the inscription was definitive. But nearly a century later, C. Grey expressed
doubts and compared it with other versions by Masson's contemporaries: G.T. Vigne, who visited Kabul in 1836 (see p. 12) and the British
officers Captain Henry Havelock, Major MacKinnon, Lieutenant William Barr and Dr James Atkinson who were there during the First
Afghan War. All their versions of the inscription were written before
Masson published his account. Unfortunately, none of them agrees
with Masson, or with each other, as to the Christian names of the deceased or of his parents. The deceased's name is variously given as
Thomas or John: his father figures as William or John, and his mother
as Elizabeth or Edith or Judith. To make matters worse, Grey mistakenly stated that Vigne had shown William as the Christian name of
the deceased whereas his transcription actually reads 'Hicks, the son
of William and Elizabeth Hicks'.[81] Grey then compounded his error
by seeking to identify the deceased with William Hicks 'a person of
desperate fortunes' who figures in the East India Company records as
having served in the rival Courteen Company at Gujrat in 1652:

*Soon after this man disappeared into Bengal and was reported dead,
which may have been merely a ruse to escape his creditors. Mahabat
Khan, Governor of Kabul in 1666, had formerly been Governor of
Gujrat, and possibly having there known Hicks, had given him shelter
and employment...*[82]

This interesting identification cannot be maintained, however, since none of the reports attribute the grave to William Hicks.

The grave was not seen again after 1841 and was probably vandalised during the Afghan uprising against the British forces of occupation. As recently as 1982, an American archaeologist reviewed all the written evidence relating to the Hicks tomb and also discovered in the India Office Library an unattributed manuscript but clearly of the period of the First Afghan War. It has a line drawing of the tomb depicting eleven lines of text spread over nine surfaces with erratic division of the words—hence Masson's 'confusedly engraved'—and partly explains the extraordinary discrepancies in the Christian names. According to this manuscript, the inscription carried the names Thomas, John and Judith which agrees with Atkinson's version. Even so, the identity of the occupant of the earliest known English tomb in Afghanistan remains a mystery.[83]

Turning to the social life of the city, Masson pays a striking tribute to the behaviour and hospitality of its inhabitants:

> *There are few places where a stranger so soon feels himself at home, and becomes familiar with all classes, as at Kabul. There can be none where all classes so much respect his claims to civility, and so much exert themselves to promote his satisfaction and amusement. He must not be unhappy. To avow himself so, would be, he is told, a reproach upon the hospitality of his hosts and entertainers. I had not been a month in Kabul before I had become acquainted with I know not how many people; had become a visitor at their houses, a member of their social parties. No holiday occurred that did not bring me a summons to attend some family circle, in some of the many gardens of the city. The stranger guest will not fail to be astonished at the attentions paid to him on such occasions. It seems as if the entertainment had been expressly designed for him, and that the company had no other object than to contribute to his gratification. The most rigid mind must admire such politeness, and the feelings which prompt its exhibition.[84]*

Masson speaks with equal warmth of the singular absence of religious prejudice against Christians:

> *... it is a matter of agreeable surprise to any one acquainted with the Mahomedans of India, Persia and Turkey, and with their religious prejudices and antipathies, to find that the people of Kabul are entirely free from them. In most countries, few Mahomedans will eat with a Christian; to salute him, even in error, is deemed unfortunate, and he is looked upon as unclean. Here none of these difficulties or feelings exist.*

The considerable Shia minority were not molested, though occasionally fights broke out between them and the Sunni majority. The Christian Armenians were treated with more than toleration; they intermarried with Mahomedans and attended each others' funerals and weddings. Though known to be a European, Masson was only once insulted in the street when he wore a Persian cap instead of the usual turban. This spirit of tolerance was confined to Kabul. Other Afghan towns, especially Kandahar, were and are prone to outbursts of fanatical religious and xenophobic behaviour.*

The Jews, however, while tolerated as to matters of faith, did not command the respect which was shown to the Armenians and Masson tells a curious tale of a Jew who was stoned to death by Moslems for denying the divinity of Christ, after the Armenians had declined to carry out the punishment.[85]

In September, Masson joined Haji Khan's expeditionary force. A soldier of fortune who had rendered Dost Mahomed Khan useful service, Haji Khan had become very influential and powerful. He was ambitious and unscrupulous; his intrigues and egregious acts of disloyalty to Dost Mahomed Khan persisted throughout Masson's time. When Masson started out for the Afghan camp, he knew nothing of Haji Khan's political views and ideas and was equally ignorant of his real character, believing the common report that he was a gallant soldier, a firm friend and a man of truth. Masson's sole aim was to examine under favourable circumstances the antiquities of Bamian. At that time Bamian was separated from Kabul territory by the whole breadth of the Besud country which was controlled by a semi-independent Hazara chief, Mir Yezdanbaksh. Beyond Bamian, the Ak Robat Pass defined the northern frontier of Kabul, beyond which again were more semi-independent chieftains, of whom the most powerful was the Uzbek, Murad Beg of Kunduz (see p. 35). Another was the wily Tajik chief, Mahomed Ali Beg of Saighan, notorious for his slave-raiding activities against the Hazaras. Masson devotes 173 pages to his experiences with the expedition, starting with an account of past events which led up to its inception. The military aspects hardly concern us; the geographical results were authoritative for at least a century. The prime interest lies in Masson's close-up view of the behaviour of the

---

* It is not fortuitous that strong Mujahideen resistance to the Soviet occupation occurred at Kandahar [nor that this was the recent stronghold of the fanatical Taliban - Ed.].

Afghans, Hazaras and Uzbeks, and the rapport he achieved with them.

Masson found it impossible to determine what were the real intentions of Haji Khan on quitting Kabul. The ostensible purpose was to collect the tribute due from the Hazaras. But Haji Khan was well aware that he had become an object of suspicion to Dost Mahomed Khan; he may have considered it possible to become independent at Bamian in alliance with Mir Yezdanbaksh or with the chief of Kunduz. His first aim was to bring Saighan under his control. Thereafter he could turn against Mir Yezdanbaksh who had become an over-mighty subject, and destroy him. Finally, if Shah Shuja were again to attempt to regain his throne, as Kabul rumour had it, Haji Khan, in possession of Bamian and commanding the resources of Besud, would be in a position to render the restored monarch an important service. An alliance with Mir Yezdanbaksh was concluded on the basis of a joint attack against Saighan and the combined force, consisting of 2,000 Hazara cavalry and 800 Afghan troops with two guns, marched through Besud.

The story of the daily progress of the oriental camp with its medley of retainers: physician, apothecary, mullas, tailors and musicians, and the nightly discussions with the talkative Haji Khan, is well told. Masson evidently exercised considerable influence over his Afghan and Hazara acquaintances, and he is no doubt justified in his claim to have prevented more than one serious row over payment for supplies demanded from the unfortunate peasants. The two guns were dragged along by forced Hazara labour, eighty men being required for the smaller, and two hundred for the larger, assisted by an elephant. In the course of its progress, the army camped in the valley containing the sources of the Logar River. Near these springs is the remarkable Azdha (Dragon) of Besud, according to legend the petrified remains of a dragon which terrified the neighbourhood until slain by Hazrat Ali (cousin and son-in-law of the Prophet)—actually a white volcanic formation stretching for about 170 yards and exhaling sulphurous odours. The vivid red rock with its springs around the dragon's head is imagined to be tinged with its blood. Another dragon near Bamian which Masson also saw is even more imposing in size, but less realistic. Both are frequently visited by pilgrims. After more long marches the force crossed the Helmand, making for Bamian. This move closed the bloodless Besud expedition during which Haji Khan increased by half the tribute paid in previous years and won the confidence of the Hazaras by his friendly manners and his gifts.

It was now early winter and the frozen snow made the passes

slippery and difficult. Masson was impressed by the mountainous landscape all around him, in particular by the Koh-i-Baba range which is crowned by a peak rising to 16,244 feet, the highest in the Hindu Kush. In the beautiful and serene valley of Bamian he camped opposite the two colossal Buddhas, 180 ft and 125 ft high respectively, carved out of the face of the sandstone cliff (see Plate A, p. 81). His stay was rather short and he had less time than he had hoped to examine the 'idols' and some of the many caves 'so much the objects of European curiosity'. On his return to Bamian from the attack on Saighan, further research was frustrated by the onset of one of the most intense winters within memory. He naturally supposed that there would be another opportunity to resume his investigations, but to his lasting regret he was never able to do so. He doubted whether the statues were Buddhas and would have been surprised to learn that Hsuan Tsang, the Chinese pilgrim, had found ten monasteries with over 1,000 monks in Bamian at the time of his visit in AD 632. Masson's views on Bamian are discussed in a later chapter.

Haji Khan, with Masson at his side, marched and counter-marched through the valleys and over the passes of the Hindu Kush. But instead of destroying the Saighan opposition, as he had frequently vowed to do, he arranged a truce with Mohamed Ali Beg and married one of his daughters. The next step was to subdue Kamard, another small khanate, but this proved unexpectedly difficult. However, the Hazara forces had made the fatal error of splitting into three detached bodies and Haji Khan jumped at the opportunity to commit an act of foul treachery. He seized Yezdanbaksh and after dragging him about under circumstances of great indignity, he finally executed him. The Hazara troops scattered; their camp was looted, whilst those captured were stripped and made slaves. The savage barbarity of these proceedings, especially the method of execution of Yezdanbaksh by means of a rope round the victim's neck the two ends of which were hauled tight by relatives under duress, disgusted Masson deeply. Thereafter he shows an obvious disposition to part company with his treacherous host.

Winter had fairly set in and Haji Khan settled down in the fort of Saidabad near Bamian, a strongly built construction of burnt bricks of immense size, which Masson believed to have been built by the Arabs. Although at an altitude of 8,200 feet, Bamian in winter is endurable, and the Afghan chief decided to remain. Masson now made strenuous efforts to get back to Kabul. His first essay, during which he experienced a very bad time, failed owing to counter orders from Haji

Khan recalling the escort. His second attempt also failed because the Hazaras holding the Shibar and Bitchilik passes barred his passage. It was a remarkable fact that he, a *feringhi*, was elected by the Afghan gang with which he was temporarily associated as their Khan or chief. He was a little better dressed than most of them in British chintzes and better mounted on Haji Khan's horses. He was rarely able to restrain their looting propensities, but he made himself popular by his civility and his small presents to the wretched Hazaras on whom they were quartered. Incidentally he gives a valuable account of an important group of Afghan passes. At last the Hazaras reopened the road and Masson was able to reach the capital by the Hajigak and Unai passes—the age-old pilgrim and caravan route between Kabul, Bamian and Bokhara.

The last part of the journey was not accomplished without great distress:

> There arose a terrific south wind, which carried the drifting snow before it. I had never in my life witnessed anything so violent, and until now had never formed a just conception of the effects of a wind-tempest during winter in these regions. I bore up, however, against it ... when my powers yielded and I found myself becoming insensible. Fortunately, at this critical moment a village was a little right of the road, to which I turned my horse, who also had become faint. Crossed the stream of the valley by a bridge, and entered the village on its bank. Threw myself from the horse and entered without ceremony the first house with open door. The master, who saw how things stood, recommended me to the masjit, engaging to take care of my horse. I replied my good man, I am a Feringhi, and what have I to do with the Masjit. On which he instantly led me into an upper apartment, occupied by a brother. There was a sandalli [charcoal brazier], my boots were pulled off, and my feet examined which had suffered no injury.

The wind continuing with unabated violence he remained at the village the next day, but the day after he was able to each Kabul where:

> My Armenian friends were rejoiced to see me again, and forgetting the perils of the road and the rigours of Bamian, I passed in their society a pleasant evening, which, by their calculation, was that of Christmas Day.[86]

From the end of 1832 until he finally left Kabul with Burnes in 1838, Masson made the city his headquarters and devoted himself to antiquarian researches in the Kohistan and in the neighbourhood of Jalalabad, though after March 1835 they had perforce to take second place to his duties as an intelligence agent. During those years he undertook no further long-distance expeditions, though he criss-crossed the Kabul province and explored the Kunar and Alishang valleys, then and for long afterwards, unknown territory. It was not until 1840 that he made another long journey, this time from Karachi to Kalat in a vain effort to reach Kabul in order to resume his archaeological and numismatic labours. But this was his third visit to Kalat and hence unproductive of new geographical information.

His major explorations having thus ended with the expedition to Besud and Bamian we can close our examination of Masson's status as a geographer by quoting Sir Thomas Holdich's considered verdict:

> As an explorer in Afghanistan he stands alone. His work has never been equalled; but owing to the very unsatisfactory methods adopted by all explorers in those days for the recording of geographical observations it cannot be said that his contribution to exact geographical knowledge was commensurate with his extraordinary capacity as an observant traveller, or his remarkable industry.[87]

To this tribute one should add that if Holdich had had access to the Masson Collection of Manuscripts (not then catalogued), he would have found many sketch maps and tables of compass bearings and distances which would have improved the existing maps of Afghanistan, if Masson had been encouraged to work out the results. In consequence Holdich might have decided that Masson's geographical observations were less unsatisfactory than he supposed.

A few days after his return to Kabul, Masson was surprised by a visit from a person announcing himself as Saiyad Keramat Ali, agent of the Supreme Government of India. He spoke of his travels as companion of Lieutenant Arthur Conolly on his overland journey in 1830, and of his adventures at Kabul. He had wished to preserve his incognito; but a letter destined for Herat having been intercepted, his existence and the nature of his employment became revealed, and he was consigned to the prison of Dost Mahomed Khan. He was rescued by the Nawab Jabar Khan who remonstrated with his brother that this was no way to treat the first agent to be sent from British India. Brought before Dost Mahomed, Keramat Ali said that his sole business was to procure intelligence of Abbas Mirza of Persia and his movements. Dost Mahomed Khan observed 'Very good, they interest me also; take care not to write anything about me.' The Nawab had joyfully carried off Keramat Ali and installed him in apartments of his own house where, under his protection, he freely reported to Captain Wade at Ludhiana.

The appointment of Keramat Ali as newswriter, originally at Kandahar but then transferred to Kabul at his own request, was the

first step in the intercourse between the Government of India and the
Barakzai sirdars. It came about as a result of the deepening concern in
Calcutta and Bombay with Russian activities in Central Asia and Persia, discussed in Chapter III. Masson was eventually to succeed the Indian newswriter, though with a wider remit. Meanwhile, Masson saw a
good deal of Keramat Ali:

> The Saiyad was more liberal in religious opinions than was, perhaps,
> necessary or decent; and, as the month of Ramazan came on, I had
> much of his company, owing to his aversion to fasting which, to save
> appearances, it was not right to display in the Nawab's house.[88]

While Masson was still absent on the Bamian expedition, Keramat Ali
had received instructions to ferret out the former's antecedents, Major Wilson's despatch to Bombay transmitting Masson's papers on his
travels having aroused curiosity about its author. Keramat Ali's report for the period 3-25 December 1832 is worth quoting for the light
it throws on a newswriter's labours and for the details it gives of
Masson's attire and possessions.

> A European arrived here in the month of May 1832 and resided for
> four months in the house of one Suliman, an Armenian from whom I
> had the following account of him. He described himself as an English-
> man by name Masson of the Sect of Priests and said that he had been
> absent from his country twelve years, during which time he had been
> travelling. He had lately come from Kurachee Bunder through Sindh
> and Candahar. He understood Persian, had with him two or three books
> in a foreign character, a compass, a map and an astrolabe. He was
> shabbily dressed and he had no servant, horse nor mule to carry his
> baggage. While at Cabul he paid his respects to Nawab Jabbar Khan,
> who pressed him earnestly to enter his service but he declined. The
> Nawab thought him a Frenchman and others thought him one also,
> but Suliman says that he had opportunities of indulging in conversa-
> tion with him and that he firmly believed him to be an Englishman.
> While living with Suliman, he had funds to defray his expenses and
> mentioned some part of his property being in Sindh. He also borrowed
> RS. 300 from a Kakuri, and sent it by a Hoondee [Bill of Exchange]
> to Sindh or Hindoostan. He had an interview at Cabul with Hajee
> Khan, Kakuri, who, on going to Bamian sent for him there. He ac-
> cepted the Khan's invitation and on 10th September having hired a
> pony for six rupees, he set out for that place. He is now with Hajee
> Khan at Bamian...[89]

Masson had evidently dropped his American disguise when he took
up residence at Kabul.

CHAPTER VIII

MASSON'S ARCHAEOLOGICAL AND NUMISMATIC DEBUT

All passes, Art alone
Enduring stays to us;
The Bust outlasts the throne
The Coin, Tiberius.

H. A. Dobson
Ars Victrix

The weather in January and February 1833, of which Masson gives a vivid account, continued exceptionally severe, and spring was slow in coming. By May, however, he was able to extend his excursions beyond the city limits and to start examining certain remains which had previously caught his attention. But he had to proceed with great caution lest he arouse animosity or cupidity in various quarters. The following passage gives a good idea of the difficulties which were to persist throughout his archaeological labours; of his methods and finds; and of the successful use he made then and later of his wide acquaintance among Afghans of all classes:

Having now resided a year without interruption, and in perfect security in the country, I was emboldened to essay whether objections would be made to the examination of some of the numerous artificial mounds on the skirts of the hills. I was unable to direct my attention to the massive topes, where considerable expense was required; still, the inferior indications of the olden times might repay the labour bestowed upon them, and by testing the feeling which my excavations created I might smooth the way for the time when I should be in a condition to undertake the superior monuments. Without asking permission of anyone, I commenced an operation upon a mound at the skirt of the hill Koh Takht Shah... Below, or east of it, was a castle and garden, belonging to Akhund Iddaitulah. I had become acquainted with his sons, who interested themselves to forward my researches... In the course of four or five days we discovered, nearly at one of the angles of the mound, a tak, or arched recess, ornamentally carved, and supported by two slender pillars. In it we found the remains of several earthen images;

the heads of the two larger ones only were sufficiently entire to bear removal. They were evidently of female figures, and of very regular and handsome features.* Affected by moisture, which had naturally in the course of centuries completely pervaded the mound, and every- thing of mere earth contained within it, we could yet from slight traces ascertain that the figures had been originally covered with layers of white and red paint, and that over the latter had been placed a surface of gold leaf. The hair of the heads, tastefully arranged in curls, had been painted with an azure colour. The recess also had been embel- lished with gold leaf and lapis lazuli tints. Accompanying the figures were a variety of toys, precisely such as the Hindus make at the present day and in no better taste, representing horses, sheep, cows etc. of cement.

The more important discovery remained. At the base of the recess were hewn stones, and on their removal he found jammed in between them Nagari writings on birch bark which had suffered badly from the all-penetrating damp. He next uncovered a suite of small apartments. In one of them, he found several images lying horizontally, one of them eight or ten feet in length. They were all of pure earth, and had been covered with gold leaf. His Moslem companions amused themselves by trying to scrape it off, but with limited success as the images were so saturated. In another apartment also decorated with mouldings, and painted with white, red and azure colours, he found three earthen lamps, an iron nail and one or two fragments of iron.[90]

His researches became the subject of conversation in the capital and the son of Akhund Iddaitulah having sold the gold leaf he scraped from the images to a goldsmith for less than a rupee, Masson's friends begged him to desist from such labours in future. They urged that the country was bad, as were the people, and that he would probably get into trouble. He pointed out that little notice would be taken of him so long as broken idols were the sole fruits of his endeavours. Mahomed Akbar Khan,[‡] son of Dost Mahomed Khan, hearing of his discoveries, sent for him and wished to see them. He was enraptured with the two 'female' heads, and lamented that the ideal beauties of the sculptor

---

* No doubt heads of Buddha which are often effeminate in appearance in Gandhara sculpture.

‡ He murdered Sir W. Macnaghten in 1881 and gave undertakings of safe con-duct to the British force which led to the notorious retreat, but did not, or per-haps in the circumstances could not, implement them.

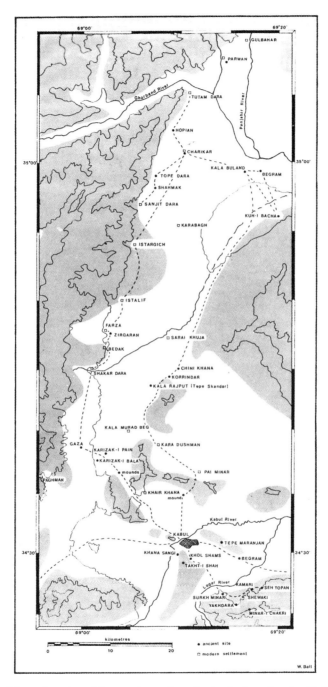

Plate 3. Map showing Masson's archaeological sites in the Kabul-Koh-Damian area

could not be realised in nature. An acquaintanceship grew up between Masson and the young sirdar who would frequently send for him. He became a pretty constant visitor at Mohamed Akbar Khan's tea-table and obtained from him an order, addressed to the various headmen and chiefs of the Kohistan and Ghorband, to assist him in any researches he might undertake in those districts, of which the sirdar was the governor. Masson was both gratified and surprised at the good sense shown by the young sirdar as to the nature and object of his researches.

His relations with the sirdar allayed the misgivings of his friends, and encouraged him to continue his researches without fear. He was, he says, always of the opinion that no umbrage would be taken, and felt assured that if he acted openly and fairly he would be fairly dealt with. Nothing further of consequence was extracted from the mound; but when Dr Gerard arrived in Kabul at the end of that year, Masson pointed out the spot to him as one likely to yield a desirable find to carry with him to India. From it he obtained the marble sculptured slab forwarded to the Asiatic Society of Bengal, an account of which, written by his secretary and companion, Mohan Lal, appeared in the Journal of the Society for September 1834.[91]

Masson was fortunate in his choice of site to make his archaeological debut, not only as regards the quality of his finds, but also in the confidence it gave him. He was fortunate too, in gaining the interest and protection of Mahomed Akbar Khan. It was not always to be so, and he had to be circumspect whenever he attacked a site in an unfamiliar district. He now started to examine the neighbourhood of Charikar in a series of trips on foot. His intention was to make a preliminary study of the local conditions and the antiquities in the area. For a stranger, travelling without tent or servants, it was difficult to obtain a lodging for the night, unless the mosque could be regarded as quarters; to pass the night in the open was neither safe nor seemly. He succeeded in forming acquaintances at all the stage villages on the several roads between Kabul and Charikar and was certain whenever he dropped in on any of them to be received with civility. In the course of these trips he visited the picturesque township of Istalif, nowadays a favourite tourist attraction,* which he lovingly describes. He also

---

* Or was, prior to the invasion by the Soviet Union at Christmas 1979, since when it has been heavily bombed.

examined the stupa at Dara which he hoped to excavate and of which he drew a sketch.

But he was looking for something much more important. Alexander the Great founded several cities in the Afghan area, one of which, Alexandria ad Caucasum, was believed to be located in the Kohistan north of Kabul and close to the Hindu Kush. Masson thought that the village of Begram and its great plain might well prove to be the site. He had previously reached the edge of the plain and had heard strange stories of the innumerable coins and other relics found on the soil but had been unable to procure a specimen, all to whom he applied, whether Hindu or Moslem, denying they had any such things in their possession. A friendly headman provided him with an escort of half a dozen horsemen to enable him to traverse and survey the plain, which was dangerous owing to the marauders infesting it. At Killa Bolend at the beginning of the Begram plain there were seven considerable Hindu traders, but no coins were forthcoming. At another village he heard fresh tales of Begram and the treasures found there. His curiosity was so intensely excited that he determined to revisit it taking along Mir Afzil, the headman's son, who had friends in the vicinity. Mir Afzil produced Baloch Khan:

> ... a fine honest young man, who brought me a present of melons and grapes. This was the commencement of an acquaintance which continued as long as I remained at Kabul; and Baloch Khan greatly assisted me in my subsequent researches, as I could always when needed call upon him and his armed followers to attend me in my excursions, and to protect the people I sent. He now exerted himself to procure coins; and at last an old defaced one was produced by a Mahomedan, for which I gave two pais, which induced the appearance of others, until the Hindus ventured to bring forth their bags of old monies, from which I selected such as suited my purpose. I had the satisfaction to obtain in this manner some eighty coins of types which led me to anticipate bright results from the future.

The fears and scruples of the owners having been overcome, he remained some time at Killa Bolend, securing their confidence. They had been anxious lest Masson should employ forced labourers to scour the plain in search of antique relics and had therefore determined to conceal from him, if possible, the existence of such objects. He took care to ascertain how and by whom these coins were found. The clue to them once discovered, the collection became an easy matter although it subsequently proved that a long time was necessary before he became fully master of the plain.[92]

His interest in finding and deciphering coins was now fully aroused:

> The discovery of so interesting a locality as that of Begram imposed upon me new, agreeable, and I should hope not unprofitable employment. I availed myself of every opportunity to visit it, as well with the view to secure the rich memorials of past ages it yielded, as to acquire a knowledge of the adjacent country. Before the commencement of winter, when the plain, covered with snow is of course closed to research, I had accumulated one thousand eight hundred and sixty-five copper coins, besides a few silver ones, many rings, signets and other relics. The next year, 1834, the collection which fell into my hands amounted to one thousand nine hundred copper coins, besides other relics. In 1835 it increased to nearly two thousand five hundred copper coins, and in 1836 it augmented to thirteen thousand four hundred and seventy copper coins. In 1837, when I had the plain well under control and was enabled constantly to locate my people upon it, I obtained sixty thousand copper coins, a result at which I was well pleased, having at an early period of my researches conjectured that so many as thirty thousand coins might annually be procured. The whole of the coins and other antiquities, from Begram, with several thousands of other coins brought to light in various parts of Afghanistan, have been forwarded to the Honourable the East India Company...[93]

It will be seen that the copper coins from Begram alone amounted to 79,735. If to this figure is added the few silver ones and the several thousands of coins, including some gold ones, from elsewhere in Afghanistan, the grand total must have been well in excess of 80,000. Yet with Masson's figures in front of them, several commentators have credited him with strangely varied totals. Hambly says 30,000; C. Grey makes it about 70,000 which is nearer the mark; Holdich merely states that the collection totalled between 15,000 and 20,000 in 1837. Even if the latter thought that the figures were cumulative instead of year by year, he would have had to give 60,000 as the final total. According to H.H. Wilson, Masson collected about 30,000 coins, but he was writing before the publication of the *Narrative of Various Journeys* and was no doubt relying on earlier figures provided by Masson. In 1839, the East India Company in a despatch to the Bombay Government, referred to the 60,000 copper coins collected by Masson of which 25,000 were still in his hands.[94] Wilson quotes Masson's estimate that for long years past Begram had yielded about 30,000 coins annually; picked up by generations of nomad herdsmen these coins had been bought by weight by local coppersmiths and melted down in the Kabul mint.

Wilson was naturally concerned with the quality of the coins rather than the quantity, and he remarks of the lost coins that:

> *The far greatest proportion, judging from Mr Masson's collection, must have been too much injured by time and corrosion to have had any other than metallic value; but from the same accumulations we may infer that great numbers of coins, of high numismatic interest, must have perished in the indiscriminate destruction to which the whole have for so long a time been condemned.*[95]

This huge collection was sent by Masson at intervals to Bombay under an arrangement with the Governor there, and shipped to the East India Company's museum in London. With the transfer of power in India to the Crown after the Mutiny, the contents of the museum became government property and many of the finer and rarer coins of the Masson collection were presented to the British Museum in 1881. In 1906 the India Office gave a number of other pieces from his collection to the Fitzwilliam Museum in Cambridge. Meanwhile its arrival in London greatly stimulated British numismatic studies: *Ariana Antiqua* to which Masson contributed a *Memoir on the Buildings called Topes*, was a first fruit. In passing it should be said that other collectors were active in West Punjab and Afghanistan at this time, largely inspired by the discoveries of General Ventura when he opened the tope at Manikyala in 1830, namely Ventura himself, Alexander Burnes, his secretary Mohan Lal, Dr Gerard, Dr Honigberger and Saiyad Keramat Ali. These collections amounted to several hundred pieces and comprised specimens of most of the types discovered by Masson, many of them in excellent preservation. Many of these items, including those which eventually reached institutions in Paris, passed through the hands of Mr James Prinsep, the erudite and energetic secretary of the Asiatic Society of Bengal, who thus in the course of a few years found himself overwhelmed by vast numbers of Bactrian-Greek, Indo-Scythic, and Kushan coins, whereas before 1830 only a handful of such coins were known to the numismatic world. Besides publishing descriptions and engravings of these collections in the Journal of the Society (Masson wrote his own articles for that Journal), Prinsep set to work to decipher the legends on the coins with considerable success: *Ariana Antiqua* is appropriately dedicated to him.

In order to judge the full impact of the coins and monuments, uncovered by Masson and others, on the study of the history of Bactria after Alexander the Great, one needs to consider the state of knowledge of that principality around 1830. *Ariana Antiqua* puts it succinctly:

A very short period has elapsed since the means of an acquaintance with the history of Bactria and Bactrian India were extremely circumscribed. It was known that after the death of Alexander, Bactria became an independent principality under Greek sovereigns, and the names of a few of them were picked out with extraordinary labour and learning from the fragmentary notices of classical authors, and one or two rare coins. It had been ascertained from the same writers, and from the Chinese authorities, that the Greek rule was overthrown by Scythian chiefs, whose sway extended to the mouths of the Indus; and from the Mohammedan historians we had learned that the Arab invaders of Sindh and Afghanistan were encountered by Hindu princes, who had therefore supplanted in those countries both Greek and Bar-

Plate B. pp. 82-83. Coins from the Masson Collection in the British Museum.

i. Bronze coin of Greek king DEMETRIUS I of Bactria, c. 190 BC; rev. showing standing figure of goddess Artemis holding bow and drawing arrow from quiver on back; inscribed **Basileos Demetriou** *(of King Demetrius) in Greek letters. 24 mm. British Museum Catalogue (BMC) 14. India Office Collection (IOC) 12.*

ii. Bronze coin of Greek king MENANDER I of N.W. India c. 150 BC; obv. showing bust of king facing right; inscribed **Basileos Soteros Menandrou** *(of King Menander the Saviour) in Greek letters. 26 mm. Registration number 1926-5-2-1.*

iii. Bronze coin of Parthian King GONDOPHARES of N.W. India c. AD 10; obv. showing figure of king seated on horseback facing left being offered a wreath by standing figure of Victory facing right; inscribed **Basileos Basileon [M]egalou Gon[do]pharou** *(King of Kings Gondophares the Great) in Greek letters; 20 mm. BMC 22. IOC 233.*

iv. Gold coin of Kushan King Wima Kadphises of Bactria and N.W. India c. AD 80; obv. showing enthroned figure of king facing left; inscribed **Basileos Ooemo Kadphises** *(King Wima Kadphises) in Greek letters; 24 mm. BMC 1. IOC 268.*

v. Bronze coin of Kushan King Kaniska I of Bactria & N.W. India c. AD 100; rev. showing standing figure of Buddha facing, inscribed **Sakamana [Bou]do** *(Sakyamuni Buddha) in Greek letters; 23 mm. BMC 38. IOC 296.*

vi. Silver coin of Chionite Huns in Bactria, c. AD 370; obv. showing bust of Sasanian king Shapur II, facing right; inscribed in Bactrian script (undeciphered); 27 mm. Registration number 1894-5-6-1293.

Plate A (right). The Large Buddha at Bamian (see text p. 70 and Chapter IX).

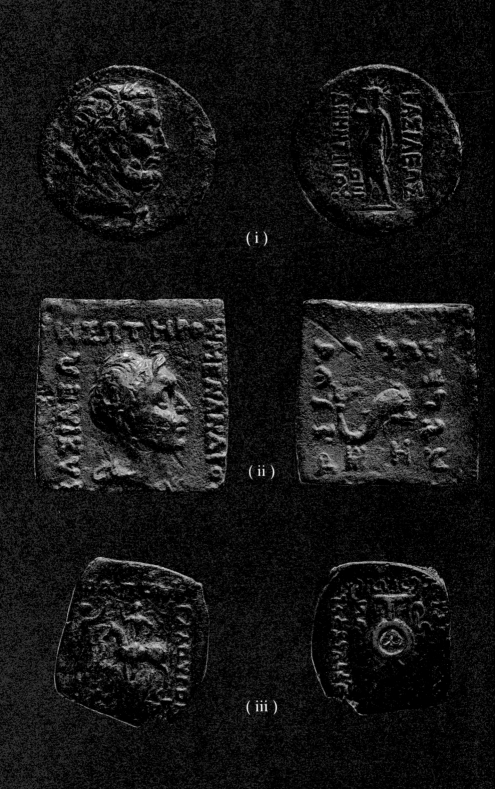

(i)

(ii)

(iii)

(iv)

(v)

(vi)

Plate C. The Great Stupa of Manikyala, Punjab (see Chapter IX).

barian kings. *These few leading facts were unaccompanied by details, and scantily occupied the interval that separated the Mohammedan from the Macedonian invasion. Within the last seven years this deficiency has been remedied, this barrenness of events has been changed to abundance. Successful research has not only corroborated all that was before imperfectly known, but has filled up the meagre outline with circumstances and persons of historical truth and importance. The hitherto unnamed or unknown members of successive or synchronous dynasties now pass before our eyes as well-defined individuals and in connected order; and revolutions of a religious as well as of a political origin may be discerned...'* [96]

Masson's own verdict on his numismatic finds runs:

It may be superfluous to dwell upon the importance of the Begram collections; independently of the revelation of unknown kings and dynasties, they impart great positive knowledge, and open a wide field for speculation and inquiry on the very material subjects of the languages and religions prevailing in Central Asia during the dark period of its history... Besides coins, Begram has yielded very large numbers of engraved seals, some of them with inscriptions, figures of men and animals, particularly of birds, cylinders, and parallelogramic amulets with sculptured sides, rings and a multitude of other trinkets and miscellaneous articles, generally of brass and copper; many of which are curious and deserve description.[97]

To this modest claim may be appended Professor Wilson's appreciation:

... in addition to new coins of Greek princes already known, he found those of several whose names are not mentioned in history as Antialkidas, Lysias, Agathocles, Archebias (sic), Pantaleon and Hermaeus. He also found the coins of the king whose titles only are specified as the Great King of Kings, the Preserver, and of others whose names assuming a Greek form indisputably denote barbaric or Indo-Scythic princes: Undapherres [Gondopheres], Azes, Azilises, Kadphises, and Kanerkes [Kanishka]. Mr Masson described the most remarkable of them and furnished linear delineations of them, which were engraved in the Journal and which, although not pretending to merit as works of art, were satisfactory confirmations of the correctness of his descriptions and decypherings. The first great step in the series of Bactrian numismatic discovery was thus accomplished, and the great object of later investigations has been to complete and extend the structure of which such broad foundations were laid.[98]

The numismatists were naturally keen to decipher and categorize the unrecorded coins. Masson realised that the pattern of their distribution was also of importance. Copper coins of hitherto unknown rulers and new varieties of known rulers when recorded in quantity at a particular place demonstrate the relative importance of the monarch in the locality. Thus as regards his Begram finds, Masson specifically states that he discovered no monies of the genuine Azes Kings there, adding that this is illustrative of the value attaching to collections of coins from a known spot.[99] He notes that copper coins of Azes are seldom or never found west of Jalalabad and only scantily there, whereas they are the most numerous of the coins met with to the north and east of Peshawar. Such a distribution naturally points to Jalalabad as the approximate westward limit of the Azes Kingdom. Furthermore, no coins of the earliest Bactrian Kings, Diodotus I and II, were found at Begram which suggests that their rule did not then extend south of the Hindu Kush. On the other hand, Kushan copper coins were found both at Kabul and Jalalabad.

Ever since Masson's time his coins and subsequent accessions have been intensively studied. Although a consensus exists in many matters, there are still gaps in our knowledge of the dynasties concerned and scholarly debate continues, in particular over the dating of individual reigns, and the exact location and extent of their dominions. Some language problems too are as yet unsolved, though here also our knowledge has greatly increased.

* (p. 87) According to Gavin Hambly's Introduction to Masson (I, pp. xxii-xxiii) Burnes and Gerard arrived together and, as Masson had just missed the party on their outward journey: 'This was therefore the first time that Masson, dining at the house of Nawab Jabbar Khan, encountered the two men who were to play a major part in shaping his life during the next few years... Burnes may have whetted his appetite for ... a pardon and regular employment in the Company's service.' This passage is fiction. Burnes did not touch Kabul on his return journey; he and Gerard separated in Persia because of the latter's ill-health. Burnes continued his journey across Persia to Bushire and thence to Bombay, landing on 18 January 1833. Gerard travelled slowly via Herat and Kandahar reaching Kabul in late November 1833. When Burnes was supposed to be dining with the Nawab, he was actually in London on leave. He did not meet Masson until he arrived in Kabul on his mission in September 1837. (Burnes, *Cabool* pp. 139-40)

CHAPTER IX

MASSON ACHIEVES RECOGNITION AS AN ANTIQUARIAN

> *The intrinsic value of Mr Masson's*
> *finds is great... I also desire to place*
> *on record my own opinion of him as*
> *a person of most superior education,*
> *and fine feeling.*
>
> Sir Henry Pottinger

If the year 1833 saw Masson fairly launched on his numismatic and archaeological researches, it also brought acquaintance with two individuals who were to influence his future, Dr Martin Honigberger and Dr J.G. Gerard:

> *On my return to Kabul from my first excursion to Begram I had the pleasure to meet M. Martine* [sic] *Honigberger, from Lahore, who proposed via Bokhara to regain his native country. My visits to this gentleman caused me to see frequently the Nawab Jabar Khan, with whom he resided; and that nobleman issued a standing order that he would be informed whenever I came, and made it a point to favour us with his company. With M. Honigberger I made a trip to Shakr Dara, with the view of ascending the high hill Hous Khast, but the season being too early we failed to do so, and I nearly perished in the attempt. M. Honigberger subsequently examined several of the topes near Kabul, and then proceeded to Jalalabad, under the Nawab's protection, where he instituted a series of operations on the Darunta group; and had not his apprehension been excited by certain rumours* [of impending hostilities] *it is possible little would have remained for my ultimate examination. As it was he precipitately retired to Kabul. His labours have had the advantage of having been made known to the European world by the late regretted Eugene Jacquet* [a French numismatist of repute]. *At the close of autumn our European society was augmented by the arrival of Dr Gerard, the companion of Lieutenant Burnes,* and a few days after his departure for Ludhiana, M. Honigberger set out with a* kafila *for Bokhara. At Ak Robat* [Pass], *a march beyond Bamian, he was maltreated and plundered. Dost Mahomed Khan, I fear, was not innocent in this matter...*

Happily, the Nawab purchased most of the stolen articles from the robbers and sent them to General Allard at Lahore for onward transmission to Honigberger.[100]

In his book of reminiscences, Honigberger confirms Masson's account of this affair and flatly blames Dost Mahomed Khan who, thinking that the Doctor was removing immense riches derived from his excavations in the Jalalabad area, had instructed the governor of Bamian to despoil him. But he adds that he had taken the precaution of handing over all the articles he had extracted locally to Gerard to carry to the Punjab. Eventually both consignments reached him in Europe.[101]

John Martin Honigberger was born at Kronstadt in Transylvania about 1795 and later became an Austrian subject. Although he may have been of Jewish descent—and his name would suggest it—he states that he was baptised in the local church which his parents attended and where they had also been baptised. Having completed his medical training in 1815, he spent many years practising medicine in Europe, Russia, the Ottoman Empire including Syria and Egypt, and briefly in Persia, before he entered Ranjit Singh's service. There he met the Reverend Joseph Wolff who noted:

> Lahore: June 19, 1832: ... Dr Honigberger, a Jewish physician from Hungary, who had seen me in Mount Lebanon, called upon me; he was employed by Runjeet Singh, first as a physician, and then in the preparing of gunpowder, and of a kind of distilled spirit, which Runjeet Singh is in the habit of drinking.[102]

This concoction consisted of raw spirit, crushed pearls, musk, opium, gravy and spices. It appealed to the Maharaja who had lost his taste for ordinary spirit which he alleged had no bite. It was so potent that two wineglassfuls knocked out even the most hardened topers among the British officers rash enough to accept it, though their host freely indulged in it.[103] This cocktail startled Lord Auckland's party during his state visit to the Maharaja in 1838. Some of his suite found it so appalling that they poured it on to the carpet but took care to do so on Ranjit Singh's blind side.

The opening of the Tope of Manikyala by General Ventura occurred during Honigberger's time in Lahore. It evidently impressed him when he visited it and led him to develop an interest in comparable monuments and in ancient coins. His coin collection created a stir in French numismatic circles when it reached Paris. Some drawings by Masson of stupas near Kabul which he gave to Honigberger appeared in the

Journal Asiatique in 1836.

During his stay in Afghanistan, Honigberger wrote to Captain Wade, the Political Agent at Ludhiana, about his archaeological activities and mentions Masson in passing:

> There is an European by name Masson. He was several years in the Punjab. It appears that he has also been to Tabriz, and has lately come to Cabul by the way of Belochistan: he resided some time at Bamian, where he amused himself in making excavations, and has succeeded in finding several idols. At Cabul, he has been engaged in the same kind of pursuit, and has been rewarded here also by his discovery of several idols quite entire.

This report was subsequently printed in the *Journal of the Asiatic Society of Bengal* for April 1834 as Honigberger's 'Journal of a route from Dera Ghazi Khan, through Veziri country, to Kabul'.[104] Unfortunately, Honigberger's memoirs, written much later, throw no further light on his own antiquarian researches in Afghanistan or on those of Masson whom he does not mention. He barely refers to the Kabul stage of his long journey home, no doubt thinking it sufficiently covered in the Journal.

Gerard, an explorer of the Himalayas and an amateur geologist, had acquired a taste for coins and stupas during his journey to Bokhara with Alexander Burnes. Although the time he spent in Masson's company was limited, he was much impressed by his personality, his researches and his knowledge of the region. He encouraged Masson to publish his antiquarian discoveries. In consequence his 'Memoir on the ancient coins found at Beghram, in the Kohistan of Kabul' accompanied by his line drawings of the more important coins appeared in the *Journal of the Asiatic Society of Bengal* in April 1834.[105] The same volume also contained Gerard's own 'Memoir on the Topes and Antiquities of Afghanistan'. Masson contributed a second and third memoir on the coins to subsequent numbers of the Journal[106] as well as articles on Bamian.[107] These articles, besides arousing much interest in cultivated circles in India, naturally drew attention to their author, but it was not till after his pardon that his fellow-passenger on the *Duchess of Atholl* could put two and two together. Brownlow was an associate member of the Asiatic Society of Bengal and in his first letter to Masson (see p. 15) he said that he had:

> ... derived much pleasure from the perusal of your antiquarian papers in the Journal of the Asiatic Society, little did I dream however that I was indebted for this to one so long and intimately known to me. Your labours are highly prized.

Important and stimulating though these papers were, Professor Wilson found them in too detailed and inconvenient a form for his scholarly purposes and prompted Masson to produce material and drawings for *Ariana Antiqua.*

Gerard, who had advanced him Rs. 1,000 for his researches, continued to exert himself on Masson's behalf, writing to Sir Charles Metcalfe in Calcutta in December 1833 on his way back to India to the effect that Masson was well qualified for any Government employment. When he reached Ludhiana in March 1834, he spoke to Captain Wade about Masson and threw new light on the value of his work.

Another well-wisher had also been active. When still at an early stage of his antiquarian researches, Masson had made proposals on 1 January 1833, to the Bombay Government for financial aid through the medium of Colonel Henry Pottinger, to whom he was apparently drawn by some complimentary remarks of Major David Wilson at Bushire.[108] This letter was the start of a voluminous correspondence over many years in which Pottinger encouraged Masson's work and writings, obtained books for him and arranged transfers of money. He also sent occasional sums out of his own pocket. On 31 December 1833, the Colonel wrote officially to Masson forwarding copies of his letter to the Bombay Government recommending a grant of Rs. 1,500 to enable him to prosecute his antiquarian researches, and of the reply from Charles Norris, Chief Secretary, sanctioning the proposal on condition that Masson handed over all his finds to government and consigned them to Bombay.[109] With the letter he enclosed Rs. 500 as an advance. Masson was later to receive further grants of Rs. 1,000 in 1835 and Rs. 2,000 in 1836.[110] From the beginning of 1834, therefore, he started to receive sums which, small though they were, enabled him to hire workmen to tackle the 'superior monuments', and so embark on a particularly busy year.

He had decided to spend the rest of the winter at Jalalabad instead of Kabul and had accepted a pressing invitation from the Nawab Jabar Khan to stay at his estate at Tatang nearby and to remain there until his host could join him. The Nawab provided a guide who proved to have escorted Gerard and his party. Masson had his own servants and a *mirza* or secretary joined them; all were mounted and armed which was as well since there were robbers about. The party took a route through Khurd Kabal, Tezin, Jagdallak and Gandamak, which later acquired notoriety as the one followed by the retreating British army in 1842: indeed Jagdallak and Gandamak were to be the scenes of desperate stands against overwhelming odds. By an ancient bridge over the Surkh Rud the party came across Khalil Khan with whom Masson had stayed at his fine house in Laghman six years previously. The pleasure of the reunion was marred by Khalil Khan's news that he had fallen on hard times and was reduced to collecting tolls from caravans at the bridge. He complained of fever and died a few days after Masson reached Tatang.

The Nawab Jabar Khan had developed his estate from scratch; it now consisted of a 'superior castle with very lofty walls and towers' which held a spacious residence for his family and about thirty-five houses for his tenants and farm workers, surrounded by large flower-gardens and park land. The Nawab took great pride in it and was never so happy as when planting trees, widening canals, or feasting upon the beauties of his flower-gardens. 'A doubtful politician and statesman, his skill as a husbandman is denied by no one,' says Masson. Comfortably installed in apartments over the principal gateway with a noble view of the valley of Jalalabad, it is no wonder that Masson enjoyed his stay in these delightful surroundings or that he spent other winters at Tatang thereafter. The Nawab had insisted that his guest should not wander far from the castle, so he confined his walks and climbs to the immediate environs, enjoying the extensive views from the hills and taking some bearings. There were also ancient structures to be examined as well as 'one of those graves of extraordinary dimensions which abound in this part of the country'. It was 108 feet in length with a crudely constructed stone wall surround; local legend ascribed the grave to the biblical patriarch Lot.

During 1833, Shah Shuja, starting from Ludhiana and encouraged by a four months' advance of his British pension and hence the tacit approval of the Government of India, had defeated a force of the Amirs of Sind and had reached Shikarpur. Men and money were flowing in and the road to Kandahar was open. Intrigues of the most tortuous kind were begun by the Kandahar and Peshawar sirdars with the ostensible object of inducing Dost Mahomed Khan to march to Kandahar to assist in repelling the menace presented by Shah Shuja's advance. The danger was manifest, yet the real purpose was to entice Dost Mahomed away from Kabul so that his territories would be open to invasion by the chiefs of Peshawar and Jalalabad. Dost Mahomed agreed to go to the aid of Kandahar provided that no advantage would be taken of his absence by the Peshawar chiefs. Sultan Mahomed Khan, the senior sirdar, had moved up beyond Jalalabad and, while declaring

his desire for a united family front to face the crisis, covertly sent agents
to subvert Dost Mahomed's supporters. The latter in turn dispatched
emissaries to Peshawar on a similar errand! Masson states that the
Nawab Jabar Khan and Haji Khan were aware of these plots and
countenanced them, hence the former's fears for Masson's safety
should he wander far from Tatang. Dost Mahomed had no illusions as
to the real intentions of his brothers and pretended to prepare for a
march to Kandahar but switched direction and sent his army toward
Jalalabad instead. Mahomed Akbar Khan, the Dost's son had been
sent to Laghman province and the two forces succeeded in taking
Jalalabad in January 1834 without a siege and without bloodshed; its
capture made the ruler of Kabul more formidable than ever.

The Nawab Jabar Khan arrived at Tatang from Kabul the day before the assault on Jalalabad, while Haji Khan took himself to Peshawar
where he entered the service of the sirdars. Immediately after his host's
arrival Masson left Tatang to work on the stupas of Darunta (Chapter
X) and was engaged there until the Nawab earnestly requested him to
accompany his son, Abdul Ghias Khan, who was to be sent to India to
receive an English education. Masson felt that he could not decently
refuse and agreed to accompany the young man to Peshawar at all
events and to Lahore, if necessary. The idea of sending Abdul Ghias
Khan to Ludhiana had originated with Saiyad Keramat Ali; it was by
no means approved of by Dost Mahomed Khan who viewed with dis-
taste a connection with the British authorities, particularly when the
interests of the family were being threatened by Shah Shuja. That threat
soon obliged Dost Mahomed Khan to return to Kabul, whereupon
Abdul Ghias Khan was secretly floated down the river on a raft to
Peshawar; on 22 March Masson followed with a 'formidable caval-
cade, the retinue of the young lad'. He found his charge lodged with
Sultan Mahomed Khan and a critical situation brewing. A Sikh army
under Hari Singh was encamped some five miles from the city and it
was feared that he would occupy it under the terms of the treaty between Ranjit Singh and Shah Shuja (see pp. 25-26).

The plots devised by the chiefs of Peshawar to ruin Dost Mahomed
Khan had recoiled upon them; his victory at Jalalabad had broken the
confederacy and they now feared lest he should attack them. In their
distress they applied to the Sikhs for assistance. Haji Khan, who was
to have been a main instrument for the destruction of Dost Mahomed
Khan, had only succeeded in alienating a section of the army and the
Shia portion of the population: both these groups and the principal

Hindu merchants also approached the Sikhs. Peshawar fell like a ripe plum.

Masson had a front row view of the action:

The morning came, when Sultan Mahomed Khan, who had always his spy-glass in hand, described the Sikh force in motion. All became panic-struck, and horses were saddled and mounted in a trice. The house was emptied as if by magic, and none remained in it but Abdul Ghias Khan, his party, and myself. We ascended the roof, and beheld the Sikhs moving forward in very respectable style. In the van was the young Shahzada [heir apparent] on an elephant, with Hari Singh and a variety of Sikh chiefs, attended by a host of cavalry. Behind them followed the battalions of General Court advancing in columns at a brisk pace... Subsequently we learned during the day that the Sikhs pressing too close upon Haji Khan, who covered the retreat of Sultan Mahomed Khan, the Khan lost patience and turned upon them. He handled them very severely... Some very splendid instances of individual bravery were exhibited by the Afghans, and one gallant fellow cut down six of his opponents.

It was to no avail and the discomforted sirdars retired to the hills.

Abdul Ghias Khan having made arrangements with the Sikhs for his departure for Ludhiana, Masson saw no reason to accompany him as his onward journey would be safe and easy. Masson was anxious to get back to his excavations, but his first stop was at the fugitive sirdars' camp. From there he took the Abkhana route, an alternative to the Khyber Pass and therefore new to him. At Minchini he was provided with an escort of Mohmand tribesmen as far as Dakka to which a certain Saleh Mahomed, a Ghilzai, attached himself. At Abkhana the party had an exciting time being ferried across the swollen and raging Kabul river on rafts of skins. They had emerged from the hills into the valley of Jalalabad when four Afghans joined them and set to work making crude sandals from the beaten stems of a plant. Presuming that Masson could not understand Pushtu they talked loudly and freely. He was not amused to discover that they intended to rob him and that their sandals were being made to follow him.

He had already become suspicious of Saleh Mahomed who had at first kept himself very much apart and had latterly disappeared. As the escort was about to return home it transpired that Saleh Mahomed had tried on several occasions to suborn them to commit, or connive at, robbery and having failed had gone off to seek more compliant associates. Masson was much concerned since his party was in a region of bad repute and was unarmed. At Bassowal, Saleh Mahomed was detected in the bazaar in the company of six other men, all with their faces muffled and wearing swords. At this awkward moment, luck came to Masson's rescue. An armed group of forty Kohistani merchants appeared from the village, about to make a night march towards Jalalabad. They agreed to allow Masson's party to join their caravan. He was soon recognised by three or four of them who had previously seen him in the Kohistan; understanding between them therefore became complete. Jalalabad was reached without difficulty and Masson resumed his interrupted excavations at Darunta. He then turned his attention to the Chahar Bagh stupas and in May to those at Hadda.

Masson subsequently ascertained that Saleh Mahomed had an evil reputation as a hired assassin. It was thought that he might have been commissioned from some high quarter, but Masson believed that Saleh Mahomed must have been among the crowd when the former showed to the fugitive sirdars at their camp the relics extracted from the Darunta stupas which he had taken to Peshawar. Seeing what he considered to be treasure, Saleh Mahomed's cupidity had been aroused. Some time afterwards at Kabul the Ghilzai tried to contact Masson who refused to see him. Several attempts to burgle his house the next year led Masson to suppose that Saleh Mahomed was the instigator.

In July Dost Mahomed Khan narrowly defeated Shah Shuja at Kandahar. This defeat was due more to Shah Shuja's defects than to his opponent's limited military skill. The ex-king was a consistent loser of battles who was always more concerned about the safety of his harem and his treasure than about achieving victory. On this occasion, Shah Shuja quitted the field while the action was still going on and Dost Mahomed Khan prevailed, in spite of the uncertain temper of his troops and the treasonable approaches to Shah Shuja of Abdul Samad,* the Nawab Jabar Khan and other leaders. His victory over a former monarch further enhanced his reputation and paved the way for his assumption of the title of Amir. Shah Shuja was not pursued and after encountering many difficulties in the Seistan, Baluchistan and Sind finally managed to return to Ludhiana whence he had started.

The dispossessed Peshawar sirdars had meanwhile again moved up to Jalalabad with a view to taking over the province in the hope

---

* The unprincipled Persian adventurer who later, when in the service of the Amir of Bokhara, was partly responsible for the execution of Colonel Stoddart and Captain Conolly in 1842.

and belief that Dost Mahomed Khan would be defeated. Disappointed in this regard Sirdar Mahomed Khan and Haji Khan made their peace with Dost Mahomed Khan. The unsettled state of the region proving unfavourable to Masson's researches at Hadda, he left to resume work at Darunta. With his workmen he then toured the Kunar river valley in August looking for monuments and inspecting the country. He found a small, but perfect, stupa with its base and drum entire—a rare occurrence—but the unfriendly landowner prevented its excavation. Finding that the inhabitants were generally ill-disposed, Masson thought it prudent to turn back.

On a second excursion to Laghman he followed the Alishang and Alingar rivers up-stream from their junction and in so doing penetrated further than any European until the present century. In the course of this trip, he visited the shrine and grave at Mehtarlam traditionally assigned to Lamech, the father of Noah; though more celebrated than Lot's grave it is much smaller, 48 feet long, but still of 'extraordinary dimensions'. Other graves of similar size in the vicinity are said to be of Lamech's relatives. Well pleased with his trips and his thorough exploration of the valley of Jalalabad 'abounding in interesting monuments, as tumuli, mounds, caves etc.'. Masson left for Kabul on 14 September 1834 to start work on stupas around the capital beginning with Guldara.

CHAPTER X

TOPES, TUMULI AND RELICS

It appeared to me to be likely that a connected description of the principal antiquities and of the whole of the coins received from Mr Masson, would be acceptable both to the cultivators of numismatic sciences, and to those interested in the ancient history of India.

H. H. Wilson
Ariana Antiqua

The Great Tope of Manikyala (see Plate C, p. 84) and its smaller neighbours proved to be of seminal importance for the study of Buddhist architecture in the Punjab and Afghanistan and of the coinage of the Kushan kings and their successors (and hence the early history of the region). It also served to demonstrate an effective, if crude, method of excavating such structures. It is a solid circular building surmounted by a dome and was first reported by Mountstuart Elphinstone on his return journey to British India in 1809 from his abortive mission to Shah Shuja at Peshawar (see p. 24). He describes the event as follows:

The most remarkable sight we met with in this part, and perhaps in the whole of our journey, was an edifice about fifteen miles from Banda, our second march from Rawil Pindee ... which seemed at first to be a cupola but, when approached, was found to be a solid structure on a low artificial mound. The height from the top of the mound to the top of the building was about seventy feet, and the circumference was found to be one hundred and fifty paces [subsequently established as 500 feet]. *It was built of large pieces of a hard stone... The greater part of the outside was cased with the* [same] *stone, cut quite smooth; and the whole seemed intended to have been thus faced, though it had either been left incomplete, or the casing had fallen down. The plan of the whole could, however, be easily discovered. Some broad steps (now mostly ruined) led to the base of the pile: round the base is a moulding on which are pilasters about four feet high, and six feet asunder; these have plain capitals, and support a cornice marked with parallel lines and beadings. The whole of this may be seven or eight feet high...*

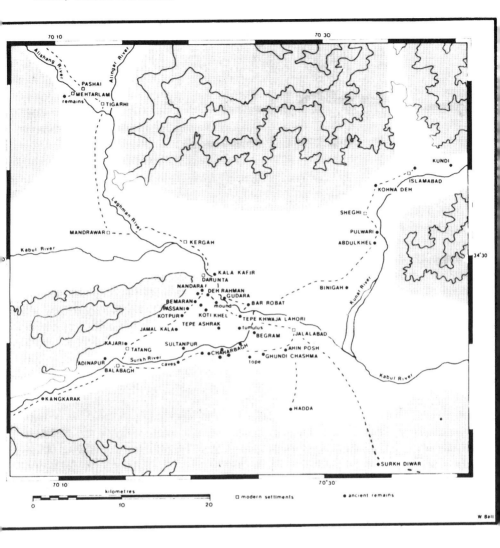

Plate 4. Map showing Masson's archaeological sites in the Jalalabad Valley.

Above this rose a perpendicular wall or drum for about six feet from whence sprang the dome. Most of Elphinstone's party thought it 'decidedly Grecian'. They had started on their side-trip in order to look for the reputed site of Taxila, but in fact Taxila lies roughly as far to the north-west of Rawalpindi as Manikyala is to the south-east. The inhabitants of the near-by village of Manikyala called the edifice a Tope, the first instance of its use in European hearing, and thereafter generally adopted in the 19th Century to describe similar structures.

Masson writes 'tope', throughout but modern usage prefers 'stupa'.

Twenty-one years elapsed before the character of the tope or stupa was ascertained by actual examination. It proved to consist of a small inner stupa encased in a much larger one. After unsuccessful attempts to penetrate it at the base of the dome, General Ventura had his soldiers start at the summit and dig downwards. Deposits of relics were uncovered at various depths. At about twenty-five feet an iron box was found containing a gold box which in turn held a gold coin, some silver ones and some jewellery. Of these coins some were Sassanian and one of Vasovarman (*c.* AD 720) suggesting that either the outer stupa was of very late date, or an earlier one had been restored at that time. At forty-five feet, a large quarried stone appeared and underneath it a similar stone with a hollow in the centre in which lay a copper vase containing a gold cylinder. At fifty-four feet and again at sixty-four feet, a few more coins and other objects were found. The principal deposit appeared at a depth of seventy-five feet: an immense stone slab covering a small cavity which yielded a copper box filled with a brown liquid; inside was a brass relic casket with a punched inscription on the lid, inside that again was a gold cylinder holding a gold coin of Kanishka and various relics together with five copper coins of Vima Kadphises and Kanishka. Outside the copper box were forty-four coins of the same monarchs. It would seem therefore that the original, smaller stupa was erected during or shortly after the reign of Kanishka.

Encouraged by the successful operations of his fellow-officer, General Court opened no fewer than fifteen smaller, but similar, stupas in the immediate vicinity of Manikyala village. In one of them he too found a small chamber underneath a massive stone slab in the centre of which stood a copper urn containing a silver cylinder with seven silver Roman coins, and further enclosing a gold cylinder holding four gold coins of Kanishka, precious stones and pearls. These coins of the Roman Republic were naturally of great help in dating the monument since, once identified, they could be dated with precision, unlike most of the Kushan coins in the then state of knowledge. The stupa evidently cannot have been built earlier than the latest of the Roman coins (Marc Antony as a Triumvir *c.* 43 BC) nor later than Kanishka's reign. However, coins of the Roman Republic remained in circulation for over a hundred years so that after allowing for a substantial period of circulation, much wear and long-distance travels, their presence would be consistent with current views of Kanishka's date of about AD 120.

Although Masson does not seem to have visited Manikyala, he would have been aware of its importance and of the technique employed in opening it from Honigberger and from the pages of the Journal of the Asiatic Society of Bengal. He profited accordingly when he started to attack the stupas in the Jalalabad valley. Occasionally he dug from the top on the Manikyala model, finding coins and relics at different levels. But usually he penetrated the monuments horizontally at the junction of the drum and its platform. Certainly he developed a keen intuitive sense of where to look for hidden relics. He too came across the 'Russian Doll' feature of cylinders within cylinders within other cylinders, ranging from a base metal to silver to pure gold. In *Ariana Antiqua* he summarises his opinions on the nature and origin of the structures he examined and thereafter discusses his find.[111]

A tope, he says, comprises two essential parts, the base, usually square, and the perpendicular body or drum resting thereon. The drum always terminates in the form of a cupola, sometimes only slightly convex, but more frequently approaching the shape of a cone. Belts of ornamental mouldings enclose the circumference of the drum frequently containing a succession of arches supported on pilasters. In some cases only the pilasters occur, and in still fewer even they are omitted, and the belts of mouldings constitute the decorative characteristics.

These monuments are substantially constructed of layers of large stones, cemented with well-prepared and beaten earth. While the interiors of stupas are immense masses of stones and earth, regularly disposed, the exterior surfaces have been objects of particular care. On the upper portions of most of them, from the lower lines of mouldings, concentric lines of fashioned stones have been continued to the summit. As the space between these concentric circles is filled up with:

> ... *dark slate, in the most curiously neat manner, such topes present a very singular and striking appearance, from the chequered arrangement of their upper surfaces* [i.e. diaper masonry]. *The mouldings, pilasters, arches, and other embellishments stand in relief, and are all formed with slate-stones in the same peculiar and neat style.*

The abundance of slate of a fine dark colour in the hills of Afghanistan has 'furnished the artists with a plentiful supply of excellent and easily worked materials, of which they have admirably profited to promote the elegance and beauty of these structures'. Originally, a surface of white stucco covered the upper portions of the stupas, including the mouldings and decorative belts, also probably the lower portions but in most cases this has disappeared.

As to their size, Masson states that they vary greatly in their dimensions but that they would appear to have been regulated, as everything else relating to them, on a fixed principle. Some of the monuments have a circumference of one hundred and forty-four feet, many of one hundred and eight feet, while others even exceed or fall short of these dimensions. Stupas must be considered as facing east, both because many of their bases have flights of steps at that point, and because others have niches fronting the east. Some of the bases of larger stupas had flights of steps at all the cardinal points, others only at the eastern and western points, and others again simply at the eastern points; some had none. Every stupa was erected on a base although from the ravages of time and the accumulation of fallen debris it cannot always be recognised as such.

Many stupas have contiguous to them large oblong areas enclosed within huge mounds of earth which may perhaps have been intended for reservoirs of water. Frequently these areas lie to the south, but also to the east or west. No Darunta stupas have these areas whereas all those of Chahar Bagh, Hadda, and the Kabul district have them. Masson notes that the favourite sites of stupas are at the skirts of hills, on eminences separated from each other by ravines. All of them have a number of caves nearby, many of which are large and all were originally lined with stucco. The largest caves have decorated and carved interiors culminating in a cupola. Stupas are always accompanied by tumuli, often by many; though frequently isolated, a tumulus is never without its cave. Tumuli abound all over Afghanistan. Water is constantly found near stupas and its presence seems to have been a governing factor in the selection of the sites. At Hadda, water had been conducted in subterranean aqueducts from remote points, through a most difficult soil, and at great labour and cost. Where water no longer exists close by, the original, but exhausted, springs are easily visible.

Masson goes on to discuss the relics hidden within the stupas and, occasionally, within the tumuli. They are, he writes, mostly discovered in small chambers formed by squares of slate, enclosed in caskets or vases of copper, brass, and steatite. These vases, sometimes

Plate D (right).   Head of Buddha; dark grey schist, Gandharan school, c. 3rd century AD, height 38.7 cm. Collected by Major-General Sir Frederick Richard Pollock and deposited in the British Museum under the Dighton Pollard Bequest. OA 1929.11-4.2. For further description. see Zwalf, Vol. I, p, 93. (See Chapter XI)

Plate E. The Bimaran Reliquary; repoussé gold, inset with amandine garnets; height 6.7 cm, base diameter 6.6 cm. British Museum OA 1900.2-9.1. For further description, see Zwalf, Vol. I, p. 348. (See text, p. 105)

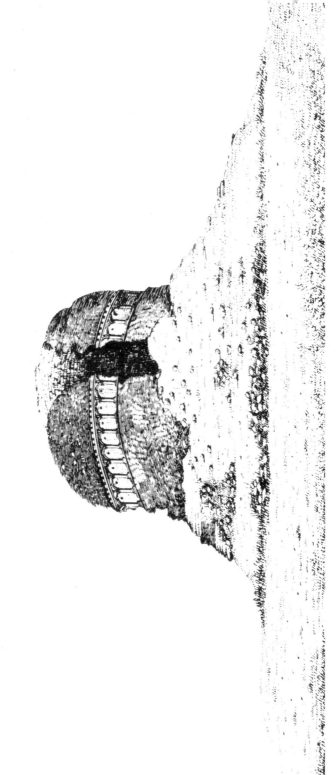

Plate 5. Masson's sketch of a Darunta Stupa in the Jalalabad Valley.

globular, sometimes cylindrical, usually contain small cylindrical cases of gold and/or silver, either separate or enclosed the one within the other. In one of these will generally be found a fragment or two of bone, and these appear to have been the essential relics over which the stupas were raised. In the larger vases is usually discovered a portion of fine pulverised earth or of ashes, amongst which have been placed burnt pearls, beads, rings, seals, and other trinkets, with gems, coloured stones, pieces of crystal, fragments of mother-of-pearl, shell etc. In some examples the deposits have been accompanied by twists of bark with inscriptions thereon. Unfortunately, these pieces of bark have disintegrated or do so when handled and what might be invaluable evidence is lost. Although relics are generally lodged in the centres of stupas on the line where the drums rest on their bases, they are sometimes found at the centre and bottom of the latter where they touch virgin soil. Very many stupas, and even tumuli, have double structures: an inner stupa enclosed in an outer one of similar form. The inner core is covered with stucco and the line of separation from the outer stupa is often marked by unburnt bricks, or by stones of a kind different from those used in the mass.

Using the Nawab Jabar Khan's comfortable country seat at Tatang as his base, Masson excavated at three localities in the Jalalabad valley: Darunta (comprising stupas at Kotpur, Bimaran, Nandara etc., 18 in total); Chahar Bagh (6 stupas); and Hadda (13 stupas), which he believed were in chronological order, Hadda being the latest settlement. At Darunta, the local landowner, considering the stupas to be his own property, sent a party of armed men to drive away Masson's workmen, but explanations led to so good an understanding that henceforth the owner's castle became Masson's advance headquarters. The Masson charm had worked again. Of the locality, he remarks that:

> The scenery of Darunta is naturally picturesque; and its interest is, of course, much enhanced by the presence of its topes. The coup-d'oeil must needs have been gorgeous when these monuments existed in their original splendour [i.e. painted and gilded].

We shall now follow the sequence of excavations described at length by Masson in *Ariana Antiqua* selecting the more important results for mention.[112] At Stupa No. 2 of Kotpur he found, apparently for the first time, an inner stupa with a diameter of twelve feet and covered with stucco. Ten copper coins with a figure of Hercules on the reverse*, a

---

* Kujula Kadphises: 2nd half of 1st century AD.

steatite cylinder containing a small one of silver, and some relics, were discovered.

Stupa No. 2 of Bimaran had been opened by Honigberger but abandoned. Reopening it, Masson made his most striking single discovery, the famous Bimaran Reliquary (see Plate E, p. 102): a round casket of pure gold with four figures, repeated, of Buddha flanked by Indra, Brahma and a female disciple, each in a cusped niche. A row of twelve garnets embellish the top and bottom while the base has a lotus-flower design. The reliquary (now in the British Museum) is considered to be a masterpiece of Gandharan Buddhist metalware; it may be dated to the late 2nd or early 3rd century AD.[113] Inside the casket were found a piece of bone, no doubt the sacred relic, and various gold objects. It had been enclosed in the usual vase of steatite but with lines of inscriptions scratched on it and on its cover. Within the vase were numerous gold ornaments, gems and beads, etc. Outside the vase were four copper coins in excellent condition of the 'horseman' type and on the obverse the titles BASILEUS BASILEON. On the reverse were characters in Kharoshthi script.[‡]

Honigberger had had better luck at Stupa No. 3 of Bimaran where he found another globular steatite vase containing a variety of trinkets and ornaments with many burnt pearls. Outside the vase, in a quantity of fine mould, as in the case of the Bimaran reliquary, was a handsome pagoda-like ornament of gold, more burnt pearls and twenty-seven copper coins with the legend BASILEUS BASILEON SOTER MEGAS.[‡]

Masson's examination of the Bimaran stupas led him to hazard the theory that while deposits of coins of the same type indicate the age of the structure, their actual number may not be accidental, but may refer to the length of life or reign. This hypothesis, he says, cannot of course apply to stupas which yield a medley of coins of all types and ages, but only to those where the coins are of a single type and of 'applicable numbers'. The twenty-seven Soter Megas coins from Bimaran stupa No. 3 depict the bust of a king at ages ranging from 20 to 50 years. They may therefore represent the regnal years of the king responsible for its erection. Masson's interesting theory has not been followed up,

---

* These coins are of billon (an alloy) copying the types of Azez II silver coins with the added *tamgha* (distinctive symbol) of Kujula Kadphises, the Kushan ruler.
‡ The King of Kings, the Saviour, the Great: known as the nameless King. His coins proved to be particularly numerous in Afghanistan.

but it should be noted that in some stupa deposits which have an inscription, the regnal year is given in the inscription. The number of coins of a ruler found by Masson do not seem to exceed the length of reigns where this is now known from deciphered inscriptions.

Stupa No. 5 of Bimaran (or Jani Tope) yielded no fewer than seven chambers carefully enclosed by slate stones, three having been found by Honigberger, three by local inhabitants, and the seventh by Masson digging down from the summit. Altogether sixty-eight coins were recovered, mostly of the 'Hercules' type in poor condition but with a few of the 'Horseman' type all in excellent preservation.

Of the stupas at Deh Rahman, No. 2 was remarkable for its size, one hundred and eighty feet in circumference, and for its situation in the middle of the village. Stupa No.1 of Nandara is considered by Masson to be the most beautiful and most tastefully executed of the whole group. Larger than most with a circumference of one hundred and forty-four feet, it rests on a magnificent base with a flight of steps on the east side. It has a belt of double lines of mouldings and a succession of finely turned arches and pilasters.[114] Above the mouldings, dark slate and white stones give a chequered pattern and 'the effect produced by this diamond or chequered, arrangement is nowhere so advantageously displayed as in this tope'. Opened first by Honigberger and then by Masson, it yielded a painted bark casket much decayed, but no relics. It is also one of the few stupas with a shaft in the centre.

Stupa Gudara produced a silver casket enclosing a smaller one of gold, together with a few ornaments and the essential relic, a fragment of bone. In this stupa Masson met with the novel circumstance of a tunnel running from the centre towards the side which he subsequently found in two other instances. He was unable to hazard a guess as to its meaning.

At Chahar Bagh the stupas proved to be of inferior appearance and smaller dimensions than those of the Darunta group, rarely exceeding one hundred and eight feet. No architectural embellishments were observable, nor any traces of the usual external coating of stucco or cement: they were 'rude, naked structures'. On the other hand, they each had a large oblong space, enclosed by lofty and ample mounds. Chahar Bagh did not prove very productive of finds, but the coins were unmixed deposits of the Kushan era, while Stupa No. 4 produced twenty-eight coins of Kanishka. The numerous tumuli which are such a feature of the area and whose purpose baffled Masson, were likewise barren of results.

The Hidda (Hadda) stupas situated about five miles south of Jalalabad also showed only bare masonry: in fact they were even then often too dilapidated to have preserved their original outlines. Nevertheless, they gave highly satisfactory results: gold and silver cylindrical cases and numerous ornaments as well as coins and bones. In Stupa No. 8 was found:

> *...a massy copper gilt lamp with stand; the upper receptacle for the oil still contained a portion of the fluid matter, and the wick was in as fresh a state, apparently, as if it had become extinguished during the night; on exposure to the air, however, the oil speedily evaporated, and the wick crumbled.*[115]

But it was Stupa No. 10, Tapa Kalan (or the Big Mound), the largest and most important of the Hadda monuments, which yielded an astonishing harvest of 329 gold, silver, and copper coins; numerous gold rings some with gems; gold ornaments; and various gems and beads. The Russian doll progression of copper, silver and gold cases was seen again: the gold case had a cover surmounted by a handsome jewel and encircled by seven small emeralds.[116] The gold coins included five of the Byzantine Emperors, Theodosius, (AD 408-450), Marcian (450-457) and Leo (457-474). All the 202 silver coins were Sassanian coins extending to, if not beyond the Hejira. This stupa cannot therefore be earlier than the 7th century AD.

At Stupa No. 13 a small earthen jar was discovered 'perhaps the most useful that any of the many topes examined had yielded, for it was encompassed with a [Kharoshthi] inscription, written with a pen, but very carelessly'.[117] Anxious lest it should suffer damage he transcribed the inscription.* Masson also dug out of a nearby mound a number of funerary jars mostly ornamented in various colours, one of which had an inscription. The same mound yielded a great number of statues of about six or eight inches in height with a strong cast head fixed on a body of earth from which only the heads could be removed. They were seated and clothed in folds of drapery with the hair in rows of curls. The bodies were sometimes painted with red lead, and occasionally covered with gold leaf.

Masson was the first to draw attention to the significance of Hadda. Although the entire Jalalabad valley is littered with countless Buddhist ruins which once held thousands of monks and were visited by

---

* A century later this Kharoshthi inscription was deciphered: 'in year 28 a relic was deposited in the king's grave in a stupa by the architect Samghamitra'.

multitudes of pilgrims, Hadda was especially sacred. The Buddha himself was believed to have flown through the air to convert a demon dragon there. The Chinese Buddhist pilgrims Fa-Hsien and Hsuan Tsang, who traversed the Jalalabad valley in the course of their extended journeys to India, have left detailed records of the Hadda shrines and their relics and have described the attendant elaborate ceremonies as they saw them in AD 420 and AD 632. In the course of the present century over 1,000 stupas, each with its Vihara and temple, have been identified—a vast complex with Hadda at the centre. French, Japanese and Afghan archaeologists have excavated more than half of these stupas which yielded rich, indeed spectacular, finds. Hadda objects date from the 2nd to the 8th century AD; the city was probably at its zenith in the 3rd century AD.

In the neighbourhood of Kabul, more particularly around Shewaki, Dr Honigberger had examined all the stupas with varying success. Masson reopened the fine one at Guldara obtaining several gold Kushan coins. He was also attracted to a column with the diaper masonry familiar from stupas, the Minar-i-Chakri ,* overlooking the Kabul plain. It is a solid Kushan Buddhist structure 85 feet high standing on a square base, possibly a victory monument and probably of the 3rd century AD. Masson's sketch of the Minar is given in *Ariana Antiqua* and may be compared with a recent photograph taken after its conservation (see Plates 7(a) and 7(b) pp. 110-111).

Of the stupas in the Koh Daman and the Kohistan north of Kabul examined by Masson, he singles out Dara as 'perhaps the most complete and beautiful monument of its kind in these countries, as it is one of the largest'. It was the first stupa he had opened (in 1833), before he had gained experience of excavations or trained a team of reliable workmen. He was anxious to resume work on Dara and grumbles that his new duties for the Government of India prevented him from visiting the spot again.

The last stupas described by Masson were those of Kohwat in the Wardak district close by the Logar river about thirty miles west of Kabul, some five or six with numerous tumuli. His operations resulted in seven vases of metal and steatite with other and various deposits.

---

* Conservation work on the Guldara monastery and Minar-i-Chakri was carried out by the British Institute of Afghan Studies in 1975-77 (see Plates 7(a) and 7(b), pp. 110-111).

Plate 6. The Shewaki Stupa. (See text p. 108)

One of the brass vases had a Kharoshthi inscription punched around it.* The coins were Indo-Scythic and Masson remarks that in the groups of stupas explored at Kabul and Jalalabad, examples of all the primary and generic Indo-Scythic coins have been found, namely of the Azes and Kushan Dynasties.

It is of course impossible to separate the coin finds from the archaeological and architectural aspects of the stupas in which they occurred. Masson speculates a good deal about the coins in attempting to date the stupas since he was grappling with so many novelties, but he does establish certain points which have not been gainsaid subsequently. Thus he states that no Graeco-Bactrian coins were found in any stupas he excavated, fair proof that they were erected long after the fall of that principality.

---

* Eventually translated as: 'in year 28 ... the Gotama's relic was enshrined'. Now in the British Museum (Konow 1929, pp. 165-70).

Plate 7(a). Masson's sketch of the Minar-i-Chakri (India Office Library).

Plate 7(b). The Minar-i-Chakri after conservation work in 1975-77.

CHAPTER XI

THE ORIGIN AND DIFFUSION OF BUDDHIST REMAINS DISCUSSED

I have very little to say [about the Buddhas at Bamian] *except that they are very large and very ugly.*

Sir W.J. Kaye
History of the War in Afghanistan

At first sight it is curious that the early 19th century travellers and explorers should have been so reluctant to believe that the monuments they examined in Gandhara, i.e. north-west Pakistan and eastern Afghanistan, were Buddhist. Yet Ceylon had already become a British dependency by 1815; the war with Burma of 1824-26 had led to the capture of Rangoon and a sight of the splendid Shwedagon Pagoda there; some intercourse with Siam had occurred during the 1820s. Ladakh and Tibet had been visited by Moorcroft in 1820. In all these countries Buddhism was a living and vigorous faith, though some followed the Mahayana form and others the Hinayana or Lesser Vehicle; the difference between the two sects tended to confuse the uninitiated. Of special importance was India, since she possessed the earliest Buddhist monuments as well as other highly important ones and some of these edifices were known and recorded. On the other hand, the practice of Buddhism had long since vanished from the subcontinent. Perhaps largely for this reason remarkably little was known by the resident Europeans of the tenets and practices of Buddhism. Furthermore, the records of Fa-Hsien and Hsuan Tsang, which were to prove so valuable a source of information about the extent of the Buddhist faith and institutions, were not yet available in the West. A translation of Fa-Hsien into French did not appear until 1836, the first in a European language.

Moorcroft had visited the Manikyala stupa in 1824 before he set eyes on any stupas in Afghanistan or on the colossal statues at Bamian. But Manikyala had not then been excavated and he may therefore be excused, in spite of his own observations in Tibet, for being barely inclined to recognise it as Buddhist:

> We could gain no satisfactory information of its origin, but it has not
> at all the character of a Grecian edifice [contradicting Elphinstone's
> impression]. It has a much greater resemblance to the monumental
> structures of the Tibetans.[118]

But he reverses himself by saying of the massive stupa on the Khyber
Pass: 'it is most probably a Hindu structure, though for what purpose
is doubtful. It is evidently of great antiquity and of the same period as
the tope of Manikyala'.[119] Writing of his visit to Bamian he says:

> My own conviction, from the characters of the buildings, of the caves,
> paintings and sculptures is that Bamian, whatever its ancient appel-
> lation, was the residence of a great Lama, bearing the same relation to
> the Lamaism of the west as Lhassa does now to that of the east...[120]

Of the caves in the cliff face containing the 'idols' he says that those
which were connected by means of galleries and staircases accommodated the higher order of the Lama clergy, while the isolated cells and
caves were used by the lower classes of the monastic society, such as
monks and nuns, and as hostels for visitors. This is as close as Moorcroft
got to ascribing to Bamian a Buddhist origin, unfamiliar as he was
with such remains, so different from the developed Mahayana art and
architecture of Tibet. Furthermore, Buddhism has never stood still; it
is continuously changing and the difference in it between 5th century
Bamian and 1824 must be considered very great. Although he describes
the colossal statues he does not suggest that they are Buddhas, nor
indeed does he venture to speculate on what they might represent.
After seeing the rock-cut stupa Takht-i-Rustam, near Haibek (now
called Samangan, its ancient name) he sums up his views:

> The excavations [i.e. caves] in the mountains, in connection with
> those in Afghanistan, at Bamian and others observed on the whole
> road hither, and with the topes of the Punjab and the figures at Bamian
> would seem to intimate its being the work of a Buddhist people. It
> differs, however, so much from anything we saw in Tibet that I cannot
> acquiesce in such an appropriation.[121]

Although Moorcroft and Trebeck were the first to observe the stupas
in north-west India and Afghanistan, they lost the credit of priority
by the delay in publishing their Travels.* The first published notice of
the stupas was Alexander Burnes's cursory account in the *Journal of*

---

* The manuscripts had been deposited in several places and the whole had to be
severely pruned by Professor Wilson (op.cit: Preface, 1ii-1iii).

the Asiatic Society of Bengal for June, 1833 and reprinted in his *Travels to Bokhara*. He and Gerard had seen General Ventura's private collection and had inspected Manikyala itself where they picked up some antiques and coins; on one of the coins the name of Kanishka was later found distinctly legible for the first time. Burnes inclined to a belief that:

> ... in these 'topes' we have the tombs of a race of princes who once reigned in Upper India, and that they are either the sepulchres of the Bactrian kings, or their Indo-Scythic successors, mentioned in the Periplus of the second Arrian. The rudeness of the coins would point to the latter age, or second century of the Christian era. [122]

However, when stating his conclusions regarding the topes he adds: 'They may, however, be Boodhist buildings.' [121]

Burnes was disposed to think that Bamian might possibly have a Buddhist origin. After saying: 'There are no relics of Asiatic antiquity which have roused the curiosity of the learned more than the gigantic idols of Bameean' which he thinks are male and female figures, he comments:

> I am aware that a conjecture attributes these images to the Boodhists; and the long ears of the great figure render the surmise probable. I did not trace any resemblance to the colossal figures in the caves of Salsette, near Bombay; but the shape of the head is not unlike that of the great trifaced idol of Elephanta. [124]

In fact it is Siva. Then on the next page he writes:

> ... it is by no means improbable that we owe the idols of Bameean to the caprice of some person of rank who resided in this cave-digging neighbourhood, and sought for an immortality in the colossal images which we have now described. [125]

He was much struck by the frescoes which decorate the niches, as was Masson.

Lieutenant J. Wood, having noted the topes seen on the previous day's march with the Burnes mission in 1837, expresses the hope soon to hear that modern research working on the recently discovered coins already in the East India Company's museum has, by deciphering their inscriptions, dispelled all doubts of the purpose for which these 'singular piles' were originally erected. [126] He also records that during a short stay at Begram he sent out some children in search of coins who returned with thirty-five copper coins, adding that 'when gleaning the surface is attended with such a result, what splendid success may be expected to crown the systematic and assiduous researches of Mr

Masson, the British Agent at Kabul!'.[127]

Masson himself, while occasionally veering towards accepting a Buddhist origin for the stupas he had examined, was far from convinced. No doubt part of the problem for him and others was the difficulty of attributing the great number and wide distribution of stupas and mounds, with their imposing size and massive construction and hence the enormous cost involved, to any but monarchs, and powerful and rich ones at that. He writes:

> Topes could only be erected under favourable and concurring circumstances of power and command of treasure, strongly countenancing the opinion that they are royal or saintly monuments in general, were other and more decided proofs wanting.[128]

The notion that a religious organisation could command such resources, however much augmented by royal contributions, was not entertained. Stupas with no coins or relics and perched on rocky eminences might, he thought, be cenotaphs dedicated to saints; and the accompanying tumuli be places of interment of the saints' followers. Even while admitting the possibility of a Buddhist origin as he calls to mind 'the chaityas or consecrated structures raised over the relics of the saints of that religion, and memorably over those of their great incarnation Sakya...'. He continues to prefer the opinion that stupas are the cenotaphs of kings.[129] Of the innumerable caves dispersed throughout Afghanistan and invariably associated with stupas or tumuli, he remarks that they all had a similar purpose being the abode of the priest or recluse attached to the funeral endowment.

Bamian, which he visited six months after Burnes, presented him with a problem. There were, he writes, no topes because the monarchs there commemorated were probably of a peculiar faith, which did not permit the burning of their bodies; therefore there was no need of the tumulus to cover the spot of cremation, or of the tope to receive some consecrated relic.[130] In his 'Notes on the Antiquities of Bamian' he says: 'We visited Bamian under the idea of meeting with Buddhist antiquities, but it became evident that they were of another character.'[131] He thought that the colossal statues not only commemorated monarchs, but that the valley was a burial place of a dynasty of kings. Recognition of the statues as Buddhas was doubtless hampered by their mutilated condition. The faces have been sliced off from the forehead to the upper lips by iconoclastic Moslems who believed that by so doing they destroyed the soul force of the hated idol. The hands and much of the arms have also disappeared. But it was the absence of stupas at

Bamian that continued to trouble Masson. In a notebook written as late as 1844 he says that it would be most surprising if Bamian without topes and without any of the symbols connected with Buddha were Buddhist.[132] He had by then read the earliest attempts to translate the Chinese pilgrims' reports, but they are inaccurate and incomplete with the result that he mistakenly thought he had found confirmation of his opinion in Hsuan Tsang's apparent omission of any mention of Buddhist remains at Bamian: later translations describe the great Buddhas in some detail.

Having found no coins in the Bamian valley to help him, Masson was forced to speculate on the dates of the Buddhas. He is not alone in antedating them by several centuries and it is only comparatively recently that archaeologists have more or less agreed that the larger Buddha may be assigned to the 5th century AD, and the smaller statue to the 3rd or early 4th centuries.

The early 19th century travellers we have been considering all attempted to contribute to the advancement of knowledge. But as far as researches on stupas are concerned it has truly been said that whereas Dr Honigberger was the first to investigate those of the western part of Gandhara (as distinct from Manikyala etc., in the eastern part), 'the first detailed account of the buildings themselves is that given by Mr Masson who, with singular perseverance and sagacity, completed what Dr Honigberger had left undone'.[133]

In contrast to the travellers of the period, the academic world had formed definite opinions on the Buddhist character of the structures in question. As early as 1821, William Erskine had written of the Tope of Manikyala that:

> ... although its origin is unknown, yet in its hemispherical form and whole appearance it carries with it sufficient proof that it was a magnificent Dahgopa or Buddhist shrine, constructed at a remote period by persons of the Buddhist faith.[134]

This view is the more commendable and surprising since he had seen only a sketch of the stupa which had not then been excavated. Other savants, notably Professor Wilson in London, had paid close attention to the evidence emerging from the Buddhist dagobas of Ceylon in particular, and from investigations of sites in India. Wilson summarises

Plate 8 (right). Model stupa excavated at Sultanpur; light grey steatite, in three parts, overall height 19.4 cm. British Museum OA 1880-94. For further description, see Zwalf, Vol. I, p. 341.

one of the conclusions of these scholarly studies in *Ariana Antiqua*: 'The topes are the shrines of the supposed relics of the last Buddha, Sakya or Gautama; and the tumuli are the tombs in which the ashes of his votaries have been buried, under the protection of his holy shrine.'[135] The first part of this statement is of course correct, but not the second. Subsequent excavations have shown that tumuli or mounds were often disintegrated Viharas (halls for the monks attached to the stupas) which commonly developed into monasteries. In some cases the mounds were chaityas or temples for worship, in others, a collapsed stupa. Since the stupas themselves were solid and any relics were well hidden, the Viharas and chaityas usually also had a fragment of bone of the Buddha which could be displayed for the edification of the monks and laity. Around AD 100 statues of Buddha and sculptured scenes from his life were added to these buildings as the primitive Hinayana school of Buddhism grew to discard the original symbols of the wheel or the footprint in favour of representing Buddha in human form.

The preservation and worship of relics of Buddha began immediately after his attainment of Nirvana about 480 BC, when eight cities contended for the honour of possessing his mortal remains. The difficulty was met by assigning a portion to each of the contending parties, who are said to have erected stupas to contain them in each of their respective localities. Thereafter fragments of bone multiplied, while his canine teeth in particular brought great renown upon their resting places, notably the celebrated Temple of the Tooth at Kandy in Ceylon. In Gandhara, a tooth was preserved at a great stupa near Jalalabad, but had disappeared when Hsuan Tsang looked for it in the early 7th century and only the foundations remained. A neighbouring stupa contained Buddha's staff, while yet another contained his robe. At Hadda, the principal shrine held Buddha's skull-bone. His begging-bowl was housed at Peshawar by King Kanishka, where it was worshipped with the greatest reverence. This relic worship gave rise to the erection of the great stupas, the most important feature of Buddhist architectural art. The worship of the stupas themselves probably arose from the popular idea that the sanctity of the relics was shared by their shrines; and gradually stupas, simply in memory of the Buddha or any of his notable followers, came to be multiplied and reverenced everywhere.[136]

Wilson's second conclusion is that the stupas of north-west India and Afghanistan are undoubtedly all subsequent to the Christian era;

but here again some uncertainty still exists today.[137] Beyond doubt, however, is the great revival of Buddhism and with it the emergence of Buddhist art and architecture in Gandhara which took place under the Kushan dynasty, especially during the reign of Kanishka (early 2nd century AD) the greatest of his line, who may have been a Buddhist himself. It was he who summoned the historic Buddhist convocation in Kashmir which adopted the more complicated and ritualistic Mahayana or Great Vehicle with its emphasis on the miraculous life and personality of the Buddha. The new doctrines were carried by missionaries to Afghanistan and thence across Central Asia to Tibet, China and beyond. They established shrines and monasteries along the route; in this way Gandhara statuary spread throughout the Kushan empire. Before long, innumerable pilgrims from countries which had adopted Buddhism followed this route in reverse on their way to India to worship at the sacred places associated with the Buddha and to study the scriptures of their new religion.

CHAPTER XII

MASSON AS INTELLIGENCE AGENT

> *It is of little consequence who or what
> Mr Masson actually is or has been, so
> long as the literary stores of our muse-
> ums are furnished with materials in
> which they are now deficient.*
>
> Sir John Campbell to Mr Secretary
> Macnaghten, dated Tehran,
> 12th January 1834

While Charles Masson was happily pursuing his antiquarian re-searches in 1834 with increasing success and growing confidence, Captain Claude Wade in Ludhiana was building up his file on the unsuspecting archaeologist. A letter from Wade to Macnaghten was to have such an impact on Masson's future that it merits extensive quotation:

> *9th April, 1834... On the 5th February 1833, I transmitted an article
> of intelligence to you from Cabul* relative to Mr Masson, and ob-
> served that the European in question had been residing about seven
> years ago in the Punjab where he was well-known to the French offic-
> ers, that I believed him to be a deserter from our artillery, either on the
> Bombay or Bengal establishment, that he was represented to be a per-
> son of good education and a good draughtsman, and that I should
> endeavour to ascertain with what views he was travelling in
> Afganistan. I accordingly wrote to our Agent in Cabul, who informed
> me that Mr Masson was engaged in exploring the antiquities of that
> country, and had lately proceeded, in company with Dr Honigberger
> then on his return to Europe from the Punjab, to excavate some ex-
> traordinary edifices in the vicinity of Cabul and Jalalabad, which had
> strongly excited their curiosity, from their general similarity to the
> Manikyala structure. About the same time I received a letter from Dr
> Honigberger, giving me a long account of his excavations, in which he
> adverted also to his companion, after which I heard no more of Mr*

---

* See Keramat Ali's report quoted on p. 72.

Masson until Dr Gerard arrived (11 March) at Ludhiana, who not only confirmed my previous information concerning the nature of his pursuits, but gave me an insight into their value and importance I had not before possessed...

Desertion is a crime which is viewed I believe by our government with a degree of rigour that scarcely ever admits of pardon but, if the severity of our laws is such as to preclude the extension of his Lordship's clemency to him, I still hope that I shall be excused for the correspondence I have opened with Mr Masson and that, adverting to his acknowledged talent and ability and the light which his interesting researches are likely to throw on the ancient history, antiquities and present state of Afghanistan, I may be indemnified by government for any small sums of money with which I may hereafter supply Mr Masson for the prosecution of his labours. I learn from Dr Gerard and others that he is not a person of extravagant pretensions and, if the occasional donation of a few hundred rupees which government can fix will secure his services, their expenditure will scarcely be thought too much for the valuable information which it is in his power to afford.

I cannot divest myself altogether of the awkwardness of opening such a communication but ... the circumstance of Mr Masson having assumed a new name may in some measure be allowed to remove the embarrassment of recognising him in his present situation when it is not necessary that his recognition should appear to emanate from Government.

It is not merely from the nature of his scientific researches that Mr Masson's services have occurred to me as likely to prove advantageous to government ... but the observations which he has made, and the information which he has collected on the government and resources of a country which is of daily increasing interest to the British Government, cannot be an object of indifference. His long residence in Afghanistan has not only enabled him to acquire a complete geographical and statistical knowledge of the country, but living like he has been like a native of it on terms of intimacy and familiarity with its inhabitants, he has enjoyed opportunities of making his observations which no other European travellers have hitherto possessed. In the course of his journeys he has visited various parts of Afghanistan which they have never seen. They have kept the beaten track and been favoured guests of its chiefs. He has entered the recesses of the country and associated day after day with its indigent peasantry which must give a value to his enquiries and ensure an accuracy of information not to be expected from those the formation of whose opinions and impressions have necessarily partaken of the rapidity of their journey.[158]

As an assessment of Masson's achievements and potential usefulness Wade's remarks could not be bettered. It is a pity that his fellow
Political officers, especially Macnaghten, did not bear them in mind
when the question of relations with Afghanistan became acute. Other
interesting points arise from this letter. It reveals in particular that as
early as February 1833 Wade was reporting that he believed Masson
to be a deserter. This plainly shows that Hambly's notion that Masson
confided his secret to Gerard or to Burnes[139] must be mistaken since
Burnes and Masson did not meet till four years later (see footnote on
p. 78) while Gerard, as has been said, met Masson for the first time in
November 1833, many months after Captain Wade had first reported
his suspicions. Who then was his informant? Gerard provides a clue.
When he reached Lahore on 30 January 1834 he learned who Masson
really was from Dr Harlan, the one man in a position to know from
having met him soon after his desertion and having accompanied him
on the road for a while. It seems certain therefore that Harlan had also
revealed the secret to Wade, but at an earlier date. Gerard took the
trouble to write to Charles Trevelyan on 8 April 1834 a long letter setting out the full facts, stressing his high opinion of Masson, and hint-
ing at the desirability of reaching an arrangement with him of the
kind that eventually emerged.[140]

In Chapter I we have seen that Harlan had had an interview with
Wade before he left Ludhiana for Peshawar and offered to keep in
touch with him, in other words to act as a spy for the British. Grey
expresses the opinion that Harlan left Ludhiana as a spy for Shah Shuja
and continued as such during his whole career.[141] This view receives
some support from another passage from the Rev J. Wolff's account of
his conversations with Harlan at Gujerat:

> Next (after Burma) he went to Khorrosaun, as agent to the ex-King
> Shah Sujah-ool-Moolk, who honoured him with the title of the 'Friend
> of the King' ... and he informs me that the restoration of Shoojah-ool-
> Moolk would be of the greatest advantage to the British Government;
> however, being no politician, I was not able to understand well the
> reasons he assigned.[142]

Once he reached Kabul, Harlan wrote frequently to Wade who
eventually suggested to his Government that no further
communication be held with him as he was merely endeavouring to
impose on the Afghans as a British Agent.[143] Clearly such a man would
not have hesitated to curry favour with the Political Agent by giving
him a tip about a British deserter. Harlan left Afghanistan in 1829 for

Lahore and entered Ranjit Singh's service at the end of the year. He first appears in the *Narrative of Various Journeys* during the Amir's abortive attempt to recapture Peshawar in 1835. Harlan was then one of the negotiators sent by the Sikhs but he infuriated Dost Mahomed Khan by his intrigues. In spite of this incident, Harlan again took his talents to Afghanistan after having been deported from the Sikh Kingdom. Masson writing to Pottinger in February 1838 calls him 'An American adventurer here in the Amir's service' and 'a violent and unprincipled man'.[144] He was also a romancer of the first order claiming grandiose Afghan titles and high military rank in the Amir's service. He went over to Shah Shuja after the outbreak of the First Afghan War, was sent to India by the British and eventually deported to the United States.

C. Grey has suggested that when Wade wrote his letter to Macnaghten quoted above, he was even then thinking of Masson as a replacement for Keramat Ali.[145] Wade had certainly laid heavy stress on Masson's potential usefulness as a high grade source of information on Afghanistan and the region generally. On the other hand, there was as yet no reason to recall Keramat Ali. In any case, Wade could not move until he learned how his hints of a pardon for Masson had been regarded by his superiors. The reply came in a despatch from Macnaghten dated Ootacamund, 26 May 1834:

> *I am desired to acquaint you that, in the present state of our relations with the countries between the Indus and the Caspian Sea, His Lordship attaches the greatest importance to the attainment [sic] and accurate intelligence of the affairs of that quarter, and it being evident that the individual to whom you allude is eminently qualified to aid in this object, your having entered into a communication with him is entirely approved.*
>
> *You will be pleased to encourage Mr Masson to furnish you by every opportunity with his notions of the prevailing state of politics and of the feelings of the people in the different countries which he may visit, especially with reference to the reported design of the Russians to obtain a footing in Persia and Afghanistan. You are further authorised to supply Mr Masson with such funds from time to time as may suffice for his support, not exceeding in any one year the sum of 1000 Rs. Should you deem this sum insufficient for the purpose, his Lordship will be prepared to reconsider this part of the question.*
>
> *It is not deemed necessary at present that Mr Masson should be recognised by Government. To secure his zealous service it will probably be enough that you afford him encouragement to maintain the*

communication. In the meantime, however, the Governor General will strongly recommend to the Home authorities that a pardon be extended to Mr Masson in the event of that individual fulfilling the expectations which are now entertained of him. The offence which he has committed is in a military point of view undoubtedly a heinous one, but it may perhaps be deemed susceptible of extenuation when reviewed with reference to the character of the individual and to its attendant circumstances.[146]

A free pardon for a deserter from the East India Company's army required an approach to the King, even though it was an independent military service. Masson's friends John McNeill and Colonel Pottinger actively supported the proposed pardon with London.

Over the next months of 1834, Wade and Masson exchanged several letters in which the latter requested books needed for his studies and gave the latest news about his finds. He also produced a paper on the political state and resources of Afghanistan. In December Wade thanked him for the paper which had afforded him the highest satisfaction, and acknowledged Masson's offer of his services in collecting and transmitting information on the state of affairs west of the Indus. He referred to Masson's desire to regain that station in society which he had had the misfortune to lose and to Dr Gerard's favourable representations about him. He added that if Masson continued to serve the Government satisfactorily, the Governor General in Council would recommend to the authorities in England that a pardon be extended to him. Wade failed to mention that such a recommendation had already been made.[147]

Meanwhile, unknown to Wade, Keramat Ali was mixing himself up in local politics. Shortly after Shah Shuja had defeated the Amirs of Sind in January 1834 at the start of his campaign to regain his throne, Keramat Ali had begun to act as an intermediary for correspondence between the ex-king and some of the perennial malcontents, particularly the Nawab Jabar Khan and Abdul Samad. Shah Shuja had always had some supporters in Afghanistan either because he was a legitimate Sadozai monarch, or because he was regarded as an instrument to get rid of Dost Mahomed Khan; his initial successes naturally encouraged renewed intrigues in Kabul. Keramat Ali's activities as a go-between did not come to light until incriminating documents fell into the hands of Dost Mahomed after his victory over Shah Shuja at Kandahar in July of that year. According to Masson, Keramat Ali, already obnoxious to many people on account of his licentious opinions on religion, was only saved from arrest by the intercession of the

Nawab Jabar Khan. This news had not yet reached Wade when he complained in a letter of 13 August 1834 to his Government of the unaccountable failure of the Kabul newswriter to report on events at Kandahar. In a reply dated 19 September he was informed that the Government would have no hesitation in removing the newswriter from his post unless his explanation should prove entirely satisfactory.[148] From that date, therefore, Wade had authority to recall Keramat Ali. The latter saved him the trouble by resigning, but was in no hurry to return to India.

In a despatch to the Governor-General of 9 February 1835, the Secret Committee of the Directors transmitted a:

> ... warrant granting His Majesty's Free Pardon to James Lewis, a deserter from the Bengal Horse Artillery. This is the same person who, under the name of Charles Masson, has been for several years past, engaged in scientific and historical researches in the countries bordering on the Indus, and who was recommended for a Free Pardon by the Government of India.[149]

Long before that despatch reached its destination, Wade wrote on 11 February 1835 a letter which Masson found awaiting him at Tatang in mid-March, announcing that the Government had at his recommendation been pleased to appoint him as 'Agent in Cabul for communicating intelligence of the state of affairs in that quarter on a salary of Rs.250 per mensem'.[150] Evidently both Calcutta and Ludhiana felt that the matter was now too urgent to await London's reactions. In August, Wade forwarded a copy of the warrant of the free pardon to Masson—the first he knew of it.[151]

Keramat Ali had indeed stirred up a hornet's nest which it was Masson's first official task to clean up. Not only had the newswriter committed treason in Dost Mahomed's eyes, but he had also imputed his misdeeds to Captain Wade's known (but unavowed) wishes. When he finally departed for India he swore that he would procure Wade's removal from his post or be himself transported. That officer was naturally incensed and Masson quotes from furious letters he received on the subject. He comments that:

> An evil, greater than irritation occasioned to Captain Wade, arose from the political lessons given by the Saiyad to Dost Mahomed Khan, and the principal people at Kabul, for he instructed them not as things were, but as he fancied them to be;* this was unfortunate, and so was

---

* i.e. that the British might be willing to persuade Ranjit Singh to retrocede Peshawar to the Amir.

*his connection with the Persian adventurer, Abdul Samad; and his
errors here were afterwards felt in their effects...*

If Wade was displeased with recent events, Masson was far from happy
about his new appointment:

> *I might have supposed that it would have been only fair and courteous
> to have consulted my wishes and views before conferring an appoint-
> ment which compromised me with the equivocal politics of the country,
> and threw a suspicion over my proceedings, which did not before attach to
> them.*

He apparently thought that he would continue to report on Afghan
affairs on an unofficial footing and had not expected an official appointment with a salary attached. But what upset him most was the
likely effect on his researches:

> *I might have also lamented that I should be checked in the progress of
> antiquarian discovery, in which I was engaged, and I might reflect
> whether the positive injury I suffered in this respect was compensated
> by the assurance that his lordship, the governor-general in council,
> 'anticipates that the result of your employment will be alike useful to
> government and honourable to yourself'.*

In a subsequent passage he remarks that the duties of agent were, 'to
use Captain Wade's appropriate term, "imposed on me"'.

Although he was not without some grounds for complaint at Wade's
lack of frankness, he seems to have conveniently forgotten the condi-
tional offer of a pardon which was part and parcel of the arrangement. It cannot be supposed that a pardon was of limited appeal to
him, rather the contrary, since without one he could not return to British India or indeed to Britain. It was unfortunate that once his private
position in Afghanistan had been eroded by becoming an employee
of a power that his Afghan friends were beginning to fear, he would
inevitably no longer be above suspicion. Moreover Keramat Ali's an-
tics had already soured the atmosphere of the Amir's court. There
was in fact an instant reaction to his appointment. The same messen-
ger who had brought Wade's letter also brought letters to the Nawab
Jabar Khan from his son Abdul Ghias Khan at Ludhiana (see p. 92) no
doubt with similar information. At any rate:

> *... this nobleman, who had hitherto been so assiduous in his attentions
> and civility, treated me with such marked rudeness, that I abruptly
> left him, and without taking leave mounted my horse. This was the
> first fruit of my new appointment; nor was it until some time after his
> return to Kabul that our intercourse was carried on in the same friendly*

manner as before. To do the Nawab justice, when he found that he had been deceived, or that he had misunderstood matters, his concessions and apologies were ample.[152]

Masson had spent the past winter (1834-35) back in Kabul intent on pursuing the study of antiquities in the vicinity of the capital. The Amir had spent that winter striving to raise money by fair means or foul (the Hindu merchants were squeezed to the limit) in order to mount a holy war against the infidel Sikhs and, if possible, to regain Peshawar. Towards the end of February 1835 Dost Mahomed Khan left Kabul for Jalalabad, his army having preceded him. Masson left shortly afterwards for Tatang. The Amir had barely reached Jalalabad when an attempt was made to assassinate him. While he was still in camp there, a letter arrived from Lord William Bentink which outlined the idea of a commercial treaty, but which gave no satisfaction so far as his quarrel with Ranjit Singh was concerned. The Afghan army received reinforcements from Bajaur and from the ex-chief of Peshawar, Sultan Mahomed Khan, who hoped to recover his former possession. Some skirmishing took place, but with the arrival of the Maharaja in person the Sikhs soon surrounded the Afghan forces and forced the Amir to retreat in disorder. This brief and inglorious campaign not only damaged Dost Mahomed Khan's reputation, but also worsened his relations with the Maharaja and, if that were possible, with Sultan Mahomed Khan who had double-crossed the Amir.

He had engaged, without allies or resources, in a struggle to which he was unequal, and the consequences of his failure proved a fertile source of subsequent embarrassment to him, while he had thrown away the advantages he possessed, and those which he might have derived from his victory over Shah Sujah al Mulkh.[153]

Moreover it irritated the British in the person of Wade and led to the renewal of his relations with Shah Shuja which had been in abeyance since the disaster at Kandahar the previous year.

Kabul, too, felt the effects of the Amir's defeat: intrigues and disorders reached a pitch of intensity remarkable even by Afghan standards of the time. The streets were the theatres of constant conflicts and slaughters, of which no one took any notice and the city appeared to be on the verge of lapsing into anarchy. The exasperated Amir concocted a scheme to rid himself of his more obstreperous relatives by a *coup*, but the names on his list were leaked and those threatened naturally took precautions:

*They kept their retainers under arms night and day, and took especial
care not to call upon the Amir together, that they might not be seized
in a mass; also, when they did attend they were numerously accompanied by armed followers. In this unpleasant state of affairs my house
in the Balla Hissar was assaulted for five successive nights by bands
of muffled villains. I quietly filled my house with armed men, and
without taking farther notice, bided in tranquillity the course of
events.*[154]

Masson suspected Abdul Samad, whom he had offended by keeping
him at arm's length, of being the instigator of the attacks on his house,
or possibly the rascally Ghilzai who had tried so persistently to murder him on his trip from Peshawar to Kabul the previous year, rumours
having been circulated that his house contained treasures and money—
no doubt a garbled report of his archaeological finds.

Taking advantage of the general turmoil, Haji Khan and Abdul
Samad, too often ready to betray the Amir, conspired with the Nawab
Jabar Khan to dethrone him. The Nawab, however, was either too indecisive or too cautious to commit himself and the conspiracy petered
out. Dost Mahomed Khan, for his part, abandoned his hopelessly com-
promised plan to destroy his disloyal relatives, but his efforts to raise
sorely needed funds aroused more discontent.

In spite of Masson's misgivings about his official appointment, he
had taken his new duties seriously, reporting at length on the political
situation in Kabul and Afghanistan generally, besides compiling detailed reports on the commerce, geography and history of the country.
There was no lack of subject matter. Quite apart from the frenzied
internal situation, the Amir's disappointment at the lack of response
from the Governor-General over his quarrel with the Sikhs, led him to
start a correspondence with foreign powers which eventually caused
him to be viewed with grave suspicion by the British authorities. A
Persian merchant of disreputable character named Mahomed Hussen
(or Hussein) who had attached himself to Captain Burnes on his journey
to Bokhara, was visiting his native land and was given letters to the Shah
of Persia. Masson also had to report that the advantages of the commercial treaty proposed by Lord William Bentinck were not properly appreciated in Kabul and that the times were unfavourable to the consideration of such matters.[155]

These preoccupations adversely affected his antiquarian researches
and he was compelled to rely largely on Afghan assistants whom he
controlled by paying flying visits to the various sites. He had already
adopted this method to some extent the previous year, before his

appointment, in order to continue collecting coins at Begram while he himself was wholly absorbed in his excavations around Jalalabad. That the system worked well is shown by the steady rise in the numbers of coins found in 1835 and 1836, culminating in the huge increase recorded in 1837. Work on stupas, however, did not lend itself to control from a distance and although he had trained men at Wardak, for instance, excavations there were less thorough than would otherwise have been the case. Nevertheless, it was not these difficulties but an acute disagreement with Wade which led to his resignation at the end of 1835. For two years he had had a happy relationship with Colonel Pottinger, forwarding his finds and receiving his stipend through that officer. Wade was aware of this arrangement. Writing on 5 December 1834, before the appointment of Masson as agent, he described it as 'one of a scientific nature and will not, of course, interfere with the connection which you have formed with me, as such a collision might prove embarrassing to all parties'. However, according to Masson, as soon as he had accepted the post and:

> ... considered me well within his grasp, I found that it was plainly his intention to interfere, and that he was very careless as to producing the collision and embarrassment he had formerly deprecated. From the correspondence which ultimately became revealed, as well as from other sources, I observed with regret that he was abetted by the then Mr Secretary Macnaghten, and that he had succeeded temporarily to embroil me with Colonel Pottinger and with the Bombay Government, who honourably supported their own officer. I saw no alternative, therefore, but to tender the resignation of an appointment which was made instrumental in promoting strife and mischief, and did so with one hand while with the other I forwarded a full explanation to Colonel Pottinger. I now felt myself at liberty, as winter had set in, to retire from Kabul; and leaving behind its politics and intrigues, repaired to the milder and serener atmosphere of Tatang.[156]

These cryptic remarks about Wade hardly serve to elucidate the quarrel, but Masson's manuscripts throw some light on it. The root of the trouble was Wade's dislike of the dual channel of communication: Masson-Pottinger-Bombay Government on antiquarian affairs, and Masson-Wade-Supreme Government in Calcutta on intelligence matters. Moreover, when Masson was still a private individual, he had sent occasional information to Pottinger. Were this to continue in the changed circumstances it would have infringed Wade's monopoly of intelligence on countries west of the Indus. After Masson's appointment, Colonel Pottinger therefore wrote to Captain Wade saying that his correspondence with Masson was of a purely literary nature. He hoped that it would be allowed to continue and that he would remain the channel for research funds and for publishing Masson's works.[157] After much trouble which involved not only Pottinger's superiors in Bombay but also the authorities in Calcutta and London, a settlement was reached on the lines originally suggested by Pottinger.

Meanwhile, Wade had exasperated Masson by his dilatoriness in remitting his official salary which sometimes fell months in arrears, and in forwarding Masson's reports to Calcutta. Consignments of coins and relics to Bombay had also suffered undue delays ever since August 1834 when Masson learned that Bombay had agreed to Pottinger's proposal that all finds should be forwarded to Pottinger's address through Wade at Ludhiana, or through Lieutenant Mackesson, another Political Officer, at Mithankote.[158] Above all it came to light that Wade had used underhand methods such as sending Pottinger a garbled quotation from one of Masson's letters, in his efforts to sow dissension between them. Masson never forgave Wade for this behaviour and later, after the failure of Burnes's mission, refused to accept any post under him. This first clash with a 'Political' augured ill for his subsequent relations with other officers of that Service.

Masson was not alone in his difficulties with, and aversion to, Wade. His former shipmate, Charles Brownlow, writing from Calcutta expressed solicitude at first: 'I am much concerned to learn that there has been a rupture between you and Captain Wade, for he possesses vast influence and has everything in his power.'[159]

But in a subsequent letter he wrote:

> I can inform you on good authority that the impressions here, in the highest quarters, regarding [Wade] are not favourable, and in your case there is a definite opinion expressed, that you have met with unfair and inconsiderate treatment... There are two or three persons about the Governor-General who have great influence, and who feel an intense interest in your researches...[160]

Dr Gerard too was critical. In a letter of 22 April 1834, written after his conversation with Wade about Masson's activities he said:

> His Political Highness is very ready to improve upon any suggestions or follow up the footsteps of others in matters of which he had before been wholly oblivious ... his ends are for an interested purpose ... he cares little for researches such as yours.[161]

In the spring of 1836 Masson returned to Kabul. At about this time Ranjit Singh, finding that the occupation of Peshawar was not only expensive but even difficult, retroceded the adjacent districts of Hashtnaggar, Kohat and Hangu to Sultan Mahomed Khan. The latter, emboldened by this development, gave a further stir to the cauldron of conspiracy against the Amir and much of the year was occupied by 'the abortive attempts of the Amir to dissipate the confederacy of his relatives, and by their measures to counteract him'.[162] Also during that spring Masson was induced to withdraw his resignation by a letter from Charles Trevelyan:

> *Your sole duty is to keep the supreme government informed of all that is going on in any of the countries beyond the Indus, intelligence of which reaches Kabul, with the addition, whenever you think proper to offer any, of your own views and comments upon the particulars communicated by you. By doing this well, as you have hitherto done, you will render an important public service, and it will be open to the Governor-General to employ you in any other way he may think proper.*[163]

One might reasonably suppose that the phrase 'important public service' coming from the Deputy Secretary to the Government of India, would be considered a proof, among others, of the value attached to Masson's reports and have saved him from the strictures of some historians, for example, Norris who refers to him as 'a traveller and archaeologist who kept the Bengal Government supplied with Kabul rumours until Burnes came on the scene and made him redundant...'.[164]

His reports were certainly in demand. For instance Wade wrote to Masson on 31 December 1836 with reference to new rumours about the intentions of the Shah of Persia towards Kandahar and Herat that:

> *... as his lordship, in council, is anxious to be kept constantly informed of the affairs of Afghanistan, I have been directed to call on you to furnish me with the earliest intelligence of all important occurrences in that quarter, for the immediate information of government.*

That he was assiduous in his duties is shown by a letter from Wade mentioning the receipt of Masson's letters of 20 September, 13 October, and 7 and 30 November, 1836. By August 1837, he was being pressed for more frequent dispatches than before, while on 15 September Wade wrote:

> *The new proofs you have afforded of your zeal and intelligence, in the performance of your special duty of keeping me regularly informed of passing events in that quarter, continues to engage the favourable notice of the Governor-General in council, and I trust that your continued industry and discrimination may secure for you a continuance of the favour of a liberal and discerning government...*[161]

Back in harness, it therefore fell to him to report the dispatch of fresh letters to the Persian Court and, more doubtfully, to the Russian Government. Equally ominous for the future was the arrival in Bokhara at the end of 1836 of the Russian Captain Vektavich (or Vitkevich) who 'gave himself out as a most important personage, and declared that Russia, being at ease as regards Persia and Turkey, intended to interfere in the affairs of Central Asia'.[166] There, in a single phrase, is the essence of the alarm felt in Britain and India over Russian designs.

Meanwhile, Masson was gratified to learn from Colonel Pottinger that his explanations as to the propriety of his conduct were entirely satisfactory. At the end of the year, he received a warning from a reliable source that Abdul Samad was again pressing for his assassination. He therefore welcomed a proposal from the Nawab Jabar Khan to accompany him again to Tatang for the winter of 1836-37.

At the beginning of 1837 Hari Singh, the conqueror of Peshawar and subsequently its Governor, occupied the fort of Jamrud at the mouth of the Khyber Pass. Fearing that this step was the prelude to further aggressive measures by the Sikhs aimed at Jalalabad, Dost Mahomed Khan felt obliged to make a demonstration with a force under his son, Mahomed Akbar Khan. The ensuing engagement in April though bloody, was indecisive but resulted in the death of Hari Singh, to the great distress of Ranjit Singh. It also proved the undoing of Abdul Samad who arrived deliberately late on the battlefield; he was disgraced and departed for Bokhara. Haji Khan, too, was disgraced for playing a double game and was ordered to quit Kabul. He went to Kandahar where he joined the Barakzai sirdars. He was destined to play a prominent part in the Anglo-Afghan war, gaining the confidence of Burnes (despite a warning from Masson) and of Macnaghten until, after a final piece of treachery, he was exiled to India.[167] Far more important was the effect which the Jamrud affair had on the framing of British policy towards the Afghan countries in general and Dost Mahomed Khan in particular. To follow its course, a look at the wider picture is necessary.

Plate 9 (left). Dost Mahomed Khan.

CHAPTER XIII

THE LOOM OF RUSSIA

If we go on at this rate, the Cossack and the
Sepoy will soon meet on the banks of the Oxus.
Baron Brunnow to Sir John Hobhouse,
March 1840

The complicated drama which now began to unfold had a main plot with several sub-plots. The main plot: tentative moves by the British and Russian Empires on the Central Asian stage to find a satisfactory defensive frontier—the Great Game. The sub-plots: Persian ambitions stimulated by Russia; Ranjit Singh still hankering after further gains, particularly Shikarpur, but restrained by British power; Shah Shuja hoping against hope to regain his throne; and Dost Mahomed Khan trying to extend his control over divided Afghanistan, beginning with Peshawar. One must therefore follow all these interlinked strands and consider the development of policies in London, St. Petersburg, Tehran, Kabul, Lahore and Calcutta, with side glances at events at Herat, Kandahar and Peshawar. The leading actors were Lord Palmerston and Count Nesselrode, the British and Russian Foreign Ministers, and the Governor-General of India, Lord Auckland. Players of the lesser roles were the three Asian leaders already mentioned, the Shah of Persia, the Barakzai brothers at Peshawar and Kandahar, and finally Prince Kamran at Herat.

Whether or not Russia was a direct, or indirect, menace the major question was, in brief, whether Afghanistan should be reunited, and if so under whose rule, in order to serve as a buffer for India in place of Persia which had failed in that role.

Lord Auckland had assumed his duties in March 1836. During the long sea voyage to Calcutta trouble had been brewing in Persia. In order to compensate for their losses of territory to Russia in the west the Persians had for several years past endeavoured to expand eastwards with expeditions against the Turcoman slave-raiders in Khorasan and had also threatened Herat. These manoeuvres, and Russian encouragement of them, were hafted temporarily by the deaths of Abbas Mirza, the heir-apparent, and shortly after of the Shah, his father. But the new monarch, Muhammad Shah, had by no means abandoned thoughts of conquest. As Henry Ellis, the British special representative sent to offer condolences and congratulations to him wrote to Lord Palmerston:

> It is unsatisfactory to know that the Shah has very extended schemes of conquest in the direction of Afghanistan and, in common with all his subjects, conceived that the right of sovereignty over Herat and Qandahar is as complete now as in the reign of the Safavi dynasty.[168]

Persian ministers went even further telling Ellis that they considered Afghanistan as far as Ghazni as part of the Shah's dominions and that the occupation of Herat and later Kandahar was intended. Such reports from Tehran, together with the arrival of an emissary from the Amir and another from the Kandahar sirdars, both seeking an alliance with the Shah against Herat and the Sikhs, boded ill for the future.

John McNeill had been assistant to Sir John Campbell when they both looked after Charles Masson at Tabriz in 1830. Campbell retired in 1835 and McNeill was appointed Minister to Persia the following year after the conclusion of Ellis's temporary mission. McNeill firmly believed that if Russian influence in Persia were allowed to become dominant, Afghanistan would be drawn in and India would be threatened. His strongly expressed views on the menace of Russia and on the counter-measures which should be taken had a considerable effect on policy in London and Calcutta.

In the autumn of 1836 Alexander Burnes was chosen to survey the Indus in greater detail than in 1831 with the technical help of Lieutenant John Wood of the Indian Navy, and this time to continue up stream as far as Attock. He was to persuade the rulers of the riverine states of the mutual advantages of establishing an entrepot and annual fair on the Indus to encourage trade with Central Asia. Thereafter he was to proceed to Kabul to discuss the commercial development of the Indus basin with the Amir in fulfillment of Lord William Bentinck's promise of the previous year. Masson first heard of the projected mission in a letter from Wade dated 30 September 1836, which set out its aims and stressed its strictly commercial character. The letter ended with a request for a report on the Amir's reactions. Masson comments sardonically:

> From this letter it will not fail to be observed that there was little notion entertained at this time of convulsing Central Asia, of deposing and setting up kings, of carrying on wars, of lavishing treasure, and of the commission of a long train of crimes and follies.[169]

Burnes sailed from Bombay in November with Wood and Lieutenant Robert Leech. Dr Percival Lord joined the party in March. When Burnes reached Hyderabad in February 1837, he wrote to Masson in terms similar to those used by Wade, stressing the commercial objects of his journey and asking him to let it be generally known that the 'main and great aim of government is to open the Indus'. Masson was sceptical:

> The main, and great aim of government, is declared to be to open the Indus. Was the Indus ever closed, or farther closed than by its dangerous entrances and shallow depth of water? Another object was to open the countries on and beyond the Indus to commerce. Were they also ever closed? No such thing: they carried on an active, and increasing trade with India, and afforded markets for immense quantities of British manufactured goods. The governments of India and of England, as well as the public at large, were never amused and deceived by a greater fallacy than that of opening the Indus, as regarded commercial objects. The results of the policy concealed under this pretext have been the introduction of troops into the countries on and beyond the river, and of some half dozen steamers on the stream itself, employed for warlike objects, not for those of trade. There is besides, great absurdity in commercial treaties with the states of Central Asia, simply because there is no occasion for them. From ancient and prescribed usage, moderate and fixed duties are levied; trade is perfectly free; no goods are prohibited; and the more extensive the commerce carried on the greater advantage to the state. Where then, the benefit of commercial treaties?[170]

Vigorous language, often quoted since. But although he was right about the exaggerated claims as to the suitability of the Indus for navigation—it was too shifting as well as too shallow—Masson in his remote spot was swimming against the strong tide of belief in England in the civilising benefits of commerce to semi-barbarous tribes, to say nothing of British merchants' hopes of supplanting Russian goods in Central Asia.

In his *Narrative* Masson describes in detail the developments and above all the misunderstandings, as he observed them from Kabul, which led to the failure of the mission. His views and his judgements have received either scant, or slight attention from some historians, largely because of his strong criticisms of Burnes, Wade and Macnaghten. If an attempt is now made to present a more balanced account it should be remembered that Masson, by common consent, understood Afghanistan and its peoples better than anyone in India;

equally important he loved the Afghans and was appalled at the total
disregard of Afghan interests and feelings shown by the British authorities. Perhaps his indignation got the upper hand, but at least it is
an emotion that does him credit.

Burnes learned of the battle of Jamrud on 2 June 1837, when he was
at Dera Ghazi Khan on the Indus. The previous day he had received a
letter from John McNeill about the desirability of re-uniting divided
Afghanistan under Dost Mahomed Khan as a firm barrier against Persian and Russian pretensions. Burnes was disturbed by the news of
Jamrud and wrote to the Amir deploring the renewal of hostilities
with the Sikhs. According to Masson, the recipient was 'sorely incensed
at the letter... I had to bear the weight of his resentment, and he was
absolutely savage.' The Governor-General, who throughout placed
great emphasis on the vital importance of preserving the friendship
of Ranjit Singh, found it even more difficult to help the Amir after this
latest attack, and in consequence was not disposed to agree with
McNeill's views. In fact, Auckland, already much irritated by Dost
Mahomed Khan's overtures to the Shah of Persia and to the Russians,
remained unwilling to do anything for the Amir vis-a-vis the Sikhs
unless he were prepared to abase himself before the Maharaja by acknowledging his faults and sending a son as hostage to Lahore. Shortly
before the Jamrud engagement the Government in Calcutta began to
realise that the commercial basis of Burnes's mission was not enough
and that he was bound to have to deal with political matters. Even so,
the instructions sent by Macnaghten on 15 May went no further than
to insist that:

> ... in any case in which specific political propositions shall be made to
> you, you will state that you have no authority to make replies, but
> that you will forward them, through Captain Wade, to the Govern-
> ment. If applied to, as you probably may be, for advice by Dost
> Mahomed Khan, in the difficulties by which he is surrounded, you
> will dissuade him from insisting in such a crisis on pretensions which
> he cannot maintain, and you will lead him, as far as may be in your
> power, to seek and to form arrangements of reconciliation for himself
> with the Sikh sovereign.

Burnes was also to gather general political intelligence and information on 'the commerce of Russia and on the measures adopted by that
power with the object of extending her influence in Central Asia'.[171] In
effect, Burnes was required to do little more than repeat his earlier
mission of 1832. No wonder that when Masson was eventually shown

these instructions he observed that they were really none at all, to which Burnes replied that Dr Lord on joining him had made the same remark.[172]

Meanwhile, Lieutenant Eldridge Pottinger, a nephew of Colonel Pottinger, had arrived in Kabul in May 1837 on leave of absence from the Army. He stayed of course with the Nawab Jabar Khan, but in July he surreptitiously departed for Herat by the inhospitable central route through the Hazarajat without telling his host or Masson. Owing to the extreme jealousy of Kamran on the part of the Barakzai chiefs, Masson was much blamed for this incident and accused of organising it. Some three months later Lieutenant Pottinger became involved in the siege of Herat and the part he played in organising its successful defence made him famous. Masson's remarks about the 'Hero of Herat' are less complimentary than has been customary:

> I have always thought that, however fortunate for Lieutenant Pottinger himself, his trip to Herat was an unlucky one for his country; the place would have been fought as well without him; and his presence, which would scarcely be thought accidental, though truly it was so, must not only have irritated the Persian king, but have served as a pretext for the more prominent exertions of the Russian staff. It is certain that, when he started from Kabul, he had no idea that the city would be invested by a Persian army; in proof of which I have letters from him soon after he reached; the first alluding to no such expectation, and the second describing the Persian advances as sudden, and wholly unlooked-for by the authorities.

Kamran had the less reason to expect to be attacked as he had gone to great lengths to assuage the Shah of Persia's anger at his attempted capture of Kandahar in the spring of that year and McNeill had commended the proffered terms to the Shah. In fact, Kamran was in a very weak position since his army had been decimated by disease during the Kandahar campaign. The Shah was not to be placated and at the end of July he started with his army on the four months' march from Tehran to Herat. When Kamran's frontier fortress of Ghorian surrendered through treachery, a siege of Herat became inevitable. For the next fourteen months till the siege was raised in September 1838, the fate of Herat was to dominate the political scene.

During Burnes's leisurely journey up the Indus to Peshawar and so through the Khyber Pass to Kabul, Masson plied him with reports on the political situation and, in response to his request, with an account of the state of the parties in the Afghan countries. As Burnes drew nearer the tempo of the correspondence quickened: there were at least six letters from Masson in August. Burnes was duly grateful; '...your competent knowledge and great local experience will, I am sure, prove at this critical juncture of great service...' He made a point of sending Masson copies of dispatches exchanged between Auckland and McNeill and other official correspondence, as well as of his own letters to the Amir and the Nawab Jabar Khan. Masson was thus kept well in the picture.

The news reaching both men from independent sources was, however, disquieting. Some two years earlier Dost Mahomed Khan had sent letters to the Shah of Persia by Mahomed Hussen (see p. 128). He had been followed by another agent, Haji Ibrahim, a brother of Abdul Samad, who now forwarded a letter from Count Simonich, the Russian Minister to the Persian Court, addressed to the Amir. As it arrived at the time of Abdul Samad's disgrace, it was generally thought to be a fabrication and Dost Mahomed Khan appeared to be of the same opinion. Masson was shown it and reported the matter to Wade:

> *The letter is written on pink-coloured paper; has no signature, but a seal stamped on it, with a legend, as Mirza Sami Khan reads it, 'Graf Ivan Simonich, Wazir Mukhtahar Bahi Russi'. The letter is addressed to Amir Dost Mahomed Khan and states that Haji Ibrahim, after his dismissal by the Shah waited on the writer; that favourable reports of the Amir and the Afghans had frequently reached him and that he was their well-wisher.*

But for the seal and Haji Ibrahim's explanatory letter there was nothing to show who wrote it.[173] Although it was the first approach from Russia, it seemed innocuous and gave Masson no particular cause for alarm. The Kandahar sirdars had also sent agents to the Shah and towards the end of June 1837 a Persian envoy, Kamber Ali, arrived at Kandahar from Tehran bearing letters and presents to the Barakzai chiefs. He was accompanied by Mahomed Hussen. As soon as Masson heard this unwelcome news, he immediately left Jalalabad for Kabul. Shortly afterwards letters arrived from Mahomed Hussen to the Amir which Masson copied to Burnes and Wade.

In the course of his correspondence with Burnes, Masson had dwelt on the subject of Peshawar which he, at least, regarded as crucial to a proper understanding with Dost Mahomed Khan:

> *My proposal was simply, that Peshawar — the assumption of which by Ranjit Singh had brought on all our evils — should be restored to Sultan Mahomed Khan; in fact, that a mere act of justice should be done.*

By this the chiefs of Kandahar would be at once reconciled, while Dost Mahomed Khan would have no alternative but to acquiesce; still, as to his exertions in some measure the restitution might be held due, I proposed that Sultan Mahomed Khan should pay annually a sum more or less, not exceeding a lakh of rupees, from his revenues, which I did not doubt he would gladly do, as the price of being relieved from Sikh control, and of the possession of the entire country.

Masson added that being perfectly aware that the occupation of Peshawar was unprofitable and troublesome to Ranjit Singh, he was satisfied that the Maharaja would relinquish it, if solicited by the Governor-General to do so.[174] He also well knew that even though the Amir had never himself possessed Peshawar, he would not relish such a settlement in his brother's favour, but was convinced that he would eventually accept it. Once the Amir had accepted, Masson believed that he would be only too glad to drop his courting of the Persians and Russians from whom he had never expected much, but to whom he had turned from lack of response from the British, and would welcome a connection with the Government of India.

Burnes responded on 4 September, having just cleared the Khyber and entered the domains of Dost Mahomed:

The view which you have taken of Peshawar being passed over to Sultan Mahomed Khan is to me very satisfactory. I am not without hope that we shall, in course of time, be able to work out this matter... Had we not had to pull the Khalsa's rein in Sinde [i.e. prevented Ranjit Singh from taking Shikarpur] *I should have said that the adjustment of it amounted to a certainty: and I now believe that the drain which Peshawar is upon his finances, his wish to please us, and other things combined, will, in the end, tend to adjustment.*

Again, in a letter dated 9 September, Burnes, who had in the meantime received an important express from Calcutta wrote: 'the adjustment of Peshawar is nearer than ever, if not mismanaged, and you well know how easy it is to do that, even without Afghans, and their proverbial stupidity'.[175] In reality, Burnes was already of the opinion that the problem of Peshawar was a minor one which could be readily solved and was thinking far ahead to the re-unification of Afghanistan under the Amir and making it into an effective buffer state on the lines proposed by McNeill. He hoped to shelve Peshawar for the present by promising the Amir moral support in obtaining that city and the territories on the west bank of the Indus as far as Shikarpur, after Ranjit Singh's death. Dost Mahomed Khan thereby relieved of his preoccupation with Peshawar, could then be encouraged to deal with Kandahar and Herat. The Governor-General's views were very different. He explicitly recognised Ranjit Singh's claims to the Peshawar district and considered that any compromise could only come from a voluntary concession on the part of the Sikh chieftain. Yet there were occasions when Lord Auckland conceded that one of the Barakzai brothers might receive Peshawar from the Maharaja in return for tribute and acknowledgement of his supremacy. But the proposition was never put to Ranjit Singh; Captain Wade, in particular, saw to that.

In the meantime, Kamber Ali's mission to Kandahar was going badly. For one thing, the Kandahar sirdars would not allow him to proceed to Kabul. For another, he had indulged in revels which became notorious. Finally, Mahomed Hussen had played a dirty trick on him. The former had borrowed Rs 800 from the envoy but had evaded repayment by a ruse and returned to Kabul where he gave Dost Mahomed Khan so extraordinary an account of his sayings and doings in Persia that the Amir and his nobles were convulsed with laughter at the lies he told. On points of business nothing could be gained from Mahomed Hussen, try as they would. The Amir slyly quartered him upon the Nawab Jabar Khan, the foreigners' friend, and occasionally sent for him, when inclined to be mirthful and to laugh at the monstrous tales he related.[176] In reply to Masson's reports of these events, Burnes, still en route to Kabul wrote:

> The audacity of Mahomed Hussein, whose letters [to the Amir] you enclosed, astounds me: he is, however, a very Persian. I translated the epistles, and sent them to the private secretary [to the Governor-General].

And again in a subsequent letter:

> The approach of the bursting bubble of Mahomed Hussein's mission is highly amusing. While seated on the Hindoo Koosh, drinking tea and laughing at the said Mirza's fibs, I little thought I was holding converse with the future ambassador of the ruler of Cabool to the King of Kings.[177]

CHAPTER XIV

FAILURE OF A MISSION

On 18 September, Alexander Burnes reached Bhut Khak, a few miles from Kabul, where Masson paid him a visit and remained the following day:

> Our conversation was nearly exclusively on political matters; and I must confess I augured very faintly of the success of his mission, either from his manner or from his opinion 'that the Afghans were to be treated as children', a remark that drew from me the reply that he must not then expect them to behave as men. [178]

Burnes own description of his arrival runs:

> ...to Bootkhak, where we were joined by Mr Masson, the well-known illustrator of Bactrian reliques. It was a source of great satisfaction to all of us to make the acquaintance of this gentleman, and we were highly gratified by our intercourse with him. On the 20th September we entered Cabool, and were received with great pomp and splendour by a fine body of Afghan cavalry, led by the Amir's son, Akhbar Khan. He did me the honour to place me on the same elephant upon which he himself rode, and conducted us to his father's court, whose reception of us was most cordial. A spacious garden, close by the palace and inside the Bala-Hissar of Cabool, was allotted to the mission as their place of residence. [179]

Masson was unhappy at the imprecision of Burnes's official instructions which were shown to him the next day; he was even more troubled by the manner and matter of the envoy's discussions with Dost Mahomed Khan. Of the manner, he writes:

> The amir had every reason to exult in the humility of his new guest, who never addressed him but with his hands closed, in the attitude of supplication, or without prefacing his remarks with 'Gharib Nawaz', your humble petitioner, which acquired for him in Kabul the sobriquet of Gharib Nawaz. [180]

Of the matter, he thought it imprudent to excite expectations in the Amir which were not likely to be realised. All this induced Dost Mahomed Khan to pitch his demands high.

Plate 10 (left). Sir Alexander Burnes in Bokharan costume.

Masson's most damaging accusation was that Burnes and his companions, instead of behaving with the degree of decorum proper in a British mission, indulged in wild revels with local ladies. The Amir received regular reports of what was going on, but forbade any notice to be taken, pleased perhaps that the envoy's intrigues were not of a political nature. Masson relates that Mirza Sami Khan, the Amir's secretary and counsellor, called on him and proposed that:

> I should follow the example of my illustrious superiors, and fill my house with black-eyed damsels. I observed, that my house was hardly large enough... I then asked, where the damsels were to come from; and he replied, I might select any I pleased, and he would take care I should have them. I told him, his charity exceeded all praise, but I thought it better to go on quietly in my old way and he dropped the subject.[181]

This accusation achieved notoriety when it was published and led to bitter criticism of Masson at the time and since. Some commentators have refused to believe the story and have accused Masson of malice and spitefulness. Others regarded it as in the worst possible taste in view of Burnes's early and gallant death. Yet the story has not been positively denied and indeed it is far from improbable: Kabul women then had a reputation for sexual licence which was enhanced during the subsequent British occupation of 1839-42.

After Burnes had had some preliminary conversations with the Amir, the latter sent Mirza Sami Khan with Mirza Imam Verdi, another of his confidential secretaries, to Masson with a proposal that Peshawar should be handed over to Dost Mahomed Khan as the *sine qua non* of any understanding with the British Government. Masson expressed strong opposition, saying that he would seek to dissuade Captain Burnes from listening to such terms. The Nawab Jabar Khan then took a hand and urged upon Burnes the necessity of firmly rejecting the proposal about to be made to him, on which so much depended. Masson did the same, feeling certain that it was a *ballon d'essai*. He suggested to Burnes that his course was a very clear one:

> ... the pleasure of Ranjit Singh to give up Peshawar afforded the opportunity of settling the Afghan question in a manner which could not have been looked for. It might be made to benefit the brothers at Kandahar and Peshawar equally with Dost Mahomed Khan, and the British Government would at all events have done their duty to them, and have fulfilled their wish to benefit the Afghan nation.

Burnes argued that the Amir would be greatly displeased were Peshawar made over to Sultan Mahomed Khan, but Masson maintained as before that the Amir had no valid claim to it and would have to swallow the proposition in the end. In the event, the Mirzas proposed to Burnes that in return for the cession of Peshawar to the Amir, one of the latter's sons should reside at Lahore with the Maharaja as a hostage for his father's good behaviour. Burnes told his colleague that he was so astonished that he made the Mirzas thrice repeat what they had said, to be sure that there was no mistake; and that, satisfied there was none, he had told them all would be settled as they wished. Masson could only express his fears that the worst results would follow:

> The Nawab Jabar Khan, and the principals of the Sunni party at Kabul, ceased to interest themselves in the success of the mission, and either seldom visited the durbar, or, when there never talked business. No person of any respectability or character ever called on Captain Burnes, and the mission was left to follow up its irregular career, and to sink into contempt.[182]

Masson also notes as a complicating factor in the conduct of negotiations, the jealousy of Burnes entertained by Captain Wade who had:

> ... informed the authorities at Kabul, through Abdul Ghias Khan, that he would have been a fitter person than Captain Burnes for the mission, and would have done more for them than he could do, on account of his influence with Ranjit Singh. I also knew that Captain Wade could depend on the support of Mr Secretary Macnaghten. On the other hand, Captain Burnes was agreeable to Lord Auckland and had the privilege of constant communication with the private secretary, Mr Colvin, sufficient to protect him from evil influence, had he used it wisely.[183]

However, it was perhaps not so much a personal matter between Wade and Burnes, but rather that the former feared lest his key position as the holder of a monopoly of intelligence on the countries west of the Indus through his chain of official newswriters and unofficial correspondents, be eroded were Burnes to bring the Amir to an alliance with the British, and Kabul replace Ludhiana as the new advance Political Agency.[184]

One of Wade's first tasks when he was appointed Political Assistant at Ludhiana in 1823, was to keep in touch with his exiled neighbour Shah Shuja-ul-Mulk. Wade became disposed to favour the ex-monarch's cause and supported Shuja's request for a four months' advance of his British pension to finance his campaign to regain his throne in 1833-34. Wade was never a supporter of Dost Mahomed Khan or of the Barakzai leaders in general. The most important of Wade's duties was to establish and maintain good relations with Ranjit Singh who regarded the Barakzai as his enemies. Ranjit Singh maintained a

Sikh agent at Ludhiana, while Wade was in effect the non-resident envoy to the Maharaja's court at Lahore. In addition, Wade was formally put in charge of all political relations with the States beyond the Indus in 1835. This combination of duties together with his long experience* and an undoubted intelligence, made him a dominant figure in the formation of British policy in the north-west.[185] His predilections had therefore a marked effect on policy.

On his arrival in Kabul, Burnes had recommended to the Governor-General that the Amir should be guaranteed the possession of Peshawar on the death of Ranjit Singh. He now forwarded Dost Mahomed's own proposal on 5 October, to which no answer could be received in less than three months. Although Burnes showed Masson all his incoming correspondence, he did not show him his outgoing correspondence, consequently despite discussions and frequent exchanges of little notes, Masson did not know in any detail what Burnes had written to his superiors. Moreover, in a letter of 19 October, Wade told Masson by direction of Macnaghten that:

> ... until Captain Burnes shall have quitted Kabul it is considered desirable that you should be subject to his orders, and discontinue your direct correspondence with me, and I beg that you will act accordingly. Captain Burnes will convey to me every week, if necessary, such information as he may collect either by his own means or those of yourself.[186]

These instructions were of course normal and proper in such circumstances, but Masson's opinions could no longer be heard.

In Calcutta, the Governor-General was led by events to give more of a political character to Burnes' mission than originally belonged to it. Macnaghten therefore dispatched new instructions on 11 September 1837, which reached Kabul on 21 October, a month after Burnes had started his negotiations. Burnes was still not given any 'direct political power' inasmuch as the injunction to report any reasonable propositions through Wade was maintained. He was to point out to Dost Mahomed the hazards of his position, the worthlessness of Persian promises and that 'under any circumstances our first feeling must be that of regard for the honour and just wishes of our old and firm ally Ranjit Singh'. If, however, the Amir desired peace with the Sikhs and abandoned any contacts with Persia, 'such good offices in his

---

* He served continuously in India from 1809 to 1844, a longer period than any of his contemporaries, except Sir Charles Metcalfe.

favour with the Maharajah as we can render would be given to him...'
These good offices might be directed towards the restoration of
Peshawar to 'a member of the Barukzye family on the condition of
tribute to Ranjit Singh'.[187] Naturally, Burnes was disconcerted and indeed 'Never can an envoy have received more obscure and unpalat-
able instructions on which to base a bid for the friendship of a foreign
potentate.'[188] It was also clear that the proposal to give Peshawar out-
right to the Amir, which Burnes should have known would be unaccept-
able, was already dead, though the crushing reply to his despatch of 5
October was not received until 21 February 1838.

The resilient Burnes persuaded himself that these instructions could
bear a wide discretion. He saw his task as the establishment of British
political influence in Central Asia. Kabul was to become the nerve-
centre of a new political system.[189] He sent Dr Lord and Lieutenant
Wood to Kunduz mainly in order to reconnoitre Badakshan. He opened
a correspondence with Eldridge Pottinger at Herat and with the Kandahar
sirdars.

By November, Kamber Ali's position at Kandahar had worsened to
such an extent that he begged the sirdars to agree to his departure.
They thereupon dictated a treaty which he was only too glad to seal in
order to get away. So apprehensive was he of being waylaid on his
journey back that he left all his property behind and 'decamped slightly
equipped' for the Shah's camp outside Herat. The day after Kamber
Ali's arrival, Lieutenant Vektavich set out for Kandahar. By this treaty,
Herat upon its capture by the Persians would be given to the Kandahar
chiefs. According to Masson, a child ought not to have been deceived
by such a document extorted as it had been, however much Burnes
might have chosen to attach importance to it, or the Indian Government to have fallen into his error. But Count Simonich soon guaranteed the treaty, which gave it greater importance than Masson had
supposed. (After the failure to take Herat the Russian Government
repudiated it and recalled their Envoy and Lieutenant Vektavich; their
gamble, if such it were, had come to nought.)

When Burnes learned the terms of the treaty he felt that it would
suffice to tilt the balance against the defenders of Herat whereupon
the Shah might well pounce on Kandahar and thereby open the door
to extensive Persian and Russian encroachments. By December,
spurred by the arrival of Lieutenant Vektavich, Burnes felt compelled
to act: he offered the Kandahar sirdars three lakhs of rupees to help
them repel any attack from Persia. Shortly afterwards, he sent

Lieutenant Leech there—yet another move well outside his instructions; designed, says Masson unkindly, for the purpose of magnifying the dangers to be apprehended from Persia, and of attaching importance to transactions at Kandahar. Masson also suspected that the information reaching Burnes from that quarter was distorted in order to spur him on, and that Dost Mohamed Khan too was manipulating Burnes in order to annex Kandahar himself.

Masson considered that Burnes was both rash in exceeding his instructions and naive in believing too trustingly in the Amir's fair words. But even had he been fully aware of Burnes's grand design he would have deplored using Afghanistan as a springboard for adventures in Turkestan. He was essentially against British interference in the affairs of the three Afghan countries and Turkestan because he was sceptical of a Russian military threat, whilst perhaps not sufficiently appreciating the effect that expansion of Russian influence alone might have on the internal stability of British India. He was, moreover, unconvinced of the ability of Persia to cause serious trouble on her eastern borders. He was particularly scathing about the calibre of the 'miserable agents' employed by the Amir and the Kandahar sirdars to negotiate with the Shah. His opinion of Kamber Ali, the Persian envoy, was little higher. All these tortuous developments and crude attempts at diplomacy fortified Masson's belief that Dost Mahomed Khan was never wholly serious in his overtures to the Persians and Russians and that his real desire was for an understanding with the British, provided always that an accommodation could be reached over Peshawar.

Lieutenant Vektavich, after a brief stay at Kandahar had, unlike Kamber Ali, successfully defied the Kandahar sirdars' efforts to prevent him from proceeding to Kabul. He arrived there suddenly on 19 December carrying a letter purporting to be from the Emperor of Russia though it lacked seal and signature. The Amir was surprised and his treatment of Vektavich in the early stages bore out Masson's view: he was accommodated in the house of Mirza Sami Khan where he was kept under surveillance and at arm's length for the next three months. His arrival, however:

> ... completely overpowered the British envoy and he abandoned himself to despair. He bound his head with wet towels and handkerchiefs, and took to the smelling-bottle. It was humiliating to witness such an exhibition, and the ridicule to which it gave rise. The Amir called on the disconcerted envoy, and Mirza Sami Khan brought over the letter

said to be from the emperor, for both of them had suspicions, in common with the Kandahar sirdars, that it might not be genuine, and so they told Captain Burnes who, however, at once assured them it was genuine, and that there could be no doubt of it... I unhesitatingly expressed my opinion that the letter was a fabrication, as far as the emperor was concerned, but that it was very probably got up in the Persian camp before Herat, because without some such document Vektavich would not have dared to show himself in Afghanistan... It may be further remarked of this document, that it was not written by the count at the emperor's command, but purported to be from the emperor himself, another proof, in my estimation, that it was not genuine—however, on that very account well calculated to deceive Dost Mahomed Khan.[190]

On 23 December, Burnes took the unusual step of writing privately to Auckland himself urging a more vigorous policy in Central Asia and putting the case for supporting Dost Mahomed Khan as strongly as he could. He rehearsed the origins of the Peshawar problem which had so upset the Amir and pleaded that its speedy settlement either in the Amir's favour or in Sultan Mahomed's would provide:

... an immediate remedy against further intrigue, and a means of show-ing to the Afghans that the British Government does sympathise with them, and at one and the same time satisfying the chiefs, and gaining both our political and commercial ends...[191]

Whether or not these arguments derived from a belated acceptance of Charles Masson's opinions which they closely resembled, they were too late. The Governor-General, influenced by Wade's contrary views, had already withdrawn his earlier suggestion that Peshawar might be given to Sultan Mahomed Khan. He was under the false impression that Herat was the strongest of the three Afghan powers and Kabul the weakest. He even thought that Prince Kamran was the most re-spectable of the rulers, whereas in fact he was dissolute, avaricious, and oppressive. British travellers had reported as much, for example, Arthur Conolly, who added that Kamran was a slave to wine and the harem. Conolly's only contact with him was an indirect enquiry whether the Englishman possessed, or could prepare, a liquor which would make the Prince drunk at once.[192] Kamran's unprincipled but clever vizier, Yah Mahomed Khan, dealt in slaves and as his power increased developed into a tyrant whose name became a by-word. A contemporary historian said of him: 'if there was an abler or a worse man in Central Asia I have not yet heard his name'.[193] Auckland also misjudged the situation at Kandahar which was in reality a poor principality, militarily weak and sadly misgoverned by the Barakzai sirdars who were in consequence highly unpopular. The Governor-General believed, too, that Dost Mahomed Khan was on the defensive whereas the Amir, though fearing that Ranjit Singh might possibly attempt to push forward as far as Jalalabad, knew full well that his opponent had neither the means nor the inclination to expose his Sikhs to the mountainous terrain further north with its harsh climate.

Auckland was concerned lest any British aid given to Kabul and Kandahar would be turned against Ranjit Singh; past events lent some colour to this view. In fact, the Amir no longer sought a military confrontation with the Maharaja. Furthermore, neither the Amir nor his Kandahar brothers trusted each other enough to combine together to wage a holy war against the infidel Sikhs, however appealing the idea might be in theory. Above all, the Governor-General 'overlooked the fact that Afghan love of independence was even greater than their love of turbulence and was thus the most effective of all safeguards against Russian domination'.[194]

In Kabul, Alexander Burnes invited the Russian officer to dinner on Christmas Day. They took to each other; both in their early thirties, both playing a lone hand: Vektavich possibly, and Burnes certainly, exceeding their official briefs. Burns writes:

> He was a gentlemanly and agreeable man, of about thirty years of age, and spoke French, Turkish, and Persian fluently, and wore the uniform of an officer of Cossacks, which was a novelty in Cabool. He had been three times at Bokhara, and we had therefore a common subject to converse upon, without touching on politics. I found him intelligent and well informed on the subject of Northern Asia... I never again met Mr Vilkievitch (or, as I see it written, Vicovich),* although we exchanged sundry messages of 'high consideration'; for I regret to say that I found it to be impossible to follow the dictates of my personal feelings of friendship towards him, as the public service required the strictest watch, lest the relative positions of our nations should be misunderstood in this part of Asia.[195]

Within four years both men had died violent deaths: the Russian by his own hand, Burnes by the mob in Kabul.

Replies to Burnes's various proposals to the Government of India now began to arrive. To his pet suggestion that a promise of Peshawar

---

* Yapp gives a fourth and no doubt correct version of the name as Vitkevich; but for convenience Masson's version, Vektavich, has been retained throughout.

should be made to the Amir on the death of Ranjit Singh, the reply deprecated speculating on the death of an individual. The Amir's own proposal that Peshawar should be given to him subject to sending hostages to Lahore, was rejected. But as neither it, nor the alternative of reinstating Sultan Mahomed Khan, had been put to the Maharaja and as Wade had not ascertained his actual wishes they were never known. Burnes was thus left without any means of softening the disappointment of the Dost. He had never been accorded any bargaining counters with which to negotiate and now the Amir had to be given a blanket negative. Furthermore his offer of money to the Kandahar chiefs called forth a severe reprimand from the Governor-General, and an order to rescind it. Burnes was in despair when he received this despatch on 21 February 1838. But he made matters worse by blaming the Amir for having made his proposals, in spite of having approved them. Masson records that:

> ... a very pretty interview necessarily passed, which a note from him to me written immediately after, will, perhaps show. 'It is impossible to write all, and for me to come to you or you to me before dinner might show our funk, I gave it fearfully and left him in a furious rage, but not a word was forgotten of which I prepared for him. He gave the old story—no benefit—no one cares for a falling nation—I offered my wares for sale, and you would not buy.'[196]

The last sentence neatly sums up the Amir's acute dilemma.

It has already been said that Masson was not shown Burnes's outward letters. When he did see them in print in the Papers presented to Parliament in 1839, a number of them heavily cut, he deplored the worthless evidence there adduced. He quotes various instances of the low grade intelligence which had been fed to the envoy and alleges that the reports of Vektavich's conversations with the Amir in Burnes's private letter to Auckland of 23 December 1837 were absolutely false, coming as they did from two sources who had been instructed by Mirza Sami Khan to delude him, the object being to 'rouse the mind of Alexander Burnes'.

The mission was now virtually at an end. But Burnes held on for two more months. For one thing Lord and Wood were still on their travels: Wood was in the Pamirs seeking the source of the Oxus in the depth of winter after stumbling across the site of Ay Khanum; he was told that an ancient city once stood there and was impressed by its fine situation, as well he might be, but naturally he had no inkling of the remarkable archaeological riches which were to be uncovered by the French in 1965.[197] For another, Burnes was hoping against hope that some event would cause Lord Auckland to change his mind. Eventually, on 21 April, Dost Mahomed Khan sent publicly for Vektavich. On 26 April, Burnes withdrew from Kabul at very short notice without waiting for his two companions who were now on the road south to join him. Charles Masson was wholly unprepared for so abrupt a departure; three of his servants were in the Kohistan and, unable to have his effects packed, he was compelled to distribute more than half of them to his neighbours. Burnes camped overnight at Bhut Khak where Masson joined him. The next morning Mirza Sami Khan visited the camp to ask if it were possible to renew negotiations, but was told it was not. He was surprised to learn that Masson too was going and tried to dissuade him saying that there was no occasion for him to leave, that no one was angry with him, that he had lived many years with them in credit, and that nothing could happen to lessen him in their estimation, and so forth. Masson, however, realised that things could never be the same again, underlined perhaps by yet another attack on his house by a gang a few days previously. As they mounted their horses, Burnes said: 'Your leaving them, Masson, is "the unkindest cut of all".' Masson continues:

> Thus closed a mission, one of the most extraordinary ever sent forth by a government, whether as to the singular manner in which it was conducted, or as to the results. There was undoubtedly great blame on all sides. The government had furnished no instructions, apparently confiding in the discretion of a man who had none... Dost Mahomed Khan and his friends were, I think, most to be pitied. They had, indeed, shown the cloven foot, but it was the general opinion in Kabul, and was mine, that had they been properly treated, they would have done as much as could have been hoped from them.[198]

CHAPTER XV

LORD AUCKLAND DECLARES WAR

There is no such thing as a
little war *for a great nation.*
Duke of Wellington

The retiring mission took the road to Jalalabad, thence dropped down the Kabul river on floats to the plain of Peshawar. Lord and Wood joined them some twelve days later. With the mission at an end, Masson's future was far from certain and his old dislike of government service reasserted itself. Already at the time of Burnes's arrival in Kabul he had told him that he felt there was no longer occasion for him to continue in hopeless and unprofitable employment. Thereupon Burnes paid a warm tribute to Masson in a letter to Macnaghten dated 9 October 1837:

> *I feel it a duty incumbent on me to report, for the information of the Right Honourable the Governor-General in Council, the great aid and cordial assistance which I have derived from Mr Masson, not only since my arrival here, but from his constant correspondence since I left Bombay. If I shall be fortunate enough to merit the approbation of his lordship in council, for what may be accomplished here, I feel that I shall owe much to Mr Masson, whose high literary attainments, long residence in this country, and accurate knowledge of people and events, afford me, at every step, the means of coming to a judgment more correct than, in an abrupt transition to Cabool, I could have possibly formed. I discharge, therefore, a pleasing task, in acknowledging the assistance which I receive from Mr Masson.*

In a despatch to Wade, Macnaghten conveyed the Governor-General's high sense of Masson's 'faithful and valuable services'. These acknowledgements of his work and a sense of duty towards the mission sufficed to shelve the question of his resignation. Masson now raised the matter again with Burnes who urged him to stay at Peshawar while he represented his case to the Governor-General at Simla. He agreed to remain because he had no wish to see any government officials in view of his poor opinion of them:

I had determined on the course to adopt, simply that of advancing no pretensions, but if still neglected, and kept in a position where I could not be useful, to clear myself from embarrassment by quitting a service which had long been disagreeable to me, and which I felt to be dishonourable besides.[199]

The pace of events was quickening. Towards the end of May, Burnes received orders to report to Macnaghten who was leading a mission to Ranjit Singh. Writing from Rawalpindi en route on 4 June, Burnes said that Colvin had expressed the Governor-General's wish that:

you will now apply yourself to the fulfilment of any new part that may be assigned to you with the same assiduity and ardent zeal which you have always manifested in the discharge of public duty... My inference from all this is that Shah Sooja is immediately to be put forward.

This was indeed the case. Two days previously, Burnes had forwarded a letter from Macnaghten to Masson dated 23 May, which read:

You will have heard that I am proceeding on a mission to Ranjeet Singh: and as at my interview with his Highness it is probable that the question of his relations with the Afghans will come on the tapis, *I am naturally desirous of obtaining the opinion of the best-informed men with respect to them. Would you oblige me, therefore, by stating what means of counteraction to the policy of Dost Mahomet Khan you would recommend for adoption, and whether you think that the Sikhs, using any (and what?) instruments of Afghan agency, could establish themselves in Cabool...*

Macnaghten sent an identical letter to Burnes. In reply Masson:

... deprecated the extravagant notion of establishing the Sikhs in Kabul, and as the lesser evil recommended the establishment of Shah Sujah al Mulkh, aware that the government had determined upon action of some kind, and never dreaming that an army of twenty thousand men was to be employed to effect an object which could have been readily accomplished without a British soldier, simply by sending the Shah to Peshawar under a proper understanding with the Maharaja.[200]

In saying this, Masson is repeating a remark he made some three years previously in a letter to Wade dated 20 March 1835, referring to Shah Shuja's campaign of 1833-34:

In the present state of Central Asia Afghanistan is the natural ally of the British Government of India... Shah Sujah's cause was not a popular one though he would have been successful had a single British officer accompanied him, not as an ally or assistant, but as a mere reporter of proceedings.[201]

Wade had resurrected this 1835 opinion in a letter to Macnaghten of 1 January 1838, as part of his persistent efforts in support of Shah Shuja. In the same letter, Wade not only played down a report of Burnes which spoke warmly of the Amir—as he did throughout the winter in his coverers to the despatches from Kabul—but also brought into the open the notion of restoring the ex-king to his throne, this time with overt British help. To Masson's annoyance, it was this earlier remark of his that Sir John Hobhouse, the former President of the Board of Control, misused in a speech to the House of Commons on 23 June 1842. The point Masson was trying to make was that the ex-king should not appear to his people as obviously dependent on British bayonets in quantity. 'It was the general opinion in Kabul', he says:

> ... that if a single British officer had accompanied the Shah in 1834, that he would have been successful—and I could understand that there was truth in it. A single British officer might have done as much in 1838; and I question whether, if Sir Alexander Burnes had been entrusted with the Shah's restoration, he would have been accompanied with more than the regiment or two which he considered necessary; but when Mr Secretary Macnaghten became inspired by the desire to acquire renown and to luxuriate in Kabul, the extensive armament was decided upon, which was utterly unnecessary, and which has conduced to the subsequent mischief as much as the incapacity of those directing it—for in the hands of abler men it might have also proved a fatal experiment... There was no reason that the exiled prince should have lost his reputation. A single British officer, or even a regiment or two might not have injured it. The envoy and minister and his host ruined it. The Afghans had no objections to the match, they disliked the manner of wooing.[202]

In his reply dated 2 June 1838 to Macnaghten's letter of 23 May, Burnes too said that Shah Shuja could easily recover his kingdom; with overt British support, substantial funds with which to attract men to his standard and one or two British regiments as a stiffener, Shah Shuja would be able to take and keep his throne. Nevertheless, in the same letter, Burnes made a final attempt to persuade his government of the merits of Dost Mahomed Khan and of his fundamental pro-British bias, saying that the Amir was a man of undoubted ability, and had at heart high opinions of the British nation. There was much to be said for him; at best he had a choice of difficulties and 'we promised nothing, and Persia and Russia held out a great deal...'.

The choice of Shah Shuja as a suitable instrument to re-unite the three parts of Afghanistan and to provide a pro-British barrier against the designs of Russia and Persia was a curious one. It is true that he was the legitimate claimant to the throne and had always had some support in Afghanistan. He had, however, been an exile for 30 years and had a long record of failures. He was intelligent but, like Charles II, he never said a foolish thing and never did a wise one. Alexander Burnes had met the ex-monarch at Ludhiana in 1832 and had not been impressed: 'From what I learn, I do not believe that the Shah possesses sufficient energy to seat himself on the throne of Cabool and that if he did regain it, he has not the tact to discharge the duties of so difficult a situation.'[203] Since then, Shah Shuja had again shown at Kandahar the irresolution that had cost him earlier battles. Even as a fugitive after that battle, his exalted notions of regal dignity had caused an ugly incident with the Amirs of Sind. Wade's part in putting forward Shah Shuja has been touched on. Masson had backed Dost Mahomed Khan until disillusioned by the latter's unwillingness to compromise over Peshawar. Burnes had no doubt that the Amir was much the abler man for the task in hand. Yet both men now thought that Shah Shuja could be successful; it was a grave blunder. Historians have criticised Burnes for trimming his sails to please his seniors, but he had tried up to the last moment to support the Amir as his letter of 2nd June to Macnaghten shows.

Lord Auckland was happy to learn of the sanguine view of Shah Shuja's prospects held by two of the 'best-informed men', fresh from Kabul itself, though he was puzzled by their belief in a small force, and still uncertain about the degree of Shah Shuja's popularity in Afghanistan. However, by then he was about to cast his habitual caution aside and adopt Macnaghten's new expansive policy of reaching out to the Hindu Kush in an effort to create a firm barrier against Persian and Russian ambitions. After prolonged negotiations between Macnaghten and Ranjit Singh, a Tripartite Treaty designed to restore Shah Shuja to the throne of Kabul was concluded in late July between the British, the Sikhs, and Shah Shuja, actually an extended version of the treaty of 1833 between the two last-named.

It was originally intended that the Sikhs should provide the troops in conjunction with a force to be recruited by Shah Shuja, with the Government of India providing financial support and some officers. By sitting tight, Ranjit Singh forced the British to commit their own troops or see the enterprise fail. An army was assembled consisting of a Bengal force and a column from Bombay, which would effect a junction at Shikarpur. The combined forces amounted to 21,000 including

Shah Shuja's contingent of 6,000, and was named the Army of the Indus.

For months past Herat had managed with great difficulty to keep the besieging Persians at bay. John McNeill had set out for the Shah's camp outside the walls in March, 1838, arriving in April but, unable to persuade the Shah to lift the siege or to give satisfaction for insults offered to his confidential messengers, had departed for the Turkish border with a view to breaking off diplomatic relations. Meanwhile, in response to appeals from McNeill to bring pressure to bear on the Shah, the Governor-General had in May sent a small military expedition from Bombay to the island of Kharg in the Gulf. Then on 24 June, a major Persian assault on Herat failed which dealt a serious blow to the prestige of the Persian monarch and Count Simonich who had followed McNeill there and had given every encouragement to the Shah to persist. The Persian army was in very poor condition, yet the siege dragged on until an ultimatum from McNeill delivered by Colonel Stoddart saved the Shah's face sufficiently to enable him to raise the siege on 9 September.

On 1 October 1838, the Governor-General issued the Simla Manifesto over the signature of Macnaghten, announcing the invasion of Afghanistan. It justified the decision to restore Shah Shuja on the grounds that the interests of the Indian Empire required a friendly ally on her Western frontier, instead of a hostile chief who had shown 'subservience to a foreign power' and had sought to 'promote schemes of conquest and aggrandizement'. For propaganda purposes Dost Mahomed Khan was thus made to appear the villain. A few days later the news from Herat reached the Governor-General. Yet the invasion plan was not cancelled as many critics, including Kaye and Masson, have thought it should have been, because to Auckland its main purpose was not to relieve Herat but to remove the Amir. Auckland published his decision to persevere with the operation on 8 November.

Charles Masson spent the hot and rainy seasons at Peshawar in a bad state of health waiting to hear what his next employment might be. Burnes had spoken to Auckland at Simla about Masson's affairs and had also raised his claims to assistant's allowances during the Kabul mission: 'His lordship admitted they were valid, but said the benefit had better be prospective.' With this letter, Burnes enclosed a note from Colvin to himself which Masson quotes:

> *You may write to Mr Masson to say that Lord Auckland is* really *sensible of his merits, and would wish to consult his convenience and*

feelings as much as he with propriety can. While the present crisis lasts, his services are too valuable to his country to admit of his being detached to a distance. He will remain, probably, so long as the rains last at Peshawar, but when the Shah [Shuja] proceeds in force towards Shikarpur he will have to move down to that quarter to join the principal officer employed. When the object of the expedition shall have been attained, Lord Auckland will gladly consider what arrangements can be made so as best to meet his views.

Masson accepted this arrangement only to find that Macnaghten had chosen to cancel it.

I now felt privileged to follow my own inclinations; I, therefore, awaited the arrival of Dr Lord [his appointed successor] and did assist him as far as information and counsel could assist such a man — and then forwarded my resignation to government, in a manner that it might be known I was in earnest. Released from the thraldom in which I had been kept since 1835, I then made an excursion to Shah Baz Ghari in the Yusef Zai districts, to recover some [Kharoshthi] inscriptions on a rock there*, and was successful, returning with both copies and impressions on calico...[204]

From Peshawar he proceeded to Ferozpur, the principal military base on the British frontier, where he had the satisfaction to be again amongst his countrymen. He declined to see any of the Politicals 'for I was abundantly surfeited with them'. Ferozpur was the scene of great activity. The Governor-General with his sisters and suite was paying a state visit to Ranjit Singh which lasted some ten days amid much pomp and ceremony. The Bengal column had gathered there and the Maharaja had brought some nine thousand of his Sikhs. Each leader reviewed the other's troops and the Bengal force marched off to Bahawalpur and Sind on 10 December. The Commander-in-Chief, Sir Henry Fane, who was on his way to Bombay and England on retirement, sailed down the river with a fleet of boats keeping pace with the Army's march. Masson went with him. When the flotilla reached the frontier of Sind he saw Lieut. Colonel Sir Alexander Burnes, as he had now become:

He informed me that Mr Colvin had written to him at Lord Auckland's request, to use his influence with me to remain in the service, and to offer me my own terms. Mr Colvin's letter had been sent to Sir John Keane [Commander-in-Chief, Bombay], therefore I did not see it...

We had also much discourse on the state of affairs. I had

---

* An Ashoka rock edict. His copy was for many years the best available to scholars.

previously learned from Dr Lord a strange account of the mode in which the amiable Lord Auckland had been driven into measures which his better judgement disapproved, and how he was obliged to yield to the assaults of certain females, aides-de-camp and secretaries; and now I questioned Sir Alexander on the part he had taken, particularly as regarded the useless expedition. He replied that it was arranged before he reached Simla, and that when he arrived Torrens and Colvin came running to him and prayed him to say nothing to unsettle his lordship; that they had all the trouble in the world to get him into the business, and that even now he would be glad of any pretence to retire from it...[205]

Strong controversies have arisen among historians over these few sentences, raising as they do the question of attributing responsibility for the decision to go to war; and reflecting on Auckland and his sisters Emily and Fanny Eden, on the two secretaries, on Burnes, and on Masson for having the temerity to print Burnes's and Lord's stories. Contemporary historians, notably Kaye, under the immediate influence of the disastrous outcome of the Governor-General's policy, broadly accepted the stories of Lord and Burnes as related by Masson. Some modern writers have thought that there was some truth in them, though exempting the Eden sisters from the imputation of exerting influence on their brother. Others have sharply criticised Masson, saying for example that he 'has done great damage to the reputation of better men.'[206]

Further down river at Bakkar, Masson:

... learned from Sir Alexander Burnes, that Mr Macnaghten, who had reached Shikarpur, finding himself entirely at fault, had written to him to send me over directly. Sir Alexander spared me any trouble on this occasion, for he answered the envoy and minister, and without my knowledge. There were sad squabbles here between these two leading politicals, and I was very well pleased to have nothing to do with either of them.[207]

These squabbles were to intensify in Kabul during the occupation and Burnes was to criticise his chief sharply in his private correspondence. As for having nothing more to do with Macnaghten or other politicals, Masson was to find at Kalat that he had been over-optimistic. In the meantime, he continued down the Indus to Hyderabad where for the first time he briefly met his patron, Colonel Pottinger, now the Resident in Sind. He went on to Karachi with Sir Henry Fane and then returned to Tatta to stay with Pottinger. He wished to return to Kabul to write, but fell ill at Bakkar and was obliged to go back to Karachi where he

spent the cold season of 1839 writing his book and his Memoir for
Ariana Antiqua. Pottinger took the manuscripts with him when he went
on leave in 1840 and offered the book to John Murray who refused to
publish it because of its intemperate criticisms of leading personalities
in India.

Masson's direct participation in the events leading up to the Anglo-
Afghan War ended when he parted from Burnes on the Indus. He was
living in Sind during the actual campaign and although he got caught
up in the revolt in Baluchistan, he had sailed for England before the
collapse of the British occupation and the retreat from Kabul took place.
Nevertheless one point should be made. Masson's bitter remark about
convulsing Central Asia, deposing and setting up of kings, lavishing
treasure, and committing a long train of crimes and follies, previously
quoted, and his lament for our loss of goodwill and prestige, were
even better founded than he could have imagined. The First Anglo-
Afghan War was the first of Queen Victoria's 'little wars' in remote
places, but unlike most of the others it was by no means of purely
local consequence. On the contrary, it cast long shadows for more than
a century. In India, the total destruction of a British army shook belief
in British supremacy. Men remembered Kabul; they knew now that
the Company did not always get its way. Its star had fallen. It was no
longer invincible.[208] In this manner the 'signal catastrophy', despite
General Pollock's successful campaign of retribution in 1842, helped
to create a climate of opinion which led to the Indian Mutiny. It is
significant in this connection that 23 of the 24 Bengal Native Infantry
and Cavalry regiments which had served in Afghanistan either muti-
nied or were disbanded in 1857. In passing, it is well to remember that
Dost Mahomed Khan, in spite of having been deposed and exiled and
finally allowed to return to his own battered country, refrained from
taking advantage of the Mutiny although pressed to do so by groups
bent on revenge. Had he encouraged his tribesmen to pour into the
Punjab, the outcome might have been very different. The ripples of
the retreat spread across Central Asia: when the Amir of Bokhara heard
the news he no longer felt any constraint and promptly executed his
prisoners, Colonel Stoddart and Captain Conolly.

The damage caused by the First Afghan War was further aggravated by the Second Afghan War of 1878-80 and kept alive by the brief
Third War of 1918 (in which, however, the Afghans were the aggres-
sors), with the result that the Afghans regarded Britain as Public En-

emy No. 1 until as recently as 1963. One of my predecessors, Sir Kerr Fraser-Tytler who served with the British Legation from 1922-41 writes:

Nearly a hundred years after the Burnes Mission, we who took up the task of British representation in Kabul after the First World War realised how much had to be lived down, and how great must be the patience and the forbearance of the British envoy and his Government if our mission was not to follow in the footsteps of Burnes and even perhaps Cavagnari.[209] *

After the Second World War, during which the Government of India had gone to considerable lengths to supply Afghanistan with scarce textiles and food, it was still only in exceptional cases that Britons, even when employed by United Nations' Agencies, were permitted to work in Afghanistan. An esoteric side-effect, but of importance to British archaeology and specifically to the Society for Afghan Studies, was that whereas in 1922 France negotiated a cultural agreement which included permission to excavate (and did so with great effect until the communist revolution in 1979), the United Kingdom failed to obtain an archaeological contract until 1974. With the fall of the Prime Minister, Prince Daoud, in 1963 a marked change took place. Social intercourse became normal and Afghans from all walks of life were at last able and willing to accept hospitality at the British Embassy. It had taken a long time to achieve; it hardly outlasted the *coup d'etat* of 1973 and the re-emergence of Daoud, this time as President of the Republic of Afghanistan. I consider myself fortunate to have served in Kabul during part of that happy decade when official and private sentiment was favourable and security of travel through the dramatic Afghan landscape was virtually absolute.

---

* Sir Louis Cavagnari with his entire mission was massacred in 1879, after a few weeks as envoy during the Second Afghan War.

CHAPTER XVI

THE 'POLITICALS'

He [Macnaghten] *is clever and pleasant,*
speaks Persian more fluently than English;
Arabic better than Persian; but for famil-
iar conversation, rather prefers Sanscrit.

Emily Eden *Up the Country*

Charles Masson's disillusionment with the Political officers with whom he had had official dealings has been touched on; worse was to come. So dire an effect did his later encounters with Macnaghten and other officers have on his personality and reputation that it is necessary to consider the 'Politicals' in more detail. The majority were ambitious young army officers who had shown an aptitude for languages in general and Persian in particular, and who preferred desk work to regimental duties, not least because the prospects of promotion were much greater. The aspirant officers together with a few civil servants were offered posts under the Secret and Political Department of the Secretariat. Some were eventually posted to Persia, the Gulf and Iraq as Envoys and Residents. In India, as red colour stole steadily across the map, so more posts were created in the newly annexed or controlled states, in order to conduct relations with the reigning princes or chiefs and to collect intelligence. Entities such as the Sikh kingdom and Sind which were still independent refused to have resident British officials, so diplomatic relations with Lahore and Hyderabad had to be conducted from a distance, in Masson's time by Captain Wade at Ludhiana and Colonel Pottinger in Cutch. These and other Political officers stationed on the frontiers of British India, of whom Wade was then the most important, exercised very considerable influence on British Indian strategic thinking through their virtual monopoly of information and the use they made of it. It was they who became the main providers of intelligence, recommendations and strategic theories to the Supreme Government.[210]

William Hay Macnaghten was in charge of the Secret and Political

Plate 11(right). Sir William Hay Macnaghten.

Department from 1833-1837 and accompanied Auckland on his extensive tour of India in 1837-38 as his chief adviser. As a young man
he had gained the highest attainable distinction in every Eastern language taught at the College of Fort William, Calcutta: Hindustani,
Persian, Tamil, Telugu etc., etc. Unfortunately, high linguistic abilities
are not always combined with other qualities such as sound judgement and robust common sense. He was essentially a bureaucrat and
was not a good judge of men. In Kabul he proved to be too impulsive,
too self-confident and incurably optimistic: for instance, his repeated
claims that the country was quiet from Dan to Beersheba were ground-
less. He was also ambitious; Masson says that he volunteered for the
post of Envoy and Minister, but he seems to have heard this from
Burnes. Macnaghten was in fact chosen by Lord Auckland though he
undoubtedly welcomed it as a stepping-stone to a Governorship which
indeed he was offered, but too late. Before he could leave Kabul to
take up his appointment as Governor of Bombay, the Afghan revolt
had broken out and he was murdered soon after.

In a noteworthy passage, Percival Spear writes that one consideration, frequently forgotten by the framers of policy, should always be
remembered:

> This was the feelings of the Afghans themselves. Through all their
> turbulence and feuds there shone one passion above all others — an
> objection to outside interference.* In this respect the Afghans are the
> Spaniards of Asia. There is evidence that Dost Muhammad would
> have preferred the British to the Russians as did his son Sher Ali later.
> But both much preferred their own independence to either. Disregard
> of this facet of the Afghan character caused much harmful exaggera-
> tion of the Russian danger in the minds of British Indian 'Politicals'.[211]

Indeed, too many of the 'Politicals' were either pursuing Utilitarian
or Evangelical nostrums for the economic regeneration or spiritual
salvation of the natives, or were unduly concerned with their own
advancement in an expanding service, to trouble themselves about
this aspect of the Afghan character.

During the campaign and the occupation of Afghanistan and
Baluchistan, the number of Political Officers was much increased. Even
junior officers were posted to large towns or troubled districts and
vested with extensive powers out of all relation to their experience,
age or rank. The list for 1841 includes, in addition to two civilians,

---

* Forgotten, too, by the framers of policy in the Kremlin in December 1979.

nine captains and seventeen lieutenants; and many of these were authorised to direct, within the limits of their charge, the most senior General Officers commanding troops.[212] The angry reactions of some of the Generals have often been quoted, William Nott, for instance:

> ... in the meantime, all goes wrong here. We are become hated by the people, and the English name and character, which two years ago stood so high and fair, has become a bye-word. Thus it is to employ men selected by intrigue and patronage! The conduct of the one thousand and one politicals has ruined our cause and bared the throats of every European in this country to the sword and knife of the revengeful Afghan and bloody Belooch...

Charles Masson would certainly have said 'Amen' to that remark could he have known it.

In another outburst, General Nott went even further:

> When we arrived here, the natives had an idea that an Englishman's word, once given, was sacred, never to be broken. That beautiful charm is gone, and every pledge and every guarantee trampled under foot. The day of retribution and deep revenge will come... I like these people, and would trust myself alone in their wildest mountains. When I was in Ghilzye, they soon found out who protected them from plunder and oppression, and who did not. My tent was always crowded with these people, begging to do something ... yet not a man could be prevailed upon to go near the Prince or the political agent... The troops I sent out today will put the government to a great expense, and the poor officers and men will have the thermometer at 108^0 in their tents ... and all because a foolish Political destroyed a small village containing twenty-three inhabitants. And why, think you? Because he thought— thought, mind you, that they looked insultingly at him as he passed with his two hundred cavalry as an escort! Had I been on the spot, he would have had eight troopers for his protection; he would have then been civil to the inhabitants, or perhaps not cruel.[213]

Even Alexander Burnes, himself a senior Political officer, wrote a few months later: 'It appears to me that wherever our Political officers are, collision forthwith follows.' In private letters he expressed contempt for 'this fry and frog spawn of Politicals'.[214] When Lord Ellenborough succeeded Lord Auckland in 1842 he spoke of the 'monstrous body of political agents' and took steps to subordinate them to the appropriate military commanders. But the damage had long since been done, not least in the Khanate of Kalat.

By no means all Political officers of the time were as blameworthy; no doubt Masson was unlucky in those with whom he had to deal.

Others were certainly men of high character and ability, some of whom befriended him. Nevertheless, the Indian Political Service then and during the next hundred years was not fortunate in its handling of India's relations with foreign countries. Two reasons why this was so are suggested by the reactions of diplomatists of the late 19th century to the appointment of Sir Mortimer Durand as Minister to Tehran. Charles Hardinge, a member of his staff, considered that his appointment was a mistake as the Persians particularly disliked Anglo-Indian officials. Horace Rumbold, another talented member of Durand's staff, recorded in his diary that the Envoy had a good deal of contempt for the Persians and the impression got around that he wished to treat them as if he had been a Resident in India in a Native State. It was precisely this habit, which persisted until the end of the Raj, of treating a proud and independent minded country as if it were a Native State in India, that exasperated the Afghans. As for Durand's contempt for the Persians, here again it was the undisguised contempt shown towards Shah Shuja and other Afghan personalities by British army officers from the General downwards, and also by some of the Politicals, that made it quickly obvious to his countrymen that he was in truth a puppet monarch.

British Ministers to Kabul, themselves seconded Indian Political Officers until 1947, have remarked on the Government of India's curious inability to appreciate the Afghan character. For instance:

> The policy of the Government of India in the 1870s, culminating in the Second Afghan War, was an unhappy blend of myopia and impatience, and there are other examples of similar ineptitude. Even Lord Curzon and his advisers showed by their attitude during the Afghan treaty negotiations of 1904-05 a failure to grasp the fundamentals of the Afghan problem or to understand the mentality of Afghan rulers.[216]

CHAPTER XVII

MISADVENTURES AT KALAT

Pudding headed Political Agents and
arbitrary Envoys and Ministers.

C. Masson
undated manuscript

Charles Masson explains his decision to resume his travels in these words:

Having despatched for publication in England a variety of manuscripts, in the early part of 1840, I found myself at Karachi, in Sind, as I supposed free to move where I pleased; and with reference to further literary and scientific projects I determined, with the unemployed materials in my possession, to return to Kabul, and the countries to which they related, judging I could there arrange them for the press with accuracy and advantage. I was also desirous to continue my antiquarian researches—with the due prosecution of which government employ had interfered—and to carry out the examination of certain points I felt assured to be within the power of verification; which, for the same reason, I had been compelled to neglect. I estimated that a period of two years in Afghanistan would suffice for my objects, and that I should be altogether about three years absent.[217]

His intention was to travel by way of Kalat but he needed to be sure that it would be safe to do so. He was well aware that a new order of things prevailed and that the recent hostilities might have caused feelings among the people he would meet, very different from those of ten years before. He was still undecided when Kalikdad, the merchant with whom he had made his first journey to Kalat and who was again on his way there, put in a timely appearance. Kalikdad was reassuring and Masson arranged to accompany his caravan, which was forming at Sonmiani. Masson left Karachi on 30 April 1840, mounted on an excellent Kabul horse with a servant and two guides. At Sonmiani he received as warm a welcome as before from his friends. Kalikdad, however, was awaiting the arrival of a ship from Bombay and a delay of a month could be expected. Masson therefore took advantage of the imminent departure of a holy man to join him, leaving his servant and baggage to follow with Kalikdad and the caravan.

While Masson had been living quietly in Karachi, the Army of the Indus with the ex-monarch Shah Shuja trailing in its wake had crossed Baluchistan on its way from Shikarpur to Kandahar. Supplies had proved hard to obtain due partly to inadequate preparations and reconnaisance, partly to the general scarcity of grain in the barren Khanate of Kalat, aggravated by a poor harvest. The lack of adequate reconnaisance could have been avoided had Macnaghten had the good sense to use Masson who knew the area better than anyone else. His good relations with the people of Kalat might have minimised misunderstandings at least. He was admirably qualified for such a job.

To make matters worse, the ruler, Mehrab Khan, had been unable to restrain the murderous and thieving propensities of the Baluch tribes nominally under his control from plundering the long columns of soldiers and their enormous baggage trains. The Army had suffered particularly during the difficult passage of the 60 miles long Bolan Pass. Macnaghten had tried to secure Mehrab Khan's cooperation with an offer of a subsidy in return for supplies, transport and recognition of Shah Shuja's suzerainty. Burnes was sent to negotiate the treaty but in spite of increasing the subsidy, only succeeded in getting the Khan to agree to pay homage to the monarch, an act which he evaded to the end. It was now felt that he was deliberately opposing the expedition; the discovery of letters allegedly from him to his agent Mahomed Hussain urging harassment of the British seemed to clinch the matter. Accordingly, both as retribution and to ensure safe communications in the future, Macnaghten proposed that the three Kalati provinces which lay along the lines of communications, namely Kacchi, Quetta and Mastang, should be annexed to Afghanistan.[218] Pending this arrangement he appointed Political officers along the route: Lieutenant Eastwick at Shikarpur, Lieutenant Loveday in the Bolan Pass and Captain Bean at Quetta. When the Bombay force had completed their task in Afghanistan they were withdrawn to India and on the return march took revenge upon Mehrab Khan by storming his capital. He and numerous tribal chiefs were killed during the fighting. His son fled to a remote spot, while a distant relative, Shah Nawaz Khan, was appointed in his stead.

The storming of Kalat took place on 13 November 1839. By the time Masson arrived there in the middle of 1840 the three provinces had been handed over to Shah Shuja, though controlled by the British, and Loveday had been transferred to Kalat. A reorganisation of the old feudal system of land tenure in the revived Durrani Empire had been put in hand by Macnaghten in Kabul. Whereas hitherto *jaghirs* (lands) had been held in return for military service, the new system substituted rents in cash, and was applied by decree of Shah Shuja to the Khanate as elsewhere. The change was regarded as an essential prelude to the general replacement of the feudal levies by a national, centralised Afghan army which should provide a disciplined support for the King. Until this could be accomplished, a British force was obliged to remain; and of course the occupation costs stayed disturbingly high. The loss of the provinces upset the balance of Kalat's economy; the demands for rents infuriated the chiefs concerned. Mehrab Khan's letters were now found to have been either forged by Mahomed Hussain or at least written by the Khan under the influence of violently anti-British reports from him. Mahomed Hussain had even succeeded in deceiving the British about his real attitude. All these factors had created a situation seething with discontent.

Masson, who had been well received by Shah Nawaz Khan when they met by chance some three days' march from Kalat, now pitched camp in the outskirts of the town where friends and acquaintances flocked to greet him. It was close to Lieutenant Loveday's tent from which he was superintending the erection of a country house. Masson was not unprepared for his meeting with the Political Agent for he had heard:

> ... *the most astonishing accounts of Lieutenant Loveday, Labadin Sahib, as he was called by the natives. Actions so singular were imputed to him, and of a nature so different from what are usually looked for from British Officers, that I was disinclined to credit them ... the alleged enormities could not have been committed without the knowledge of his superiors; and it was inconceivable to suppose that, with such knowledge, they would tolerate them. Still, the reports were so universal, in all places and with all parties, that it was difficult to avoid the suspicion that he must be a strange person.*[219]

When Masson paid his call there was only one chair in the tent and Loveday told him to sit on the ground as he was used to it. Their conversation did not go well. The Lieutenant dwelt on the men he had either blown from a gun, or would do, if and when he caught them; Masson regretted the dismemberment of the Khanate. They discussed the policies which had led to the occupation of Afghanistan and Masson freely stated his opinions on the blunders and mismanagement which had spoiled everything, and on the fearful confusion that must inevitably at some period follow. Such talk lacked tact coming from a wandering civilian to a representative of the criticised government. Invited to dine at his town residence that afternoon, Masson 'found him in a spacious apartment, hung round with suits of armour, and the corners filled with pikes, halberds, battle-axes, and warlike weapons, the spoil of the late khan's armoury'.[220] Having reflected on the nature of Loveday's reception, his objectionable remarks and the strangeness of his manner and conversation, Masson decided not to trouble him further with his company.

Masson was distressed by the changes in Kalat wrought by the war. In an unusually emotional passage he writes:

> Kalat presented in aspect and condition a melancholy contrast to the tranquil and flourishing state in which I had formerly beheld it. The greater part of the town was uninhabited, and the little bazaar, once busy and well supplied, was now nearly deserted. The inhabitants them-selves were oppressed with gloom and despondency, as they were clad in the coarse and abject garb of poverty. All of my old acquaintances had suffered most cruelly in the spoil of their property, and I was hurt to see those who had so recently been affluent and comfortable, present themselves before me necessitous and destitute. The sky, indeed, was as serene as ever, the orchards displayed their verdure, and the valley, as before, was adorned with cultivation, yet there was a loneliness, real or imaginary, on my part, cast over the scene, that was infectious, and with every disposition to be cheerful, I was, in despite of myself, dejected and sorrowful. A notion I had entertained at Karachi of re-maining here two or three months to arrange some of my MSS for publication, had been dissipated on arrival, as I plainly saw that the Brahui capital was no longer the abode of peace and security it had formerly been and it was, moreover, painful to witness the desolation and misery around me. But it was necessary to await my servants and effects coming with Kalikdad and his kafila.[221]

He used his enforced leisure to investigate the various charges which had been brought against Mehrab Khan and found to his dismay that as in the case of the forged letters already mentioned, he had been the victim of treachery by those whom he had unwisely trusted. Masson remarks bitterly that even when the truth began to emerge no effort was made to rectify matters at least to the extent of restoring the son to his father's estate and returning the jewels and other personal prop-erty looted from the palace:

> ... it was necessary to preserve unsullied the reputation of Lord Auckland's political clique, and, to conceal their incapacity, the injus-tice shown to the father was to be perpetuated by that offered to the unoffending son.[222]

About a week after Masson's arrival, Loveday sent twenty-five of his guard of sixty sepoys to Mastung together with his *munshi*, in pursuance of orders from Captain Bean at Quetta. The party was to demand rents from certain chiefs in respect of their jaghirs which they had hitherto held rent-free, as we have already noticed. Infuriated by this unprecedented demand, one of the chiefs of Sarawan roused his tribesmen and killed the *munshi* and all his escort. This success precipitated the Brahui revolt on behalf of Mehrab Khan's son who was at once summoned to head the insurgents.[223] However, Masson, who was unaware of the reason for the expedition to Mastung, was inclined to think that the revolt was caused by one of Loveday's peculiarities. He was reputed to have set his ferocious bulldogs on various individuals to the horror of the local inhabitants, but had desisted because of Masson's presence. This tale was of course heard with appalled incredulity, but then another such incident occurred which led to the death of the man who had been savaged:

> The consternation excited by this man's unhappy fate amongst the community of Kalat, to be conceived must have been witnessed; the dread of vengeance limited the expression of public feeling to low and sullen murmurs, but rumour spread the catastrophe with rapidity over the country, and there indignation was loudly avowed, and revenge determined upon.[224]

The allegation against Loveday has been denied by some, but Colonel Stacy, who made subsequent inquiries on the spot, was obliged to report that at least one of the many instances cited was true—the victim very probably the man named by Masson. Clearly Loveday must have been subject to some peculiar form of mental derangement, of which his superiors remained unaware until after his death.[225]

Some days afterwards a force collected by the chiefs and the late Khan's son appeared before Kalat. It was of no great size, about 1,200 men, poorly armed and ill-provided with ammunition, but determined to avenge the wrongs they had suffered. Charles Masson, finding that Lieutenant Loveday seemed overcome by indecision and a strange lethargy, busied himself in strengthening the defences of the city and setting men to work on casting bullets. He also:

> ... took a cursory view of the guns, and I was extremely sorry to find them useless; the largest, indeed, might be considered a curiosity, for it was cast at Modena in Italy, and above three centuries old. There were three of small calibre... It was a sad pity the guns were unserviceable: they were fixed on their uncouth carriages by rolls of cords, in-

tercepting the sight, and rendering it impossible to point them with
any tolerable precision. In place of vents were apertures as large as the
palm of the hand, and the chambers were so honeycombed, that it
startled me to think how they could stand being fired.

The former artilleryman is speaking here though he is careful to re-
frain from showing more expertise than he must. He managed to fire
a few rounds with the antique Modenese gun with little effect and
then tried to use the small guns: 'I could do no more than fire random
shots amongst the garden, and as nearly as I could, direct them towards that occupied by the khan and the *elite* of the insurgents.'[226] He
found later that a shot had passed close to the young Khan's tent and
that another had killed the charger of one of the chiefs which so terrified him that he removed from the garden to a suburb. Throughout
the siege, which lasted some six days, Masson was indefatigable, constantly on patrol encouraging and directing the defenders and remain-
ing on duty all night.

At the end of three days of fighting, a vigorous attempt to scale the
walls was defeated in spite of treachery by some of the defenders who
pulled a few of the attackers into the city. But just when it looked as
though the insurgents were beaten and ready to retire, a sudden change
of mood on the part of one of the chiefs attached to Shah Nawaz Khan
infected others. Before long, communications were opened with the
insurgents and further resistance petered out despite the Khan's best
efforts to conciliate the disaffected chief. Loveday's native staff, in
whom he had unwisely reposed the fullest confidence, were themselves active in promoting talks with the leaders of the insurgents and
gave him plenty of bad advice, at the same time disclosing information to the enemy and deceiving that officer with forged letters promising peace and good treatment. It was afterwards discovered that
one of them, Nazrulah, had long been in league with the Darogah Gul
Mahomed, the principal adviser to the young Khan. An agreement
was drawn up whereby Shah Nawaz Khan was to retire from Kalat,
while Loveday was to be escorted in safety to Quetta. Masson had no
faith whatever in the second part of this agreement and both he and
Shah Nawaz Khan deployed every argument to persuade Loveday to
leave with the latter who was after all the Indian Government's ap-
pointee. The Political Agent, still believing in the loyalty of Nazrulah
and the others, could not be moved:

The fatal consequences attending Lieutenant Loveday's placing him-
self in the power of the insurgents proclaim more forcibly than words

can convey the extreme folly of the step. Inexplicable is the infatuation which induced the resolve, as there were none of the chiefs who had not, in some mode, been personally aggrieved, and for the lives of some of them even premiums had been offered; a fact spoken in sorrow, yet in truth.[227]

The citadel was now occupied by the insurgents while Loveday's residence came under attack. It was eventually rushed and looted with the result that Masson suffered the serious loss 'not only of what other property I possessed, but of a large accumulated stock of manuscripts and papers, the fruit of above fifteen years' labour and inquiry'.

Masson had wished to leave with Shah Nawaz Khan who had abdicated and departed, but felt it his duty to remain with Loveday. Both men were now removed to the citadel and confined to the Chamber of Blood, so-called from the executions of state-offenders which had taken place there. During the siege and its aftermath, letters had passed between Loveday and Bean; unfortunately Baluchistan had been denuded of troops and neither Quetta nor Shikarpur could hold out any hope of assistance, facts which were soon known to the insurgents. Even when Captain Bean, 'a remarkably prudent man' according to Masson, received reinforcements which might well have sufficed to move against Kalat, he was under the impression from faulty intelligence that the enemy were too thick on the ground to risk an expedition.

Correspondence with Bean was resumed after an interval with a view to reaching an accommodation with the insurgents and releasing the two prisoners. Masson too was ordered to write and did so on a fragment of native paper with a native pen, in support of Loveday's wishes for peace. Inasmuch as it denounced the whole conduct of relations with Kalat during the previous eighteen months, allegedly contrary in many respects to the Governor-General's intentions, and revealed some of the deceits which had been practised on Mehrab Khan and on the Political Agents, it cannot have endeared him to the Captain. It is, however, a tribute to Masson's strength of mind that he wrote in such a fashion in the very ugly situation he was in. Lambrick relates that he came upon this letter in the Pakistan Government's archives, and will always remember the thrill he felt 'when taking into my hands this scrubby piece of paper covered with Masson's neat handwriting, brown with age; while imagining the scene in the Chamber of Blood as he plied that native pen'.[228]

The Brahui chiefs at Kalat having decided to advance to Mastung carried the two Europeans with them under a strong guard. Although their worst fears had not been realised during their detention in the Chamber of Blood, it had been a severe ordeal not only because of the threats of the leaders of the insurgents, but also because of the volleys of abuse, jeers and menaces of the infuriated crowd who flocked in to look at them. These scenes were repeated at Mastung. On the march there, Loveday was manacled to the tent-pole at night. His servants were sent away and extra guards were stationed within and without the tent; their situation began to look desperate. Letters arrived from Captain Bean addressed to the Darogah and to Loveday. The concluding paragraph of the official letter to the Lieutenant is quoted by Masson:

> The mystery of Mr Masson's appearance at Kalat at the period of the present outbreak, combined with his clandestine residence at that place, has given rise to suspicions, in my mind, of that individual, which I have not failed to communicate to government.[229]

It was evident from Loveday's embarrassment that he had earlier written in disparaging terms to Quetta. Masson thought that it was also Bean's way of acknowledging the receipt of his 'native pen' letter. From the moment of his arrival at Kalat his old friend Faiz Ahmed had gone to great lengths to look after his welfare; after the capture of the city, he had risked his life to protect Masson and persuade the Darogah to release him. He was on the point of success when a story became current that Masson possessed bills of exchange for a large sum of rupees which the Darogah was determined to wrest from him. Faiz Ahmed now sent their mutual friend Kalikdad to Mastung who took up the task of working on the Darogah. After days of rigorous treatment, the Brahuis decided to kill their prisoners and advance on Quetta, but suddenly changed their minds and sent the surprised Masson there to represent the views of Loveday and the rebels to the Political Agent.

At Quetta, Masson was taken first to Lieutenant Hammersley and then to Captain Bean with whom he had a long conversation on the affairs of the Brahuis, as well as on the critical situation of Loveday:

> I regretted, for the latter officer's sake, that I was too plainly addressing a weak man, puffed up with absurd conceptions of his official importance, and so uninformed of the nature of things, that it was wasting words to speak to him. He had not the politeness to ask me to be seated, and gave audience much in the same way as a heavy country magistrate in England would do to a poacher.

Bean ignored Masson's suggestion that Rehimdad, a prisoner at Bakkur in whom the insurgents were much interested, should be released in exchange for Loveday; refused to allow him to return to the rebel camp; and put him under house arrest:

> *I could not, indeed, forbear to reflect that I had met with an odd reception in the camp of my countrymen, after conduct which Lieutenant Loveday had been compelled to own was 'devoted and noble', after long endurance of outrage and suffering in the bondage of the Brahuis, and after most serious losses; all of which evils had been incurred through the desire to be useful to the very government whose servant had ventured upon so indecent a step.*[230]

Unable to extract verbally from Bean the reason for his arrest other than that a letter from Major Outram about a Russian agent had aroused suspicion,* Masson wrote to the Captain who merely replied that he was detained by 'authority which authority had been applied to for further instruction'. Aware that the 'authority' was Sir William Macnaghten, and realising that the order for his arrest must have been received at Quetta prior to his arrival there, it occurred to him that the Envoy might have ordered his detention from resentment at the liberty he had taken to prosecute his archaeological researches independent of official patronage. Such researches might also be thought to interfere with others working in the same field under Macnaghten's favour.[231] Much more serious was the implication in Bean's letter to Loveday quoted above that Masson's presence at Kalat had been directly connected with the revolt. For such an intrigue, had it been true, he might have been charged with high treason. He therefore wrote to Macnaghten:

> *... considerable self devotion and an entire self sacrifice during the recent affairs at Kalat I should have thought would have ensured my reputation from any foul and ungenerous suspicions, and assuredly it is a singular requital for having, with feelings purely English, associated myself with Lieutenant Loveday in the hour of danger, to be placed, when I find myself in the camp of my countrymen, under surveillance, and to be treated in a manner of which I have just reason to complain.*
>
> *... It appears too absurd to suppose that Captain Bean or any other person could believe.that I was a Russian Agent ... while I am satisfied that no combination of circumstances can make me any other than an English subject and a loyal one too, I must crave of you in what mode*

---

* This story was later refuted by Outram himself.

these unfavourable suspicions have originated, for whether they owe
their existence to an excess of simplicity or to the secret influence of
private pique and personal jealousy, I have still rights as an individual
and an Englishman, and on that account it behoves me not only to
clear my reputation from injurious suspicions, but to resent the injus-
tice of those who from whatever cause venture to asperse it. [232]

He wrote similarly to the Secretary to the Government of India. He
also wrote to John Colvin requesting the Governor General's permission to travel, if such permission were required, and explaining that
he would have asked for it before leaving Karachi had he had any
inkling that it would be expected.

While awaiting replies to these letters he lingered for several weeks
in confinement, which Captain Bean's inhumanity made as annoying
as possible. His first intention seemed to be literally to starve him and,
on one occasion, he passed two entire days and three nights without
food. Hearing of this circumstance, Colonel Stacy made representations to the Political officers with the result that two cakes of dry bread
were brought to him morning and evening from the bazaar:

On this fare I subsisted several days, until a second representation
from Colonel Stacy procured me the addition of three-farthings' worth
of sheep's entrails, also from the bazar, and brought in an earthen plat-
ter; a mess, certainly, which any dog in Quetta might have claimed for
his own. I thought this kind of insult was carried too far, and sent the
foul mess to the camp.

Colonel Stacy sent it to Hammersley who hurried to Masson but only
to berate him for having shown up the Political officers by sending
the foul mess first to the military. Masson also suffered from the cold,
Quetta having an altitude of 5,500 feet, and again Stacy came to the
rescue. [233] Towards the end of October 1840, a reply came from
Macnaghten which Masson found extraordinary. It stated that he had
authorised Bean:

... to detain you at Quetta, until the pleasure of the Governor-General
in council should be ascertained as to your being permitted to pros-
ecute your travels in countries subject to the crown of Caboul, since,
so far as I know, you are without permission to do so, either from the
British Government, or from His Majesty Shah Sooja ool Moolk.

This claim to control travel in the Durrani Kingdom was indeed novel
and lent colour to Masson's notion that personal jealousy was involved,
but it was the absence of any reference to Bean's suspicions which
upset him. He therefore wrote again to the Envoy. At this time, a force
from Kandahar under Major-General Nott marched to Quetta and

thence to Kalat to suppress the revolt. The insurgents, who had dragged the hapless Loveday from place to place during the previous long weeks, having been defeated at Dadar, broke up their camp and murdered their prisoner. Masson thus had his highhanded gaoler, Captain Bean, to thank for having unwittingly saved him from a similar end.

General Nott found Kalat deserted. He left a regiment there and returned to Kandahar. Colonel Stacy was temporarily appointed to take political charge at Kalat where in due course he was able to be of further service to Masson by recovering some of his belongings. In reply to Masson's communication, the Secretary to the Government of India informed him that Ross Bell, the Political Agent for Sind and Baluchistan, had been instructed to make a formal investigation into his case, while Bean was directed to furnish the evidence against him. Obstinate to the last, the best that Bean could do was to write to Ross Bell that since his previous communication 'nothing further had transpired by which the disloyalty of Mr Masson as a British subject could be established'. And this, remarks Masson, after the collection of a host of depositions at Kalat and after the examination of Loveday's sepoys and servants. Ross Bell also received first-hand evidence from a number of Brahui chiefs and others who had been present at Kalat throughout Masson's stay there, whilst important testimony and an offer to stand surety for his release on parole came from Stacy. In consequence Ross Bell wrote to Masson that he was cleared of all suspicion and that his conduct towards Loveday had indeed been actuated by a desire to be of service to that officer.[234] In his report to the Government, Ross Bell stated that he could not trace any specific ground of suspicion attaching to him; and as the result of the enquiry had fully cleared his character he begged to submit that Masson appeared to have some claim for remuneration on account of the inconvenience and delay to which he had been put. Macnaghten, while endeavouring to shield Bean, likewise recommended that he should receive compensation.

Masson was released at last in January 1841 and immediately set off for Shikarpur. Of that journey he writes:

> So entirely had the country been devastated, that I could no longer recognise it to be the same I had traversed some fourteen years before. Villages, then flourishing, had ceased to exist; those remaining were destitute of their attendant groves of trees, and even the very waste had been denuded of the jangal of small trees and shrubs, once spreading over its surface. There was no fear, indeed, of losing the road, as

*formerly, for that was now well marked by the skeletons of camels and
other animals, whose bleached and bleaching bones too well described
it, and the nature of the operations which had been carried on. I passed
two days the guest of Mr Bell, who made an unreserved offer of anything
in his camp; and, on parting, I received from him many assurances of
his good opinion, and even of his esteem.*

He dropped down the river to Karachi: 'whence I had started the year
before, on an excursion, which had turned out more pregnant with
singular incidents than any other I had made throughout my career'.[236]
From there he sailed to Bombay where he spent several months.

He wrote to newspapers in Calcutta and Bombay complaining in
violent terms of his treatment in Quetta and attacking the 'Politicals'
involved. His friends Brownlow and Jephson in Calcutta tried hard to
persuade him to moderate these tactless criticisms of government officials, while commiserating with him on his misfortunes. In one of
his letters Jephson wrote: 'I wish you had not gibbetted Macnaghten
quite so high.'[237] Both men supported Masson's efforts to obtain compensation and Brownlow, who was well-acquainted with members of
the Governor-General's staff, managed to put the case to Auckland
privately.

Sir Henry Pottinger, as he had now become, broke the news of John
Murray's refusal to publish his book in a letter dated 25 July 1841,
written at sea on his way to take up his post as Envoy to China:

> *No one of the respectable Booksellers in England will publish any work
> (at their own risk) animadverting on public men or measures. They
> justly say, that that is the duty of the daily Press and that such criti-
> cisms are quite out of place in Books of Travel.*[238]

In consequence, Masson wrote a new and enlarged version of the *Narrative of Various Journeys*. Presumably he pruned it of the earlier excessive criticisms, though it remained severe enough. For relaxation he
paid visits to the renowned cave temples in the neighbourhood of
Bombay and made a number of drawings of the great figures there.

He was waiting to hear further from the Government of India about
his claim for compensation, but that matter was not going well. In a
letter to Macnaghten of 1 February 1841, the Governor-General had
written that although he was happy to find that Mr Masson stood
acquitted of any improper conduct, a British subject travelling, however innocently, without official permission in countries which become
the scene of intrigue and rebellion may come under suspicion and is
not on that account entitled to be reimbursed from the public purse

for losses or detention which have been the consequence of his own unauthorised and imprudent proceedings. So much for the Supreme Government's sense of justice. Not having heard of this decision, he submitted a petition with a list of the property he had lost: his horse, apparel, books, instruments and a variety of sundry articles, besides a small quantity of plate and a small amount of specie to a total value of Rs. 5,000. These details incidentally reveal a very different style of living and travelling from when we first met him. Among the books he listed were works on Greek and Roman Antiquities; Natural History and Medicine; a Geological Manual and a Grammar of Botany; Quintus Curtius; and volumes by Smollett, Dryden and Pope. After referring to the loss of his manuscripts and papers, which could not of course have a value placed on them, the petition further stated that these losses were entirely due to the assistance he had rendered to Loveday, and asked whether he was not entitled to expect that measures be taken for the recovery of his property, or for compensation in lieu.[239]

In reply, Mr Secretary Maddock in a letter dated 18 October 1841, informed him that his application was rejected, though for reasons different from those given to Macnaghten:

> His Lordship in Council could not feel himself justified, with reference to the information in the public records as received from Lieutenant Loveday, and to the orders of the authorities in England, in granting you a compensation for losses incurred by your finding yourself in an embarrassing position which your own disposition to travel under such circumstances had placed you. It would give him pleasure to learn, as the country becomes more settled, that any portion of your lost property has been recovered.[240]

And so Loveday, even in death, succeeded in further damaging the man who had done so much to support him, whilst the overwhelming evidence in Masson's favour was simply set aside. In official eyes this discreditable behaviour no doubt had the merit of saving the faces of the Politicals concerned. As for Bean, the last word may be left with George Buist, the editor of the *Bombay Times*:

> The continuation of Captain Bean in office, and the obtaining for him of a badge of the Dooranee empire—the last that was conferred—is, after the repeated disapproval of his acts and proofs of his incompetence, one of the numberless illustrations of Lord Auckland's character... Captain Bean had friends in the Secretariat, and Beloochistan was kept twelve months at war on this account.[241]

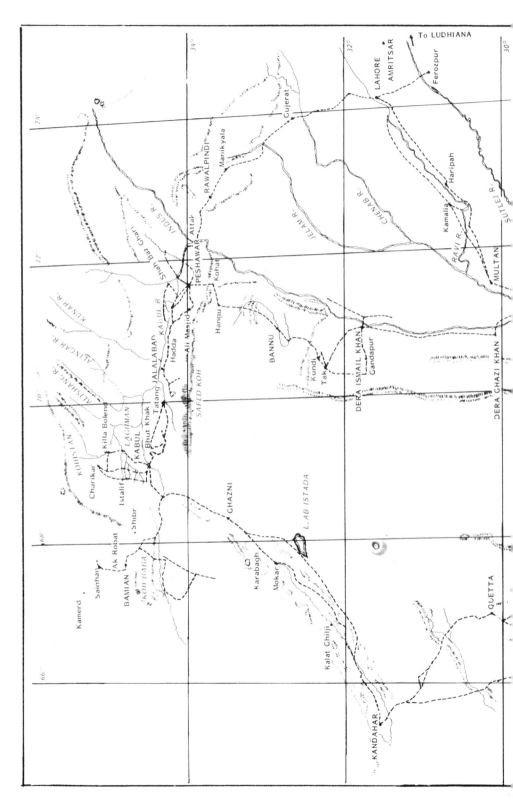

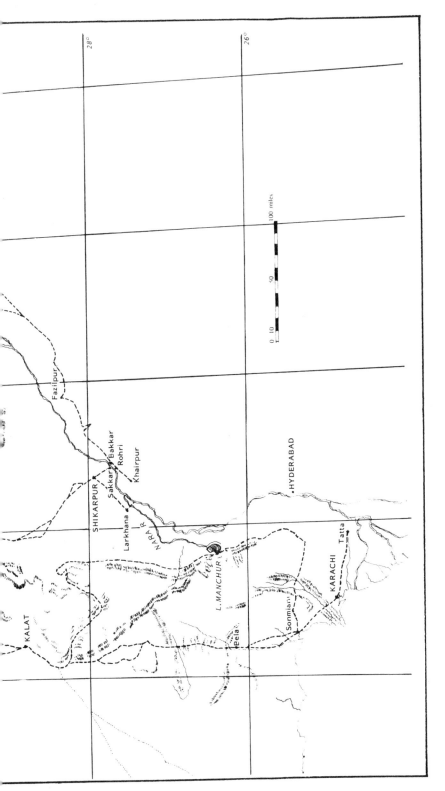

Plate 12. *Simplified version of Masson's map of his journeys.*

Masson gives the entire credit for the subsequent pacification of Baluchistan to the exertions of Colonel Stacy who secured the submission of the young Khan and his reinstatement at Kalat. Stacy, for his part, used that noteworthy event to write to Masson thanking him for his kind advice when in prison which had led to so satisfactory a result and adding that: 'My Success I attribute to the Advantage I gained by learning from you the different characters of the Chiefs and of the various tribes.'[242] Advice of similar worth would have been available to Macnaghten had he cared to evoke it.

In the belief that he might be able to prosecute his case more effectively in England, Charles Masson decided to return to London. He sailed from Bombay to Suez, crossed Egypt overland, thence to France with a stop in Paris and eventually reached London in March 1842. He was soon involved in a nice example of bureaucratic shufflings. A Memorial to the Court of Directors asking for the papers connected with his arrest and imprisonment was disallowed on the ground that it should have been forwarded through the channel of the Government of India. A second Memorial claiming the compensation recommended by the Court's own officers, Macnaghten and Ross Bell, was referred back to India, allegedly because the necessary documents were not available in London. With a final blast at the 'shallow and misguided men' who had heaped insults and injuries on him, Masson brings his *Narrative of Various Journeys* to a sad, indeed sour, close. Masson, the polemicist, is a less attractive figure than Masson, the stoical traveller and antiquarian. But he had suffered much from the Politicals and other officials and the resentment and bitterness of the concluding pages of his *Narrative* were more than justified. However, it was less his personal injuries than the immense damage inflicted by the Anglo-Afghan War on his beloved Afghans as well as on Britain's reputation in Central Asia that aroused his indignation.

He had spent over twenty years in India and the countries west of the Indus during which he had had many strange adventures and had made notable contributions to our knowledge of Central Asian life and antiquities. One thread runs throughout—Charles Masson's remarkable capacity for making friends among all classes of the country people wherever he went. Without the deep loyalty he inspired in these men he would never have survived.

CHAPTER XVIII

POSTLUDE

Of Charles Masson's life in England after his return from India in 1842 little can be told owing to the scantiness of the records. We have seen that his first twenty-one years are a complete blank: the eleven years that now remained to him are only comparatively better chronicled. His father had died but his mother apparently lived with him till about 1848, even after his marriage to Mary Anne Kilby at St Mary's Church, Stoke Newington in 1844. She was only 18 at the time and 26 years younger than her husband. He moved house with great frequency, but always in the outer London suburbs: Stoke Newington, Kentish Town, Upper Mitcham and Lower Edmonton amongst others. This constant change of residence suggests the last flickerings of his old restlessness and wanderlust.

Professor H.H. Wilson's *Ariana Antiqua. A descriptive account of the Antiquities and Coins of Afghanistan: with a Memoir on the Buildings called Topes, by C. Masson Esq.* was published in 1841 at the expense of the East India Company. Masson's *Memoir* was illustrated with a number of his drawings of his finds and the stupas he had excavated. Engravings of his coins and others were accompanied by a detailed analysis of each type by Wilson. *Ariana Antiqua* was in effect an impressive tribute to Masson's labours. Out of the edition of 500 (priced £5), 300 were placed at the disposal of Mrs Lewis, Masson's mother. This arrangement had been foreshadowed by the Court of Directors at the end of a long despatch of 2 May 1838 to the Governor of Bombay, rehearsing the entire history of the uneasy financial transactions with Masson. The despatch stated that by then the grants made to Masson by Bombay and Calcutta and sanctioned by London amounted to Rs.4,500 to which the Directors were apparently disposed to add a further Rs.2,500 (though Rs.2,000 is pencilled in the margin with a question mark). Assuming that the final total was Rs.7,000, the East India Company received not only Masson's collection of coins but also relics of the highest importance for the sum of £700—a remarkable bargain. In fairness it should be added that the decision to defray the cost of publishing *Ariana Antiqua* with its numerous engravings was taken because the Directors realised that the expense would be so high that little profit would be left for Masson.[244]

A copy of the despatch to Bombay was passed to Professor Wilson who drew on it in his Preface to *Ariana Antiqua*. After praising Masson as one of the most active and successful discoverers of coins and antiquities in Afghanistan, Wilson referred to Masson's proposal to the Government of Bombay through Colonel Pottinger to transfer his actual and all future collections to the East India Company on condition of their defraying the cost of his operations. Wilson continued:

> This proposal was favourably received, and from the year 1834 until 1837 Mr Masson was sedulously employed in the pursuit, in which he had engaged with equal intelligence and zeal, on behalf and at the expense of the East India Company.

But in Masson's own copy of *Ariana Antiqua* (now in the Indian Institute Library, Oxford), he has written in the margin against the phrase 'at the expense of the East India Company' the words 'a falsehood'. In the opposite margin, he wrote:

> Mr M. proposed to the Bombay Government if furnished with funds to expend such funds in researches on account of the Government, of course to hand them over the results. When eventually Mr M. learned that the Government consented to advance money, Mr M. voluntarily transferred to Government the collections made at his own expense and those in his possession... The Bombay Government was willing to have defrayed the cost of the operations and authorised Mr M. to appropriate for such purposes one half of the sums remitted to him — but the interference of Captain Wade prevented this arrangement being available to Mr M. — consequently Mr M. conducted his researches throughout at his own cost.

The last phrase does not tally either with the above-mentioned despatch or with the other records already noticed (see p. 90). It ignores the sums he undoubtedly received from Bombay despite the delays created by Captain Wade, and the contributions of his well-wishers, Colonel Pottinger, Sir John Campbell and others.

Another passage by Wilson in the Preface to *Ariana Antiqua* also aroused Masson's ire:

> ... it appeared to me to be likely that a connected description of the principal antiquities and of the whole of the coins received from Mr Masson would be acceptable both to the cultivators of numismatic sciences, and to those interested in the ancient history of India. I accordingly offered my services to the Honourable the Court of Directors to prepare such an account... The suggestion was most cordially and liberally approved of, and as profit was not the aim of either of the parties, the Court resolved that after appropriating such a

portion of the edition as they should think fit to require, the remainder should be presented to the mother of Mr Masson as an additional mark of the sense they entertained of the merits of her son.

Here Masson's marginal note reads:

As Librarian to the Court, it was proper that he should prepare such an account—but it would have been better that he had done so, without mixing it up with the consideration of Mr M.'s case. This arrangement seems very fair, and may be, so far as the Court is concerned. But Mr M. looks upon it very differently. Professor Wilson hands 300 copies of this work over to Mr M.'s mother, an aged woman of above sixty years of age, to dispose of as best she may, and draws up a Prospectus making Mr M. and his mother objects of sympathy and compassion. In other words Professor Wilson made Mr M.'s mother a beggar and dared to thrust Mr M. upon the notice of the world as an object of pity. He moreover furnished Mr M.'s mother with a Court Guide in which she was to find out the names of people to whom she was to go begging.

These strictures make sad reading and show Masson at his worst. Presumably his marginalia were written on first seeing *Ariana Antiqua* in print on his return to England. Professor Wilson seems to have pruned Masson's contribution of the extraneous speculations in which he was prone to indulge, hence his displeasure. Prickly and over-sensitive to slights, real or imaginary, as he was inclined to be, the combination of failure to obtain an official post, imprisonment in Quetta, the loss of his effects and papers in Kalat and his dispute with the East India Company over compensation, appears to have produced in him a form of persecution mania. In the event, his 'begging mother' must have coped successfully with the Court Guide since the list of subscribers printed at the front of some copies of *Ariana Antiqua* is headed by Queen Victoria, the Queen Dowager, H.R.H. Prince Albert and the Archbishop of Canterbury.

In spite of his prolonged efforts, Masson obtained no redress for his losses at Kalat. Eventually the Government of India paid his arrears of salary and allowances, whilst the Court of Directors gave him £500 and a pension of £100 per annum, but for his finds, not as compensation.

The *Narrative of Various Journeys in Balochistan, Afghanistan and the Panjab* was published by Richard Bentley in three volumes in 1842. It was well-timed inasmuch as it followed hard on the news of the disastrous retreat from Kabul with the destruction of the entire force of 4,600 men and 12,000 camp followers and, most damaging of all to British prestige in some eyes, the capture of a number of British officers' wives. The Duke of Wellington in particular was upset at the thought of ladies in the hands of Mahomed Akbar Khan. The 'Kalat' volume was published the next year. It is primarily a supplement to the three-volume work, but it includes a substantial Memoir on *Eastern Balochistan* which became a standard work of reference till the end of the century; a combined edition in four volumes appeared in 1844. Also in 1843 he drew up a final account of his travels in Persia, but it does not appear ever to have been published.[245] He gave a lecture to the Royal Asiatic Society in January 1844 entitled 'Narrative of an Excursion to Shahbaz Ghari' dealing with the inscription there; it was printed in the Society's *Journal* in 1846.[246] Another article 'Observations on the route of Isidore of Charax' was printed in the same *Journal* in 1850.[247]

It is evident from his manuscripts that he occupied much of his time preparing a major work expounding his views on the ancient history and archaeology of Afghanistan and neighbouring countries in which he indulged in rather wild speculations. In reality he had neither the academic training nor the languages needed for such scholarly labours. By 1847 he was trying to sell his private collection of duplicate coins which he had been permitted to retain and was proposing new explorations under Austrian auspices.

Throughout his time in the East, Masson made drawings and sketches, some of which were poorly reproduced in his book and in *Ariana Antiqua*; the rest, numbering several hundred, are in the Masson Collection of Manuscripts. Though of little artistic merit they have a permanent value as a record of much that has disappeared. The architectural drawings are better than his topographical ones, which tend to be wooden. He spent the last years of his life from about 1850 working up many of his original drawings but in so doing they lost their spontaneity.

From time to time writers in the 'Calcutta Review', reflecting the strong prejudice felt in India against him for his outspoken attacks on highly placed persons and his merciless exposure of their weaknesses, coming from a pardoned deserter, had accused him of being unreliable, mendacious and spiteful. But it was in a review of his book of verse *Legends of the Afghan countries, in Verse - with Various Pieces, Original and translated by Charles Masson, etc.* published in 1848 that Sir Henry Lawrence chose to launch a violent attack on its author:

> *We knew him to be the most poetical of prose-writers—the most fabulous of historians. But it remained for the present volume to demonstrate that he is the most prosaic of poets—the most matter of fact fabulist in the world... Well knowing the amount of poetical licence which Mr Masson has always allowed himself when dealing with*

matters of fact, the student of these legends will be startled to find the
chastened fancy of the writer so conspicuous in every page... There is
no abandon — no fine mystic enthusiasm. Even the giants and
giantesses are very commonplace mortals — not half as genuine ogres
as Mr Masson's friends, the Sindh politics ... keeping fierce hell-
hounds to hunt down human game...

This last phrase refers of course to Masson's acccount of Lieutenant
Loveday and his dogs. As an example of the poor quality of the verse,
Lawrence quoted these lines:

Some o'er the saddled camel stride
That carries two or carries one.

and added: 'This last line our readers will agree with us in considering eminently poetical.'[248] In truth, the verses are commonplace and
unworthy of ten pages of sardonic comment and, it may be thought,
unworthy of the Christian hero of Lucknow. But Masson was an obsession with Lawrence who lost no opportunity of ridiculing or condemn-
ing him. C. Grey's own verdict is very different: 'Masson who, despite Sir
Henry Lawrence, nothing extenuates nor sets down ought in malice.'

Not only were the attacks by Lawrence and others unsubstantiated
and the episodes to which they objected not explicitly denied, but in
fact Masson was an observer of remarkable accuracy on matters within
his knowledge. When he recounts a story he gives his source, e.g.
Burnes for the account of the alarm expressed by Colvin and Torrens
at Simla lest he should say anything that might serve to change
Auckland's mind about going to war. It is unfortunate that the resentment Masson aroused cast a shadow over his reputation in his proper
field, namely as a pioneer of Central Asian antiquarian research. As
an archaeologist he suffered more neglect than might otherwise have
been the case. Yet he undoubtedly laid the foundations upon which
almost all subsequent archaeological work in Afghanistan has been
based. He had, for example, amply demonstrated the importance of
the Begram site, but it was not until 1939 that the French archaeological delegation uncovered the magnificent hoard there and identified
the extensive ruins as Kapisa, the summer capital of the Kushan Empire.

There is still a tendency to criticise Masson for his alleged crude
methods of excavation and magpie-like approach to the rich field before him. He has even been accused of being a treasure hunter. But his
methods were no cruder than those of his contemporaries, or indeed
of, say, Schliemann at Troy 40 years later. It is interesting to note that
even at the time Gerard drew a sharp distinction between Masson's
methods and aims, and those of Honigberger. The latter, he says, had

'ransacked and destroyed a vast number of Mausolea' and had failed:

> ... *to pursue enquiry beyond the mere collection of the remains which I imagine are designed to be put up to the highest bidder among the eminent literati of his country. Mr Masson's objects were of a higher order and embraced the identification of ancient sites and their connexion with historical records...*[249]

In any case, the development of archaeology into a science with rigorous disciplines belongs to the 20th century. Strictly speaking, Masson and his contemporaries and successors over several decades should not properly be called archaeologists, but rather antiquarians. It is as a pioneer that he must be assessed. Besides, had he not excavated in the 1830s it is certain that some of the monuments he opened would have disintegrated with the flux of time and the attentions of local treasure-hunters, or would not have been tackled until the 1920s when it was again possible for Europeans to undertake sustained excavations in Afghanistan.

For the historian, Masson is the best authority on the politics of Afghanistan during the decade preceding the First Afghan War. As an explorer, his contributions to the geographical knowledge of the region had to wait many years before they could be properly evaluated. As a numismatist, the value of his work was acknowledged from the beginning and is today as highly regarded as ever.

In June 1853, he gave his landlord notice of intention to quit on or before 25 December the house in Church Street, Lower Edmonton which he had taken only six months previously. Before this move could take place, he died there on 5 November 1853 at the early age of 53.[250] The East India Company made his widow a donation of £100 by order of 15 March 1854. She died in 1855, still under thirty, leaving young children. The Minutes of the Court of Directors for 11 February 1857[251] recorded a resolution to pay to the legal guardian of the orphan children of the late Mr Masson the sum of £100 for the papers, drawings and coins left by him at his death, as recommended by Professor Wilson, when these effects had been deposited in the Company's Library.* This extraordinary medley of letters, drafts, notebooks, journals, newspaper cuttings, drawings and sketches was admirably catalogued in 1937 and the full details of the mystery surrounding Masson brought to light.

There is no known portrait of Charles Masson.

---

* I am indebted to Dr R.J. Bingle of the India Office Library for this reference. Prior to his discovery it was not known how the Masson Collection came into the possession of the Library.

NOTES

1. Mss. Eur. E. 161.
2. Masson: *Legends of the Afghan Countries, in verse with various Pieces, Original and translated by C. Masson etc.*
3. C. Brownlow to Masson 7 April 1841, Mss. Eur. E. 161.
4. Guildhall Library Ms. 3572/2.
5. Mss. Eur. B. 191, 648.
6. Embarkation Lists, Vol. 17, p. 182.
7. Bengal Muster Rolls.
8. Wade to Macnaghten 9 April 1834, Bengal Secret Consultations, 19 June 1834, Vol. 380. See also p. 120.
9. Wolff: *Researches and Missionary Lobours among the Jews, Mohammedans and other Sects*, (2nd Edition 1835) p. 258.
10. Quoted by Grey: *European Adventurers of Northern India* p. 253.
11. *Asiatick Researches*, Vol.6.
12. Johnston: Introductory Essay to Masson Collection. Catalogue of Mss. in European Languages, Vol. ii, Part ii, Section ii, p. 1273.
13. Masson: *Narrative of Various Journeys* with an Introduction by Gavin Hambly I, p. xi.
14. Mss. Eur. E. 161, 635.
15. Mss. Eur. E. 163, 640.
16. Hambly: Introduction to Masson I, pp. xi and xv.
17. Idem: I, p. vii.
18. Masson: I, p. 443.
19. Osborne: *Court and Camp of Runjeet Singh.*
20. Emily Eden: *Up the Country.* I, p. 284.
21. Spear: *Oxford History of Modern India*, 1965, p. 154.
22. Idem: p. 155.
23. Sir Olaf Caroe: Introduction to the 1972 reprint of Elphinstone's *Account of the Kingdom of Caubul*, I, p. xx.
24. Masson: III, pp. 34-35.
25. Masson: III, pp. 227-9.
26. Masson: III, p. 36. (He provides a list of the Barakzai brothers on pp. 36-37).
27. Masson: I, p. 286.
28. Spear: p. 157.
29. Ingram: *The Beginning of the Great Game in Asia 1828-1834*, p. 54.
30. Quoted by Ingram, p. 54.
31. Yapp: *Strategies of British India: Britain, Iran and Afghanistan 1798-1850*, p. 15.
32. Ingram: p. 54.
33. Quoted by J.A. Norris: *The First Afghan War 1838-1842*, p. 38.
34. Quoted by Ingram, p. 67.
35. Idem: p. 76.
36. Copied to Governor, Bengal, under cover of despatch from Secret Committee about Russian spies in Asia: L/PS/5/545.
37. Quoted by Ingram, p. 153.
38. Secret Committee to Governor-General, 12 January 1830, L/PS/5/543.
39. Nesselrode to Pozzo di Borgo, 20 October 1838, *Correspondence relating to Persia and Afghanistan.*
40. Mouraviev, *Voyage en Turcomanie et à Khiva fait en*

1819 et 1820 quoted by Norris op. cit. p. 19.
41. Meyendorff, *Voyage d'Orenbourg à Bokhara fait en 1820* (Paris, 1826) p. 303.
42. Mss. Eur. E. 163, 640, ii.
43. A. Conolly, *Journey to the North of India, Overland from England, through Russia, Persia and Afghanistan*, 1834.
44. Burnes: *Travels into Bokhara*, I p. xxxi.
45. Masson: I, p. 146.
46. Honigberger: *Thirty-five years in the East*, p. 44.
47. Masson: I, pp. 80-82.
48. Masson: I, p. 244.
49. Holdich: *The Gates of India*, pp. 345-8.
50. Masson: I, p. 31.
51. Masson: I, pp. 32-33.
52. Masson: I, p. 85.
53. Masson: I, p. 124.
54. Holdich: p. 354.
55. Masson: I, pp. 157-8.
56. Holdich: p. 352.
57. S. Mizuno, 1965.
58. Masson: I, pp. 184-5.
59. Masson: I, pp. 252-3.
60. Masson: I, p. 258.
61. Masson: I, p. 310.
62. Masson: I, pp. 316-17.
63. Masson: I, pp. 337-9.
64. Holdich: pp. 361-2.
65. Masson: I, p. 402.
66. Idem: I, pp. 453-4.
67. Idem: I, pp. 408-37.
68. Burnes: III, p. 15.
69. Masson: II, p. 2.
70. Forrest: *Selections from the Travels and Journals preserved in the Bombay Secretariat*, pp. 106-107.
71. Mss. Eur. E. 162, 630.
72. Masson: II, p. 4.
73. Masson to Sir J. Campbell, 6
July 1834, Mss. Eur. E. 161, 637.
74. Masson: I, p. 361.
75. Masson: II, p. 16.
76. Mss. Eur. E. 163, 640.
77. Masson: II, pp. 219-22.
78. Wolff: *Researches and Missionary Labours* p. 216.
79. Masson: II, pp. 230-233.
80. Masson: II, pp. 275-7.
81. Vigne: *A Personal Account of a visit to Ghuzni, Kabul and Afghanistan*. p. 287.
82. Grey, p. 191-2.
83. W. Trousdale: *Chowkidar*, BACSA 1982.
84. Masson: II, p. 243.
85. Masson: II, pp. 244-7.
86. Masson: II, pp. 463-4.
87. Holdich: pp. 407-408.
88. Masson: III, pp. 1-4.
89. Abstract of intelligence from Cabul from 3rd to 25th December 1832, Bengal Secret Consultations: 19 March 1833, Vol. 372.
90. Masson: III, pp. 92-95.
91. Masson: III, pp. 96-98.
92. Masson: III, pp. 140-143.
93. Masson: III, pp. 148-9.
94. Mss. Eur. E. 160, 655.
95. H.H. Wilson: *Ariana Antiqua; a Descriptive account of the antiquities and coins of Afghanistan: with a Memoir on the Buildings called Topes, by C. Masson, Esq.* p. 12.
96. Wilson: pp. 2-3.
97. Masson: III, pp. 149-50.
98. Wilson: p. 12.
99. Idem: p. 73.
100. Masson: III, pp. 171-2.
101. Honigberger: pp. 60-61.
102. Wolff: p. 265.
103. Grey: p. 235.
104. *JASB*: Vol. III, No. xxviii, April, 1834, pp. 175-8.

105. *JASB:* Idem, pp. 150-175.
106. Idem: Vol. V No. xlix, January 1836, pp. 1-28 and No. lvii, September 1836, pp. 537-47.
107. Idem: Vol. V No. li, March 1836, p. 188 and No. lix November 1836, pp. 707-20.
108. Masson: III, p. 366.
109. Mss. Eur. E. 161, 631.
110. Idem: E. 160, 655.
111. Wilson: pp. 55-61.
112. Wilson: pp. 62-118.
113. Rowland: The Art and Architecture of India, pp. 78-79.
114. Wilson: pp. 73-74.
115. Wilson: p. 107.
116. Wilson: p. 109.
117. Wilson: p. 111.
118. Moorcroft and Trebeck: *Travels in the Himalayan Provinces of Hindustan,* Ed. H.H. Wilson, 1841 (reprinted Delhi 1971) II, p. 311.
119. idem: II, pp. 349-50.
120. Idem: II, pp. 391-2.
121. Idem: II, pp. 405-6.
122. Burnes: I, pp. 72-73.
123. Burnes: I, p. 109.
124. Burnes: I, pp. 184-7.
125. Burnes: I, p. 188.
126. Wood: *Journey to the Source of the Oxus,* (2nd Edition 1872), p. 103.
127. Idem: p. 114.
128. Wilson: p. 92.
129. Idem: p. 78.
130. Idem: p. 98.
131. JASB Vol. V No. lix, Nov. 1836, pp. 707-20.
132. Mss. Eur. B. 99, 652.
133. James Fergusson: *History of Indian and Eastern Architecture* (reprinted Delhi 1967) p. 88.
134. See also Elphinstone op. cit. I, p. 108 footnote dated 1838.
135. Wilson: p. 50.
136. Fergusson: pp. 62-66.
137. Wilson: p. 322.
138. Wade to Macnaghten. 9 April 1834, Bengal Secret Consultations, 19 June 1834, Vol. 380.
139. Hambly: Introduction to Masson I, p. xxiii.
140. Gerard to C. Trevelyan, Calcutta, 8 April 1834, Bengal Secret Consultations, 19 June 1834, Vol. 380.
141. Grey: p. 254.
142. Wolff: p. 256.
143. Quoted by Grey, p. 254.
144. Mss. Eur. E. 161, 637.
145. Grey: p. 195.
146. Macnaghten to Wade, 26 May 1834, Bengal Secret Consultations, 19 June 1834, Vol. 380.
147. Wade to Masson, 5 December 1834, Mss. Eur. E. 161, 632.
148. Bengal Secret Proceedings, 1834.
149. Secret Committee to G.G. 9 February 1835. L/P & S/5/ 547.
150. Wade to Masson, 11 February 1835: Mss. Eur. E. 161/ 2, 632.

151. Wade to Masson, 19 August 1835: Mss. Eur. E. 161/2, 632.
152. Masson: III, pp. 321-5.
153. Masson: III, p. 348.
154. Masson: III, p. 361.
155. Masson: III, p. 355.
156. Masson: III, pp. 366-7.
157. Pottinger to Wade, 27 February 1835, Mss. Eur. E. 160, 631.
158. Pottinger to Masson, 6 August 1834, Mss. Eur. E. 160, 631.
159. Brownlow to Masson, 28 March 1836, Mss. Eur. E. 161, 635.
160. Brownlow to Masson, 22 September 1836, Mss. Eur. E. 161, 635.
161. Gerard to Masson, 22 April 1834, Mss. Eur. E. 161, 637.
162. Masson: III, p. 369.
163. Idem: III, p. 376.
164. Norris: p. xv.
165. Masson: III, p. 418.
166. Idem: III, p. 378.
167. Masson: III, pp. 398-9.
168. Ellis to Palmerston, 13 November 1835, Correspondence relating to Persia and Afghanistan.
169. Masson: III, pp. 405-406.
170. Masson: III, p. 432.
171. Macnaghten to Burnes, 15 May 1937: Parliamentary Papers Vol. XX V 1859.
172. Masson: III, p. 451.
173. Masson: III, p. 414.
174. Masson: III, pp. 448-9.

175. Masson: III, p. 444.
176. Masson: III, p. 422.
177. Masson: III, p. 440-442.
178. Masson: III, p. 445.
179. Burnes: Cabool, pp. 139-40.
180. Masson: III, p. 452.
181. Masson: III, p. 453.
182. Masson: III, pp. 454-7.
183. Masson: III, p. 447.
184. Yapp: Strategies of British India, p. 228.
185. Idem: p. 191.
186. Masson: III, p. 419.
187. Macnaghten to Burnes, 11 September 1837, Parliamentary Papers Vol. XXV 1859.
188. Fraser-Tytler, Afghanistan, (3rd edition 1961), p. 93.
189. Yapp: p. 232.
190. Masson: III, pp. 463-4.
191. Burnes to Auckland, 23 December 1837. Parliamentary Papers Vol XXV, 1859 (heavily pruned in Parliamentary Papers 1839 as too favourable to the Dost).
192. Conolly, II, p. 21.
193. Kaye: The War in Afghanistan, 1851, I, p. 209.
194. Spear: p. 160.
195. Burnes: Cabool, p. 262.
196. Masson: III, p. 469.
197. Wood: p. 259.
198. Masson: III, pp. 478-9.
199. Masson: III, pp. 484-6.
200. Masson: III, p. 487-9.
201. Mss. Eur. E. 165, 641.
202. Masson: I, xxxv-vi.
203. Burnes: Travels into Bokhara III, p. 185.

204. Masson: III, pp. 491-3.
205. Masson: III, pp. 494-5.
206. Norris: p. 188.
207. Masson: III, p. 496.
208. Philip Mason: *A Matter of Honour*, p. 225.
209. Fraser-Tytler: *Afghanistan*, p. 94.
210. Yapp: pp. 9-10.
211. Spear: p. 157.
212. H.T. Lambrick: Introduction to Masson, IV, p. viii.
213. Quoted by Kaye: II, pp. 350-351.
214. Lambrick: Introduction to Masson, IV, pp.viii-ix.
215. Wright: *The English Among the Persians*, p. 30.
216. Fraser-Tytler: p. 85.
217. Masson: IV, pp. 1-2.
218. Yapp: p. 264.
219. Masson: IV, p. 67.
220. Masson: IV, p. 71.
221. Masson: IV, p. 77-78.
222. Masson: IV, p. 110.
223. Buist: *Outline of the operations of the British troops in Scinde and Afghanistan*, p. 175.
224. Masson: IV, pp. 118-19.
225. Lambrick: Introduction to Masson, IV, pp. vii-viii.
226. Masson: IV. pp. 137 and 148-9.
227. Masson: IV, p. 178.
228. Lambrick: Introduction to Masson, IV, pp. xii and footnote 9.
229. Masson: IV, p. 276.
230. Masson: IV, pp. 253-5.
231. Masson: IV, p. 258.
232. Quoted by Lambrick: Introduction to Masson: IV, p. xv.
233. Masson: IV, pp. 259-60.
234. Masson: IV, p. 268-9.
235. Lambrick: Introduction to Masson, IV, p. xvii.
236. Masson: IV, p. 272-4.
237. G. Jephson to Masson, 27 March 1841, Mss. Eur. E. 161, 637.
238. Mss. Eur. E. 161, 631.
239. Mss. Eur. E. 169, 656.
240. Lambrick: Introduction to Masson IV, pp. xx-xxi.
241. Buist, p. 210 and footnote.
242. Mss. Eur. E. 161, 634.
243. General Register Office, London.
244. Court of Directors to Governor, Bombay, 2 May 1838, Mss. Eur. E. 160, 655.
245. Mss. Eur. E. 163, 640.
246. *JRAS* 1846, pp. 292-302.
247. *JRAS* 1850, pp. 97-124.
248. Calcutta Review VoI.XI. No. xxi 1849 pp. 220-230.
249. Gerard to C. Trevelyan, 8 April 1834, Bengal Secret Consultations, 19 June 1834, Vol. 380.
250. General Register Office, London.
251. IOR/B/233.

SELECTIVE BIBLIOGRAPHY

MANUSCRIPT SOURCES

India Office Library & Records:
> Bengal Secret Consultations.
> Bengal Muster Rolls, 1822-27.
> Embarkation Lists (East India Co.) Vol. 17.

Manuscripts in European Languages: Minor Collections & Miscellaneous Mss:
> Masson Collection (Mss. Eur. E. 161 etc.)
> Wilson Collection (Mss. Eur. E. 160 etc.)
> Board of Control's Secret Letters & Despatches (L/PS/5/545 etc.)
> Guildhall Library Ms. 3572/2.

PRINTED SOURCES

(Where unstated the place of publication is London)

Parliamentary Papers. Vol. XXV. 1859.

BEAL, S. *Buddhist Records of the Western World*. 1969.

BUIST, George. *Outline of the operations of British troops in Scinde and Afghanistan*. Bombay 1843.

BURNES, Alexander. *Travels into Bokhara*, 3 Vols. 1834 (re-printed Karachi 1973).

— *Cabool* 1842 (reprinted Lahore 1961).

CONOLLY, A. *Journey to the north of India, Overland from England, through Russia, Persia and Afghanistan*. 2 Vols. 1834.

DUNBAR, Janet. *Golden Interlude*, 1955.

DUPREE, Nancy Hatch. *An Historical Guide to Afghanistan,* Kabul, 2nd Edition. 1977.

EDEN, Emily. *Up the Country*. 1866.

ELPHINSTONE, Mountstuart. *An Account of the Kingdom of Caubul*. 3 Vols. 1815. (reprinted Karachi, 1972 with an Introduction by Sir Olaf Caroe).

FERGUSSON, James. *History of Indian and Eastern Architecture*. 1876 (reprinted Delhi 1967).

FERRIER, J.P. *Caravan Journeys and Wanderings in Persia, Afghanistan, Turkistan and Baloochiston*, 1857.

FORREST, George W. *Selections from the Travels and Journals Preserved in the Bombay Secretariat*. Bombay, 1906.

FORSTER, George. *Journey from Bengal to England*, 2 Vols. 1798.

FRASER-TYTLER, Sir W.K. *Afghanistan. 3rd Edition*, 1967.

GREY, C. *European Adventurers of Northern India 1785 to 1849*. Lahore 1929.

HOLDICH, Sir Thomas. *The Gates of India*. 1910.

HONIGBERGER, M. *Thirty-five years in the East*, 1852.

INGRAM, Edward. *The Beginning of the Great Game in Asia 1828-1834*. Oxford, 1979.

KAYE, Sir W.J. *The War in Afghanistan*, 2 Vols. 1851.

— *Lives of Indian Officers*. 2 Vols. 1904.

KEAY, John. *When Men and Mountains Meet*, 1977.

MACLEAN, Fitzroy. *Person from England*. 1958.

MASON, Philip. *A Matter of Honour*, 1974.

MASSON, Charles. *Narrative of Various Journeys in Balochistan, Afghanistan and the Panjab, including a residence in those countries from 1826 to 1838*. 3 Vols. 1842 (reprinted Karachi 1974 with an Introduction by Gavin Hambly).

— *Narrative of a Journey to Kalat, including an Account of the Insurrection at that Place in 1840; and a Memoir of Eastern Balochistan*. 1843. viz. Vol IV of the *Narrative of Various Journeys* (reprinted Karachi 1977 with an Introduction by H. T. Lambrick).

— *Legends of the Afghan Countries, in verse; - with Various Pieces, Original and Translated by Charles Masson, etc.* 1848.

MEYENDORFF, Baron Georg von. *Voyage d'Orenbourg à Bokhara fait en 1820*. Paris 1826.

MOHAN LAL. *Life of the Amir Dost Mohammad Khan*. 2 Vols. 1846.

MOURAVIEV, Count N.N. *Voyage en Turcomonie et à Khiva fait en 1819 et 1820*. Paris 1823.

MOORCROFT, William and TREBECK, George. *Travels in the Himalayan Provinces of Hindustan*. Edited by H.H. Wilson. 2 Vols. 1841. (reprinted Delhi 1971).

NORRIS, J.A. *The First Anglo-Afghan War 1838-1842*. Cambridge 1967.

OSBORNE, W. G. *Court and Camp of Runjeet Singh*. 1840.

ROWLAND, Benjamin. *The Art and Architecture of India*. 1954.

STOCQUELER, J.H. *Memorials of Afghanistan 1838-1842*. Calcutta 1843.

SPEAR, P. *Oxford History of Modern India, 1740-1947*. Oxford 1965.

VIGNE, G.T. *A Personal Account of a Visit to Ghuzni, Kabul and Afghanistan*. 1843.

WILFORD, Col. *Asiatick Researches*. Vol. 6.

WILSON, H.H. *Ariana Antiqua. A descriptive account of the Antiquities and Coins of Afghanistan: with a Memoir on the Buildings called Topes, by C. Masson Esq.* 1841. (reprinted Delhi 1971).

WOLFF, J. *Researches and Missionary Labours among the Jews, Mohommadans and other Sects*. 2nd Edition 1835.

WOOD, Lieut. J. *Journey to the Source of the Oxus*. 2nd Edition 1872.

WRIGHT, Sir Dennis. *The English Among the Persians*. 1977.

YAPP, M.E. *Strategies of British India; Britain, Iran and Afghanistan 1798-1850*. Oxford 1980.

ZWALF, W. *A Catalogue of the Gandharan Sculpture in the British Museum*. Volumes I & II. London 1996.

Articles in: *Journal of the Asiatic Society of Bengal (JASB)*.

Journal of the Royal Asiatic Society (JRAS).

Calcutta Review. Vol. XI. 1849.

INDEX